Prais
Wisdom

M000213185

"Riz brings his scientific mind to the heart-centric subject of the spiritual search, revisiting classic tales from Autobiography of a Yogi for the modern world. Wisdom of a Yogi is a book with heart, mind and spirit!"

—**Dannion Brinkley**, international New York Times
bestselling author of *Saved by the Light*

"How well I remember reading Autobiography of a Yogi by Swami Yogananda, and what it meant to me as a young man just beginning the spiritual journey that would become my life. And now Riz Virk comes out with this inspiring book of insights into Yogananda's great classic. It has moved me deeply and brought me the excitement of new discoveries in what is now a search that has been going on for over 60 years. The lessons he has crafted and the wisdom he has brought are a joy to experience and savor."

—**Whitley Strieber**, Author of *Communion* and
A New World

"I absolutely loved Rizwan Virk's "Wisdom of a Yogi"! Swami Yogananda's autobiography was transformational to my life as a young person and a graduate student, and Virk has done a remarkable service to all seekers of truth. This book is an update and an elaboration on the most important aspects of Swami Yogananda's life and teachings. Virk tackles the hard questions of his life events and teachings and frames them in a way that is relevant and helpful to twenty-first century readers. This book has my highest recommendation."

—**Diana Walsh Pasulka**, Professor of Philosophy and Religion,
University of North Carolina Wilmington author of
American Cosmic: UFOs, Religion, Technology

"Distills the very essence of Yogananda's Autobiography, thus making the great monk's work, life and teachings accessible to a wider universe."

—**Ashwin Sanghi**, author of *The Magicians of Mazda*

"The world is a cosmic motion picture, Yogananda told us, melding his yogic understanding of illusion and divine play with technology that was fresh in his day. Rizwan Virk suggests a 21st century metaphor and thinks the great yogi would approve. In line with his brilliant previous book The Simulation Hypothesis, he suggests that the world is a video game in which we are invited to become conscious role players and programmers, and gather our points so we can rise to higher levels of choice and perception and even create our own scripts. Riz mines Autobiography of a Yogi for lessons for our daily lives. He encourages us to commit to a simple everyday practice to calm the "whirlpools" of thoughts and feelings every day. He spurs us to make time for "little pilgrimages" to places where we feel close to heaven and earth. He reminds us that setbacks may confer opportunities. He invites us to track meaningful coincidences as clues in a treasure hunt. He recounts the tales of superpowers and wonder-working that make the Autobiography spiritual thriller - tales of a tiger swami and of yogis who can appear in two places at once - but reminds us that the real game is not about showing off siddhis but awakening to the larger reality, and embracing its light, and living from that. Wisdom of a Yogi is highly recommended both for those who have cherished Yogananda from childhood and those who are discovering him only now."

—**Robert Moss**, bestselling author of *Conscious Dreaming* and *The Secret History of Dreaming*

Praise for *The Simulation Hypothesis and Other Books by Rizwan Virk*

"Virk ... makes a cogent, clear-eyed guide to the head-spinning science of parallel universes, quantum indeterminacy, and the possibility—terrifying or relieving—that our perceived reality is in fact part of a great simulation."

—*Publishers Weekly*

"MIT scientist's '*Simulation Hypothesis*' makes compelling case for The Matrix."

—*The Next Web*

"*The Simulation Hypothesis* presents a radical alternative to current models of reality ... The result is a stunning reappraisal of what it means to be human in an infinite universe."

— **Jacques Vallée**, venture capitalist,
author of *Forbidden Science*

"How am I unreal? In *The Simulated Multiverse*, Riz Virk counts the ways. So many ways we might all live in one (or more) simulated worlds .... And just like Galileo did, Virk may help open our eyes to a greater (if humbling) cosmology."

—David Brin, author of *EXISTENCE*,
The Postman and *EARTH*

"Perhaps *The Matrix* is more than a science fiction film ... Read this book ... if you dare."

— **Tessa B. Dick**, wife of Philip K. Dick and author of
Conversations with Philip K. Dick,

"So exciting that someone from the tech world is speaking up about signs, synchronicities, and spiritual guidance. Thanks, Riz, for *Treasure Hunt*, a compelling guide for finding the map we all contain inside."

— **Pam Grout**, #1 New York Times bestselling author of
E-squared

ALSO BY RIZWAN VIRK

The Simulation Hypothesis:
An MIT Computer Scientist Shows Why AI, Quantum Physics and Eastern Mystics Agree We Are in a Video Game

The Simulated Multiverse
An MIT Computer Scientist Explores Parallel Universes, The Simulation Hypothesis, Quantum Computing and the Mandela Effect

Startup Myths & Models:
What You Won't Learn in Business School

Treasure Hunt:
Follow Your Inner Clues to Find True Success

THE ZEN ENTREPRENEUR SAGA
Zen Entrepreneurship:
Walking the Path of the Career Warrior

The Zen Entrepreneur and the Dream:
Further Adventures in Business and Consciousness

visit
www.zenentrepreneur.com

WISDOM
OF
A
YOGI

BAYVIEW

BOOKS

Originally Published in
India by

WISDOM
OF A YOGI

LESSONS FOR MODERN SEEKERS
FROM *AUTOBIOGRAPHY OF A YOGI*

RIZWAN VIRK

BAYVIEW
BOOKS

First published in India by HarperCollins *Publishers* 2023.
This international English reprint is a complete reproduction, authorized by
the original publisher, HarperCollins *Publishers*, and the author for worldwide
distribution (except the Indian subcontinent).

This edition (v .5) published in paperback by Bayview Books, LLC.
www.bayviewlabs.com/bayviewbooks
2 4 6 8 10 9 7 5 3 1

Publisher's Cataloging-in-Publication data

Names: Virk,
Rizwan, author.
Title: Wisdom of a Yogi : lessons for modern seekers from 'Autobiography of a
Yogi' / Rizwan Virk.
Description: International English reprint edition. |
Tempe, Arizona : Bayview Books, [2023] | "First published in India by Harper-
Collins Publishers 2023"--Title page verso. |
Includes bibliographical references and index.
Identifiers: ISBN: 978-1-954872-10-3 (paperback) |
978-1-954872-09-7 (epub/kindle)
Subjects: LCSH: Yogananda, Paramahansa, 1893-1952. Autobiography of
a Yogi. | Spiritual direction-- Study and teaching. | Spirituality--Study and
teaching. | Spiritual life--Study and teaching. | Karma--Study and teaching. |
Yoga--Study and teaching. | Meditation--Study and teaching. | Yogis--India. |
Gurus--India. | Siddhas. | Spiritual biography.
Classification: LCC: BP605.S4 V57 2023 | DDC: 294.5/44--dc23

For my father, Muhammad Yaqub Virk (1937–2022),
who represented the best of East and West
and who is now reading this in the library beyond
the simulation

Contents

Editorial Notes

A Note on Swami Names

Paramahansa Yogananda was born Mukunda Lal Ghosh. It was after he graduated from Serampore College, West Bengal, that he was ordained as Swami Yogananda, by his guru, Sri Yukteswar Giri. Many of the events recounted in *Autobiography of a Yogi* (mostly referred to as 'the *Autobiography*' henceforth) occurred when he was young and still known as Mukunda. In this text, when summarizing stories from the *Autobiography*, I may refer to him as Mukunda or Yogananda, depending on how old he was when the relevant events occurred. When discussing events that occurred during his adulthood, I will generally use Yogananda. There are multiple spellings of 'Paramahansa' and 'Paramhansa'—for simplicity, I have chosen the one used by his organization (Self-Realization Fellowship): Paramahansa.

On the other hand, when relating stories about other swamis or adepts, such as Sri Yukteswar or Lahiri Mahasaya, I will use the names by which Yogananda referred to them in the *Autobiography*, regardless of their age during those stories. Sometimes this is an ordained name ('Sohong Swami'), sometimes a given name ('Ram Gopal'), sometimes it is a designated name that disciples use ('Bhaduri Mahasaya') and at other times it is simply a nickname that Yogananda invented ('The Tiger Swami', 'The Levitating Saint' and 'The Saint with Two Bodies'). Babaji's case is unique, as we do not know his given name or whether he had an ordained or designated name. I will refer to him simply as Babaji or, more formally, Mahavatar Babaji.

A Note on Editions, Quotes and Page Numbers

Multiple versions of *Autobiography of a Yogi* have been published, starting with Yogananda's original text, published in 1946 by Philosophical Library. This version had a blue cover and the complete text is available online, courtesy of Crystal Clarity Publishers. The text is also freely available online on Project Gutenberg and many other platforms. The most popular printed version is no doubt the Self-Realization Fellowship edition, which was first printed in 1953 and has undergone various updates since then.

When quoting from the *Autobiography* in the notes, I have included both the page number and the chapter title, so the quote can be easily located whether one is reading a physical copy or an online version of the book. The page numbers will generally be from a particular Self-Realization Fellowship version (typically my old paperback version—twelfth edition, twelfth paperbound printing, 1993; see the bibliography for other versions I may have used). The exact quotes have typically been sourced from one of the freely available online versions, most likely the Crystal Clarity Publishers online edition; I have tried to link the quotes to page numbers in the paperback, but there may be a few cases in which the quote has been taken from the online edition and differs from the Self-Realization Fellowship paperback edition.

INTRODUCTION

Ancient Wisdom for Modern Times

By the time he completed his masterwork, *Autobiography of a Yogi* in 1945, Paramahansa Yogananda had been away from India for twenty-five years, teaching yoga and meditation in the United States. He had tirelessly given lectures and classes all across the North American continent or, as we Americans like to say, 'from sea to shining sea', covering the distance between Boston on the Atlantic seaboard and San Diego on the Pacific coast. He had called on many dignitaries, including the President of the United States and the President of Mexico, and experienced both success and bitter disappointment in his lifelong mission to introduce yoga and meditation to the West's mostly Christian population.

With the publication of the *Autobiography*, I think we can agree, he accomplished his mission. The book opened the floodgates and inspired a much larger number of Westerners to undertake the spiritual quest than Swami Yogananda could ever have done in person. The success of the book over the years would bring many aspirants onto the path of yoga and transform Yogananda from a mere man into an icon. This was not only true in the West but also in his homeland, where, because of his unofficial role as an ambassador of Indian philosophy, he became a distinguished and well-known figure. This was evidenced by the 2017 issuance of commemorative stamps honouring Yogananda by the Government of India, even though Yogananda emigrated in his twenties and spent most of his adult life in the United States.

You might say that the book transformed Yogananda from a person who embodied the ordinary meaning of the word 'guru', which is defined as an 'expert, teacher', into someone who exemplified the ancient Sanskrit meaning of the word—'one who is a dispeller of darkness'—for millions.

How does one dispel darkness? With light, of course.

Yet the *Autobiography* contained no yoga or meditation techniques, referring only cryptically to the practice of kriya yoga. Instead, it was a series of stories about Yogananda's life and the lives of the spiritual masters, sadhus and holy men he encountered or had heard of from his teachers. These stories were sometimes fantastical, sometimes humorous and almost always inspiring. Even three quarters of a century ago, when the *Autobiography* was first published, these stories were already thought to be of a land that barely existed or few had seen—the book had become a window into 'old India', a time and place full of wonders and miracles that was quickly fading with the rise of modernity.

The real impact of Yogananda's classic book, in both East and West, was an inspiration, perhaps the first and most important step to opening the door and glimpsing the light as a spiritual seeker. This impact has been visible in every generation since. In fact, Western interest in yoga deriving from the popularity of Yogananda's book can be clearly traced across the decades—starting in the 1940s and 1950s and through the cultural upheaval that occurred in the 1960s and 1970s, which caused many Westerners to turn towards Eastern traditions (then known as the 'counterculture movement'). Although Yogananda wasn't alive during this latter period, his book was one of the most popular among young counterculturalists, becoming a doorway to Eastern wisdom for an unbelievably large number of Westerners, a passport to a strange new way of looking at the world, which, as we know, wasn't new at all, but a new spin on incredibly ancient teachings.

This passport in the form of a paperback book was a frequent gift, freely passed on from one person to the next. It was as if a flame had been lit in each reader, who felt compelled, in turn, to light the next candle by giving away copies of the book to friends and acquaintances who might find in it the inspiration to get on the path to self-discovery and God. It is important to note that, according to Yogananda, 'God' was not some external entity; God was self-realization, something that happened inside us as we lifted the veil between the material and the spiritual worlds.

Yogananda's emergence in the West and the publication of the book were collectively one on a string of great Indian twentieth-century exports that passed along embers of the ancient flame of yoga and consciousness. And those who received the embers passed them along, again and again. George Harrison, the guitarist of the Beatles, was known to be a big proponent of the book after it was given to him by Indian musician Ravi Shankar in 1966. Ravi Shankar said that it was George's introduction to Eastern mysticism. Harrison, in turn, passed on his new favourite book to his bandmates and to many others in the artistic world, including fellow musician Gary Wright, singer of the well-known song 'Dreamweaver'. Harrison kept a stack of copies of the *Autobiography*, ready to give them away to anyone he thought needed 're-grooving', to use the language of the 1970s. Today, the book has found its way back to Yogananda's homeland and has gained a special status all its own.

To paraphrase the words of Buddha—a single candle can light a thousand others without itself being diminished.

Is the *Autobiography* Still Relevant?

The impact of the *Autobiography* wasn't limited to musicians or spiritual seekers. Steve Jobs, co-founder, chairman and CEO of Apple Inc., which became the world's most valuable company, was a big fan and went so far as to say it was one of his favourite books. Jobs first read it as a teenager and claimed to have re-read it every year since then. Walter Isaacson, author of a well-known biography called *Steve Jobs*, tells a story from March 2011, the day after a launch event for the iPad 2, when Jobs showed him his iPad. According to Isaacson, the only book downloaded on it at the time was *Autobiography of a Yogi*.[1] Later that year, according to Marc Benioff, co-founder of SalesForce.com,[2] at the reception following Jobs's memorial service held at Stanford, Benioff received a small brown box, which, he later found out, contained a copy of *Autobiography of a Yogi*. This story (which the Jobs family hasn't commented on publicly or confirmed because this was a private affair), if true, would be yet another example of a prominent individual passing on the *Autobiography* to others.

But as inspirational as the *Autobiography* is (it was named one of the top 100 spiritual books of the twentieth century by a panel of theologians and luminaries convened by HarperSanFrancisco in 1999), it isn't unreasonable to ask if this 500-page book containing Yogananda's teachings and stories, which can seem antiquated in today's hi-tech world of short attention spans, is still relevant.

Yogananda's stories of India's saints are charming, eye-opening and, even awe-inspiring, but, to a modern reader, the India that he describes may seem to have long since faded into the past. Thus, these stories may be a little difficult for us to relate to. It is reasonable to ask if new generations, raised on television and video games, smartphones and social media, and instant streaming and communication across the globe, might derive inspiration differently.

In Yogananda's day, the way to achieve spiritual enlightenment was to find a guru and to pledge oneself to his lineage (normally, the adept was male, with a few well-known exceptions). Today, the idea of committing oneself fully to a single guru or lineage may seem a little out of date. We can get on YouTube and watch well-known gurus discuss miracle healing, provide modern commentaries on the *Yoga Sutras of Patanjali* and demonstrate pranayama exercises, maybe even the hidden kriya yoga techniques that Yogananda only taught to the 'initiated'.

For one thing, a modern seeker today is likely to encounter many different teachers through the course of their career and learn something from each of them. This was definitely true for me as I journeyed through my career as a computer programmer, a tech entrepreneur and an investor.

In short, the big question this book begins with is: is Yogananda's book (and its stories and underlying lessons) relevant to modern seekers today?

Lessons for the Modern World: The Wisdom of the Yogi

I wrote this book to say, emphatically, that Yogananda's book, his stories and lessons, are as relevant today as they were in the previous century. I wanted to write about some of the stories that inspired me to demonstrate that the lessons are timeless. Even for someone like me, raised and well-versed in the use of modern technology, the *Autobiography* continues to be a reminder—to bring Yogananda's eternal spiritual wisdom into the modern world, every single day.

Being successful in the world and pursuing a yogic path of self-discovery is not easy. In fact, today yoga seems to have been compressed—at least in the West—into only the physical asanas, which represent only one of the eight limbs of yoga as defined by Patanjali. Yogananda, whose spiritual name literally translates to 'bliss of yoga', recognized this. His book, despite being the first introduction to yoga for many westerners who now practise yoga poses, wasn't really about asanas at all. It was about the ancient meaning of yoga, of union with the self and with the Divine. Yogananda, unlike some modern writers, wasn't afraid to use the word 'god'.

The Universal Search

One of the first things that stands out when it comes to the teachings of Yogananda is that he emphasized the universality of yoga; it was, Yogananda asserts, a path that allowed one to seek God no matter what one's religion or lineage. This had been emphasized by his guru, Sri Yukteswar, who had been recruited by his teacher's guru (Babaji) to write a book about the unity of the Vedic scriptures and the Bible.

This influence wasn't lost on Yogananda, who saw what he called the pursuit of realizing God not as the domain of any particular group or religion and often quoted from the Bible and other scriptural sources to make his points more accessible to his audience.

Though Yogananda was ostensibly concerned about recruiting students via his organizations (the Self-Realization Fellowship in the US and Yogoda Satsanga Society in India) into his lineage (which, according to Yogananda, originated with the enigmatic figure referred to as the Mahavatar Babaji, about whom we will speak later in the book), the broader effect of the *Autobiography* has been to encourage spiritual seekers of all creeds and nationalities to set off on their own paths of self-discovery and, once on the path, to light the flame in others.

And this is what makes the book unique—it goes beyond any one organization, spreading the light of meditation and yoga as an equal opportunity flame. Steve Jobs studied and practised zen meditation, not exactly the same practice as Yogananda's kriya yoga. The Beatles studied with Maharishi Mahesh Yogi, founder of the Transcendental Meditation (TM) movement, before a very public falling out with him. Speaking of famous musicians, Elvis Presley received a copy of the *Autobiography* from his hairdresser and friend as an introduction to the yogic path. His copy of the *Autobiography* was rumoured to be present in his room when he died.

It almost doesn't matter which lineage, guru or religion you belong to—the reason the *Autobiography* has persisted and continued to influence people is that it has the ability to light the fire of self-discovery, to inspire would-be seekers to get on the path to self-realization and to remind those who have strayed from the path, in the face of a world that unceasingly diverts our attention to other pursuits, to return to meditation and yoga as paths to god realization.

My Own Strange Encounters

The universality of Yogananda's book is borne out in my own story, although at first glance I would seem like a strange choice for the task of writing about the *Autobiography* and the lessons contained in it. For one thing, I am not a renunciate who has forsaken the world for spiritual growth, nor do I claim to possess a title like 'swami'. Rather, I have lived in the world as a businessman and author, and have considered the challenges that I have come across in the material world as part of my personal spiritual path. Throughout my career, first as a computer programmer, then as an entrepreneur and creator of video games and finally as an investor and author, I have found others turning to me for advice related to material success much more than spiritual pursuits.

On the other hand, though I was born outside of Lahore, where, coincidentally, Yogananda's family spent a few years early in his life (and where an important incident involving a magical amulet took place, which will be related later in this book), I spent most of my life ensconced in the West. My Muslim parents weren't exactly thrilled to see me studying 'Hindu' teachings like those in the *Autobiography*. Later, in a trajectory similar to Yogananda's own, I took up residence in Boston after going to MIT to study computer science, then drove across the continent to attend graduate school (studying management at Stanford University) and settle in sunny California, in the region that has become known as Silicon Valley to the world.

I am not ashamed to admit that in the early days of my spiritual search, I was (I'm guessing, like many of you) simply looking for ways to increase my capacity for success in the material world. I turned to meditation and yoga for help— less stress and better concentration would lead to writing better computer programs, I reasoned; greater equanimity would help me deal with chaotic business situations and better visualization abilities would help me manifest the worldly success I so desired. Like many others, I turned to meditation and yoga without regard for their underlying spiritual content. This is common even today—tens of millions turn to hatha yoga primarily for its physical benefits and to meditation and mindfulness because of its stress-reducing effects.

Illustrating how the flame of Yogananda's wisdom went from the East to the West and then spread back to the East again, it was, oddly enough, a Caucasian Buddhist meditation teacher with an adopted Indian spiritual name who first recommended that I read *Autobiography of a Yogi* as part of my quest to integrate my spiritual search with the search for career success as a tech entrepreneur. I wrote about some of these experiences, which took place in the 1990s, in my first book, *Zen Entrepreneurship*, and have written more about them in its sequel (forthcoming).

Like millions of others, I was affected by the *Autobiography*. This was partly because of its authenticity (W.Y. Evans-Wentz, the Oxford professor who translated much Tibetan work into English, wrote in the foreword to the *Autobiography* that this was one of the 'few books in English about the wise men of India which have been written, not by a journalist or foreigner, but by one of their own ... in short, a book about yogis by a yogi'), but mostly because of its ability to inspire through memorable stories, each of which contained multiple spiritual lessons. Some of these lessons are only grasped through re-reading the story many times.

As one embarks on the journey of self-discovery, no matter what one's initial motives are, one cannot escape the underlying truth once the flame is lit. Even a worldly materialist like myself realized that I had it backwards. Meditation and yoga weren't there just to help me with samsara (the trials and tribulations of the world). Rather, the waves of samsara were there to help me with my own path of self-discovery and meditation. Over the years, whenever I found myself straying from the spiritual path, I have found myself drawn, like Steve Jobs was every year, back to Yogananda's classic, and each time I learn new details and gain a better insight into depths that eluded me in the past.

Magic and Miracles in the *Autobiography*

The *Autobiography* is chock-full of stories about the miracles and magic of saints and sadhus in the Himalayas and all over India. These are, perhaps, for a first read, some of the most memorable stories in the book—they certainly were for me!

In Yogananda's recollections of India at the beginning of the twentieth century, magical deeds seem as much the rule as the exception: saints appear in multiple places at once, materializing as physical bodies that can be seen and talked to by their compatriots; mind reading by swamis is constant; advanced yogis and those with access to spiritual entities (like jinn) make objects appear and disappear at will. Even more surprisingly, miraculous beings, like the seemingly immortal Mahavatar Babaji and his disciple, the Christ-like nineteenth-century guru of Benares, Lahiri Mahasaya, can supposedly send messages (and teleport their own bodies) to any part of the physical world in an instant. There are levitating saints, perfumed saints, and much more. On top of everything else, the Divine Mother appears to Yogananda often during his childhood, seemingly granting his every wish!

What are we to make of these stories in the twenty-first century?

The more religious-minded would take them as gospel, while the more scientific-minded among us might scoff at them and dismiss them as evidence that Yogananda was, at best, exaggerating and, at worst, making the stories up. Yet, when telling these stories, Yogananda is careful to point out the provenance—some were witnessed directly by him and some were witnessed by people whom he knew and implicitly trusted, such as Sri Yukteswar. Some of the stories were of public figures who were widely known and written about at the time.

We must remember that Yogananda, born in 1893, and his book serve in a way as a bridge between the stories of 'old India' and the modern world, which didn't arrive until well into the twentieth century (and in some parts of the subcontinent, is still in the process of arriving). When I was born, in a small village in Punjab almost three quarters of the way through the century, we still didn't have running water or electricity (though that has now changed).

These stories are meant to hook us, to light the flame of self-discovery. The modern mind, like the ancient mind, still needs stories like these to inspire, to evoke awe and wonder, to take us out of our day-to-day concerns.

In the modern world, our engineers and scientists are so convinced that we have the physical world mostly figured out that it takes something truly unusual to shake us out of that world view, to realize that there may be more at work in the universe than that which we can directly perceive with our senses or our scientific instruments. In short, not only did these colourful stories of swamis and their superpowers stand out in my memory, they kept me interested in coming back for more. Only in subsequent readings would the more spiritual meanings and lessons embedded in these stories become clear.

During his decades of travelling and speaking all over the US, Yogananda wasn't above using a hook to get sceptical Westerners to attend his talks. The titles of his talks make this clear, ranging from 'Power of Mind and Manifestation' to 'Science of Religion'. On the one hand, I believe Yogananda thought of these stories as ways to get people to take the initial sips of self-realization and to open their minds to the possibility that there is more than the physical world around us. On the other hand, these stories reinforce the timeless message that the physical world around us is maya, an illusion, a dream-world—and that we all take what happens in the physical world too seriously. Yogananda himself explains how these miraculous phenomena work in the book, combining ancient Indian teachings with the modern scientific concepts and technologies percolating at the time.

For a modern technologist like me, the idea that we live in an illusory world was one that I only fully embraced after considering the virtual worlds that we are now creating in cyberspace. If our lives are like movies (which Yogananda suggests), then they are movies that we can affect—the choices we make can change our script. I believe if Yogananda were alive today, he would use updated terms, saying that we are in an 'interactive movie', or, if he were really attuned to the young people and technology of today (as he was in his time), that we are inside a multiplayer video game!

I came to this analogy myself when writing my book, *The Simulation Hypothesis*, to show that the metaphor of a video game, complete with challenges and quests, was a better way to explain to modern audiences the ancient Indian concept of the lila or the grand 'play' of life. We will discuss this further in several chapters in this book.

The Purpose of this Book

In this book, then, my purpose is to highlight some of the lessons in the *Autobiography* by delving into some of the spiritual, amusing and fantastical stories that have captivated audiences for the better part of a century. I also want to relate these stories and lessons to our experience in the modern world.

More specifically, I want to demonstrate that these lessons are as important today as they were when Yogananda was a child growing up in Calcutta or when he roamed American cities in the first half of the last century. I will attempt to do this by describing how the lessons manifested themselves in my own life and how, sometimes, I had to come back to them again and again before they did. Along with stories from my own life, I have included some anecdotes from others who say that the *Autobiography* had an impact on them (usually that of getting them onto, off or back on to, the spiritual path).

I hope that the stories I recount in this book will help you to light (or re-light) the flame of self-realization. Like the famous Swami, my goal in this book is not to discuss specific meditation or pranayama techniques, but to provide Yogananda's colourful stories with a modern interpretation and spin. In doing so, I will highlight several aspects of Yogananda's life that may have been only briefly touched on in or completely left out of the *Autobiography*.

Whether you have never read Yogananda's book, read it once and put it aside, or, like many, have read it over and over, I hope this book will help you to go deeper in your own personal search. Finding your own path, lighting your inner candle, is the only real way to dispel the darkness.

You can read this book straight through, though it may perhaps be more effective to read the lessons, which are organized into parts, one or two at a time. That gives you time, if you are so inclined, to check out (or go back to) the corresponding stories in the *Autobiography*. For those that have never read the *Autobiography*, the stories that I reference are summarized, so you can digest the lessons easily; I hope these summaries will inspire you to read Yogananda's book for the first time.

The East and the West

Rudyard Kipling's famous quote, 'East is East, and West is West, and never the twain shall meet', is relevant today for not being relevant at all. We are as likely to find materialists looking for worldly gain in the streets of Mumbai or Shanghai as in New York or Los Angeles. Philip Goldberg, who wrote a biography of Yogananda, points out that Yogananda was one of those who bridged this gap, calling him the 'first modern guru'. Today, those in the East and the West find ourselves in a connected, materialistic, digital world, and it turns out we are all in need of Yogananda's inspiration and lessons more than ever.

I hope this book will inspire you to pursue that inspiration and apply those lessons even in the midst of the mechanized, computerized world that we live in today.

PART I

Finding Your Path

LESSON #1

You Don't Need to Go to the Himalayas

I felt powerfully drawn to the Himalayas ... I listened eagerly to his tales about the high mountain abode of yogis and swamis.

— YOGANANDA[1]

Mountains cannot be your guru ... As soon as the devotee is willing to go even to the ends of the earth for spiritual enlightenment, his guru appears nearby.

— RAM GOPAL MUZUMDAR, the Sleepless Saint [2]

When I was younger, I had (at least) two noteworthy but fanciful dreams, both of which were based on youthful notions of how the universe works. One was very spiritual and the other was very materialistic. On the one hand, I dreamt that I would start a software company and make millions of dollars, rising above my middle-class upbringing and becoming a success story in the conventional sense. The other dream was of someday escaping to the Himalayas and finding a master who could show me the mysteries of the spiritual universe, thereby allowing me to leave the cares of this materialistic world behind.

Though both were, in their own ways, noble goals, they were both predicated on the idea that someone or something 'out there' would satisfy me and bring an end to my cravings; in this case, cravings for both material and spiritual success. Both were based on the delusion that we have to 'chase' our destiny and that it won't find us wherever we happen to be.

In *Autobiography of a Yogi*, we find that Yogananda (referred to by his given name, Mukunda) also had boyhood dreams of escaping to the Himalayas. In fact, you might say that, at a very young age, he became *obsessed* with the thought of running away from home and going to the revered mountains to live in spiritual isolation with the masters.

Yet his destiny took him on a different road. While he did become a renunciate and a monk, Yogananda's adult life was spent in the world rather than running away from it. It is a strange fact that we often get glimpses of our future life when we are young; the trick is to use the essence of those visions, not their literal content, to guide us.

In the *Autobiography* there are many different stories of Mukunda trying to flee his home for the Himalayas; each is a colourful adventure occurring at a different age, first as a precocious young boy, then as an ambitious teenager and later as a monk-in-training. In each story, Mukunda nurtures an idealized image of living among the magical, almost mythical, swamis who reside in the caves of the Himalayas.

In these stories, one can sense the deep spiritual longing felt by the young man, by all accounts already a spiritual prodigy.

It was a call to escape ordinary life and to fulfil his karma as a yogi. But we also see the folly of trying to rush into finding one's destined path by 'running away' prematurely from one's life and obligations. In fact, Yogananda eventually finds his guru not in the exalted, rarefied air of the mystical peaks, but much closer to his home.

While he spent much of his youth dreaming of running away (with each attempt thwarted by his family), his spiritual education nevertheless proceeded apace thanks to the plethora of gurus and saints that were in the city where he spent much of his childhood—Calcutta. Even as an adult, Yogananda ended up spending very little time in the Himalayas; his destiny was to take him elsewhere—to the West.

Let's look at these stories, which appear at the beginning of the *Autobiography* and see if they contain any valuable lessons for seekers today.

An Early Attempt and Glimpses of the Future

Mukunda had a particularly powerful spiritual vision when he was just eight years old. In this vision, he saw yogis seated in meditative postures in a cave, the space beyond them illuminated by a great light.

'Who are you?' I spoke aloud.
'We are the Himalayan yogis.' The celestial response is difficult to describe; my heart was thrilled.[3]

The 'wonderful glow' (as Yogananda describes it) behind the yogis was the Divine, a manifestation of the Light, he is told.

From that point onwards, Mukunda had a strong urge to flee to the Himalayas, to be a wandering ascetic and to meditate in caves. This was a powerful longing, what I call a 'Big Clue' about the future, an idea we will talk more about in 'Lesson #10: Getting Help and Following the Clues'. In some ways, the vision was emblematic of his future life as a monk of the swami order, but it was wrong in its specifics even while its essence rang true.

Before we get to the story of how he found his guru, Sri Yukteswar, let's briefly summarize some of Mukunda's thwarted attempts to run away to the Himalayas. The first instance: they were living in Bareilly and a young Mukunda was plotting with his landlord's son, Dwarka Prasad, to run away to the mountains. These early attempts were easily thwarted by his older brother, Ananta, who jumped with considerable gusto into his role as enforcer of their father's wish, namely that Mukunda was not to leave home, forsaking his education and family, until he was ready.

When his young friend Dwarka told Ananta about Mukunda's not-so-secret plan to run away, Ananta asked his brother, almost derisively, 'Where is your orange robe? You can't be a swami without that!'

Although this early plan to run away was unsuccessful, Ananta's question made an impression on Mukunda. It created a clear image in his mind that stayed with him for the rest of his life, suggesting that even thwarted attempts to rush towards our destiny can bring unexpected benefits. Decades later, in the *Autobiography*, Yogananda wrote:

> But I was inexplicably thrilled by his words. They brought me a clear picture: that of myself as a monk, roaming about India. Perhaps they awakened memories of a past

life; in any case, I realized with what natural ease I would wear the garb of the anciently founded monastic order.[4]

When we are young, we often cultivate images of ourselves as adults that aren't quite right in the finer details, but we often get the 'big picture' right. Somehow these glimpses not only get us excited, they 'feel right'. This means that there is probably something for us in these visions.

These glimpses are clues, or guideposts, but we have to be careful not to take them too literally. In Yogananda's case, he did, in fact, become a wandering monk eventually. Only he was wandering around America for most of his adult life, and not India—something he certainly did not foresee in those early years!

Yogananda was no doubt correct about having been a monk in his previous life, wandering around India. In that sense, it could have been an image of a 'past life', or an image of a 'possible future'. It could also have been just the fanciful imaginings of an adolescent mind obsessed with the spiritual search.

I would suggest that it doesn't really matter; what matters is that this glimpse was a clue. Following that clue took Mukunda down his future path in life to become Swami Yogananda. We'll talk more about paths in life, which relates closely to our karma, and how they are often determined by 'tasks' that are placed in front of us, in 'Lesson #2: Sometimes, the Universe Unexpectedly Gives You an Important Task'. Sometimes, they are more than glimpses—we are literally given tasks to perform, whether we think we are qualified to do them or not.

Speaking of glimpses, in my own case, I saw myself as a scientist when I was in grade school, and this image somehow always 'felt right' but not exact. As I went through middle school and high school, this image transformed into that of a computer engineer and programmer. When I worked on the TRS-80 that our math teacher kept in his lab behind our classroom, it was obvious that I had a natural talent for it. Our teacher even let my best friend and I skip math lessons so we could experiment with programming by modifying a text adventure game that was popular in those days.

While that image of the future started in a general manner and became more accurate over time, there was no doubt that even as a teenager I had a sense of my forthcoming path. If you had asked me in high school or when I first arrived at MIT to study computer science what kind of career I would have, I would have told you that I would be a 'computer entrepreneur' first, and after becoming successful at it, I would become a writer.

Those early impressions proved to be generally prescient, even if the details and timing were off. But how could I possibly have known this? It just 'felt right', as if it was pre-ordained, a script that had been placed in front of me. I still had to do the work to make the image a reality—I still had to get my computer science degree and write my books, for example, before I could be either an entrepreneur or a published author.

As with Yogananda's glimpse, the big picture was right, but not necessarily in the details. For example, the timing was all off. I thought that I would be an entrepreneur in my twenties and then, at the ripe old age of twenty-eight, shift to becoming a writer. I did in fact, start writing my first book, *Zen Entrepreneurship*, at the age of twenty-eight (while taking time off after my first start-up failed), but it would take another twenty years of working as an entrepreneur and investor in the software and video game industries before I primarily shifted to being an author, and it would take a personal tragedy to finally get me there, but more on that later.

Second Attempt and the Mysterious Amulet

Now, back to Mukunda's next attempt to flee his home and fulfil his vision of becoming a holy man. Young Mukunda was deeply affected by the death of his mother when he was eleven years old, and the family was still living in Bareilly. His mother was in Calcutta attending to the wedding of his older brother Ananta. To say that this event was life-changing for the boy is no understatement.

A year after her death, Mukunda decided again to run away to the Himalayas. He was yet again intercepted by Ananta, who, to both pacify his restless younger brother and to fulfil the wishes of their late mother, gave Mukunda an object that their mother had entrusted to his care before her death accompanied by a strange story. This object, an amulet, that would turn out to play an important part in Mukunda's eventual discovery of his guru while he was still, in a way, trying to run away to the Himalayas. This is a prime example of how the miraculous is intertwined with the quotidian in Yogananda's autobiography, and it is hard to separate the two.

Now back to the story their mother told Ananta, which he related to Mukunda on this occasion: one morning when the family had been living in Lahore, a strange sadhu had appeared at their house, insisting to see the 'mother of Mukunda'. Mukunda was still an infant and too young to remember this incident. The sadhu had informed Mukunda's mother that she would be departing the earth soon due to illness, but that she would find a silver amulet materializing in her hands the day after his visit.

He had then instructed the mother to give the amulet to Ananta when she was ill and to instruct him to give it to Mukunda one year after her death. The aspiring monk would 'receive it about the time he is ready to renounce all worldly hopes and to start the vital search for God. When he has retained the amulet for some years, and it has served its purpose, it shall vanish. Even if kept in the most secret spot, it shall return whence it came.'[5]

The very next evening after the sadhu's visit, while Mukunda's mother was meditating, a silver amulet materialized in her hands, just as the holy man had foretold (Yogananda himself called it an 'astrally produced object'). Mukunda's mother had carefully guarded the amulet for several years before her final illness and then passed it on to Ananta at her deathbed, with instructions to give it to Mukunda one year after her death.

Ananta had, at first, been hesitant to give young Mukunda the amulet and to relay the strange story, because he was afraid it would simply 'inflame' the restless boy's desire to leave home and become a monk, a task for which Ananta and their father thought he was still much too young and unprepared.

Receiving the amulet seemed to satisfy Mukunda's immediate craving and to give him yet another glimpse of the future and perhaps of past lives, just as Ananta's earlier derision at his lack of an ochre robe had done. As Yogananda would write in the *Autobiography* many decades later: 'A blaze of illumination came over me with the possession of the amulet; many dormant memories awakened.'

A Colourful Interrupted Flight to the Himalayas

Before we continue the story of the amulet and how and when it vanished, we need to fast forward to Mukunda's next unsuccessful attempt to flee home for the call of the exalted peaks on his spiritual path; perhaps his most colourful attempt to run away yet.

Some years later, when Mukunda was in high school and living in Calcutta, he was meditating in the little attic that he had taken over as his personal ashram. Once again, the old desire to run off to the Himalayas surfaced. This time, being older, he schemed with a high school friend, Amar, and with his cousin, Jatinda Ghosh, and they made a secret plan to undertake the long train journey to the foothills of the great mountains.

The appointed morning arrived with what Yogananda later called 'inauspicious rain'; nevertheless, after tossing his pack of belongings from his attic room window down to the street, he snuck away with Amar to meet Jatinda at the local train station. In order to throw off the authorities (who would no doubt be notified by Mukunda's overly vigilant guardian Ananta as soon as they were discovered missing), they donned European clothes and took the train to Burdwan, from where they planned to board the train to Hardwar, located at the foothills of the glorious Himalayas.

But immediately things went wrong. Jatinda abandoned his two earnest companions in Burdwan, suddenly frightened by the stories of tigers wandering in the mountains that they had been discussing on the train ride. Mukunda somehow convinced Amar to keep going. Meanwhile, Ananta discovered their plot, telegraphed officials to 'intercept three Bengali boys running away from home in English clothes' and gave chase. He offered an ample reward to whoever detained the boys until his arrival.

The two boys managed to outwit a European train official who suspected them of being the runaways by claiming their names were Thomas and Thompson, insisting that there were only two of them so they couldn't be the three Bengali runaways indicated by Ananta's telegram. The official felt sorry for them and even got them upgraded to the European section of the train. They finally arrived near the mountains. Yogananda writes: 'The train bore us triumphantly into a dawn arrival at Hardwar. The majestic Himalayas loomed invitingly in the distance.'

From Hardwar, the duo bought tickets to go north to Rishikesh, where their Himalayan spiritual search would begin in earnest, but they were prematurely detained by an official who recognized them. The officer took them to a police station to await the arrival of Ananta, who was on his way and arrived the next day. Eventually, Mukunda agreed to go back to Calcutta with his older brother, though not before collecting several interesting stories involving sadhus and holy men.

The Two Sadhus

The following stories, which end the chapter titled 'My Interrupted Flight to the Himalayas' in the *Autobiography*, illustrate more than just a conclusion to yet another of Mukunda's attempts to run away. Rather, I think they reveal an important point about Yogananda and how his future is interwoven with his precocious encounters with holy men. It seemed to be Mukunda's karma to not just to collect stories everywhere he went as a boy (even when running away from home!) but also recollect them clearly decades later while writing the *Autobiography* in America.

The first is an almost unbelievable story narrated to the boys by the policemen holding them in Hardwar (we'll discuss in more depth the miraculous nature of some of these stories in 'Lesson

#7: The World Is Like a Movie, a Dream, a Video Game'). Once, the policeman, who had been in search of a criminal, incorrectly cornered a sadhu and in the altercation that followed, severed part of the sadhu's arm with his axe. Horrified when he realized his mistake, the police official prostrated himself at the feet of the sadhu, begging for forgiveness. To his surprise, the yogi picked up the arm and attached it to his body, telling told him not to worry, that it was an understandable mistake and that the arm would be completely healed in three days. According to the policeman, when he met the sadhu three days later, the arm bore 'no scar nor trace of hurt!'

In the second story, Ananta asked Mukunda on the trip home to stop in Benares to visit a scriptural authority (a meeting Ananta had pre-arranged) to convince Mukunda that his future lay not as a renunciate but as a man in the ordinary world. The so-called authority warned Mukunda that he would meet 'continual misfortune and be unable to find God' if he went off to become a monk and shirked his ordinary responsibilities.

Mukunda, shaken by the 'forceful prognostications' of this pundit, made a silent prayer to God, asking for a sign. Just then, another sadhu, who had been just outside the pundit's house and overheard the conversation, summoned him. The calm sadhu then told Mukunda not to 'listen to this ignoramus' and reassured him that his path was in fact that of a renunciate.

Here we see an important pattern that is at work in Yogananda's life and in the *Autobiography*, a pattern that holds a lesson for us all. We are often given advice, bad advice, from people who have their own agendas. Mukunda, a mischievous though spiritual boy, often found himself in sticky situations that he needed to get out of. A brief prayer asking for some kind of sign often resulted in the discovery of a way out, usually involving a spiritually attuned stranger. We'll talk more about this process of asking for help and for signs from the Divine in 'Lesson #10: Getting Help and Following the Clues'.

After this, perhaps his most elaborate attempt to run away yet, the teenager then promised his father that he would at least finish high school in Calcutta before trying to become a monk. As a reward, his father agreed to get him a Sanskrit tutor, who ended up being a fellow disciple of Lahiri Mahasaya. However, rather than diligently practising Sanskrit, Mukunda, as was his inclination, spent many hours asking this teacher stories about yogis and spiritual masters, getting what was perhaps a different kind of education than his father intended!

Leaving Home for the Ashram

After graduating from high school, Mukunda finally left home with a friend to join an ashram in the holy city of Benares (also known by its ancient name, Kashi). Though he was not in the Himalayas, Mukunda should have felt that he was finally fulfilling his lifelong dream: to become a monk and dedicating himself to the search for God rather than worldly concerns.

But it was not to be. For one thing, Mukunda was disappointed to find that the ashram required him to perform mostly organizational duties and little meditation. The other students even mocked him for retreating to meditate when he should have been taking a more active role in the ashram; and far from feeling that he had finally found his path, he became dissatisfied. Another disappointment to the young monk was the lack of regular meals, though it would turn out that even this uncomfortable aspect of the experience would serve the adult Yogananda in later years when he wandered in foreign lands. He found that he was able to go long periods without a meal if necessary.

It was around this time, amid his growing dissatisfaction with the ashram, that the tide turned. Mukunda had brought a 'sole treasure' with him from home—the mysterious silver amulet. He had kept it in a sealed envelope and checked on it every morning. One day, it suddenly vanished out of its sealed envelope. Mukunda prayed for clarity on the next steps in his path while meditating that day.

Ironically, a fellow disciple who had chided him for spending too much time meditating, summoned him to help in running an errand for the ashram in the city. It was while running this errand that, on an inconspicuous street in the Bengali section of Benares, the young monk felt drawn to a 'Christ-like man in an ochre robe' standing at the end of the street.

Mukunda initially convinced himself that this was just wishful thinking on his part and moved on, leaving the man standing at the end of the alley. But his conscience pulled at him, as it often does when we receive a clue but ignore it, and he went back to the alley, abandoning his errand. The man was still standing in the same pose. He now recognized the face of the man as one he had seen during his meditations many times. It was, in fact, Sri Yukteswar, who was destined to be his guru and show him the path to god-realization. Reciprocally, the holy man recognized him at once and, right there, promised to show him the path to God.

In a strange twist of fate, Yukteswar was in Benares visiting his family home, but his ashram was in Serampore, only twelve miles from Calcutta. Not only that, but Yukteswar had also been a disciple of Lahiri Mahasaya, just like Mukunda's father, making them brother disciples!

Yukteswar somehow seemed to be aware of the mysterious silver amulet that had disappeared and told Mukunda not to worry. The object had 'served its purpose' now that he had found his guru. Yukteswar invited him back to Serampore but suggested that he return and live with his family in Calcutta for some time.

This last suggestion irked Mukunda, since he had made such a show of leaving his family. It would only give Ananta, who had triumphantly predicted the young monk would come back home before long, satisfaction. Ananta's words still stung the young man: 'Let the young bird fly in the metaphysical skies. His wings will tire in the heavy atmosphere … we will yet see him swoop towards home.'

In fact, just as his father had counselled Mukunda to finish high school, his new master made him promise that he would finish college, which seemed like an almost insurmountable task for the restless monk who wanted to spend his days searching for God, not reading books.

Yukteswar told him that he had an inkling that the young monk would go to the West, where education was much respected, and the guru considered a college education and working knowledge of English would be essential to succeed in this mission.

One Last Attempt and the Sleepless Saint

You would think that, with finding his guru, the young Mukunda, now well on his way to becoming the monk Yogananda, would have abandoned the quest to flee to the mountains. Yet, even after a few years at his master's ashram, he continued to feel the old call to flee to the Himalayas, a 'growing impatience with hermitage duties and college studies.'

Mukunda asked his guru for permission to go to the Himalayas, where he hoped 'unbroken solitude' would allow him to achieve continuous divine communion.

Sri Yukteswar admonished him: 'Many hillmen live in the Himalayas but have no god-perception.' He went on to explain to the young monk, 'Wisdom is better sought from a man of realization than an inert mountain.'

But Yukteswar did not forbid him from going, which Mukunda took as permission, hoping to meditate in silence amongst the majestic peaks. This resulted in perhaps his last official attempt to run away to the Himalayas.

Mukunda had tracked down the whereabouts of another disciple of Lahiri Mahasaya, Ram Gopal, who was called the 'sleepless saint' because he was 'always in an ecstatic consciousness.'[6] The sleepless saint, according to Mukunda's Sanskrit teacher, was now living in a small village called Ranbajpur, near Tarakeswar.

Tarakeswar was the site of a temple where numerous healings had miraculously occurred, including one that had happened to Yogananda's aunt,[7] which he recounts in the *Autobiography*. The site, Yogananda reminds us, is akin to Lourdes, a small village at the foothills of the Pyrenees in France, which had become a holy pilgrimage site for Catholics.

In arriving at the temple in Tarakeswar, which consisted only of a single round stone altar, symbolizing infinity, the young monk didn't stop at the temple to pray or even bow to the Divine. Mukunda, as revealed in the *Autobiography* (see 'Lesson #9: Go Out of Your Way for Little and Big Pilgrimages'), normally recognized the Divine in all temples and took time to stop and pray in temples big and small. He was eager to find Ram Gopal and so skipped this important rite.

After a series of mishaps, including a night spent in a local peasant's hut, the next day he ran into a man who was 'physically unimpressive except for dark piercing eyes'. The man came right up to him and told him that he had decided to wait for the young monk because his purpose was good; otherwise, he would have left Ranbajpur and Mukunda would never have found him. It was, in fact, the same Ram Gopal he had been seeking. The adept miraculously seemed to know all about Mukunda's trek to visit him, including the fact that he had not bowed at the temple in Tarakeswar.

His first question for the young monk was: 'Where do you think God is?' When Mukunda answered that God was 'within me and everywhere', Ram Gopal asked him why he hadn't taken the time to bow before the symbol of the infinite at the temple in Tarakeswar. He then informed Mukunda that it was this show of pride that was the source of his inability to find Ram Gopal for a whole day.

This is the first (though perhaps not the most important) lesson that Ram Gopal has for Mukunda: sometimes, when we are in a hurry, we let our pride and arrogance cause us to skip steps, and this make our journey longer than it needs to be. Approaching the Divine with a sense of humility is as important as not skipping steps in order to 'go quickly'.

To use a more modern example, in *Star Wars: The Empire Strikes Back*, Master Yoda tells the young apprentice, Luke Skywalker, 'Action. Adventure. A Jedi craves not these things,' and admonishes him for not paying attention to where he was and what he was doing. In the modern world, we want results, and we want them as quickly as possible. The idea of meditating and praying at a temple for days on end for a result seems antiquated.

Ram Gopal correctly surmised that in taking this trip, Mukunda was running away from his master to look for a shorter, perhaps simpler, path to enlightenment than the one fate had in store for him. Mukunda had heard that Ram Gopal has spent many years meditating in caves in the exalted mountains, and that was how he had become the sleepless saint, and still had the nagging suspicion that this might be an easier, simpler path for him. Ram Gopal then instructed the young monk, using the words that I quoted at the beginning of this chapter:

> The Himalayas in India and Tibet have no monopoly on saints. What one does not trouble to find within will not be discovered by transporting the body hither and yon ... As soon as the devotee is willing to go even to the ends of the earth for spiritual enlightenment, his guru appears nearby.

Ram Gopal then asked Yogananda if he had a small room where he could shut the door and meditate, to which the answer was yes, since he had such a room in his attic in Calcutta (and later in Yukteswar's ashram in Serampore).

'Let this be your cave,' the sleepless saint told the young seeker. 'That is your sacred mountain. This is where you will find the kingdom of God.'

Yogananda tells us, decades later, that these 'simple words instantaneously banished my lifelong obsession with the Himalayas. In a burning paddy field, I awoke from the dream of mountains and eternal snows.'

Does This Lesson Still Apply Today?

Although this exchange occurred over a hundred years ago, I believe this is good advice that still applies to our lives today. Like I did when I was younger, like Yogananda did in his youth, we might fantasize that we need to go to the ends of the Earth to find enlightenment, or to a cold Himalayan cave to find a master. But it is best to start with where we are, and to find what might not be so far away from us. In a sense, we can look at what clues the universe is already giving us, today, right where we are.

Does this mean we don't need to travel? Not at all. Yogananda was perhaps one of the most well-travelled monks of his generation. What it does mean is that we shouldn't skip steps, that would fulfil our obligations and responsibilities in the world even while we tend to our spiritual ideals and goals. We should look for enlightenment both at home and also abroad.

In my own case, I ended up learning meditation from a white guy with curly blonde hair in Boston, a story that I fictionalized in my book, *Zen Entrepreneurship.* At that point in my life, when I had just graduated from MIT and was considering starting my very first software company, I needed mentors in the realms of both business and spirituality, two avenues that would strangely intertwine themselves in my life for many years. The teacher that I needed and was ready to listen to, was someone who showed some wisdom and experience in both of these areas—but there were few teachers like that. His stated intention was to combine spirituality with business—to use the arena of the modern world as a way to deal with our karma and to advance on the spiritual path.

Moreover, when I had quit my job while travelling in Europe to come back to Cambridge, Massachusetts, to work for a small start-up spun out of the MIT Media Lab, one of this teacher's disciples turned up teaching basic meditation just next door to the start-up's office! This disciple introduced me to his teacher, who was within driving distance of Boston, without requiring a long journey to the Himalayas or even to California, which might be thought of as a spiritual cauldron in America.

While I have had many teachers since then, he remained perhaps the most influential on my own unique spiritual path and it all started by paying attention to what was nearby—right next door to our office, less than a mile away from MIT.

This teacher also assigned me the 'homework' of reading *Autobiography of a Yogi*. While I had picked up the book and browsed its pages in bookstores, it had never really called out to me and I had never purchased a copy or read it. I needed someone to describe its overall message in a way that I could relate to in order to be receptive to its manifold spiritual messages.

Finding Yogananda's Book as a Passport

Unsurprisingly, modern stories of people finding their spiritual path through Yogananda's book, which serves as a passport to the spiritual worlds for so many, are not that uncommon. These stories don't need to have the drama of Mukunda's flight to the Himalayas, with his older brother giving chase across cities and railway lines. In fact, the US is filled with stories of modern seekers going to India, only to find their path bringing them back to a spiritual practice or teacher in the US.

Steve Jobs famously went to India when he was nineteen to 'look for spiritual enlightenment'. When he arrived, he found, in the room where he was staying, a copy of *Autobiography of a Yogi*. While he had come across the book before, it was from this point that he started reading it every year up until his death. Finding the copy of the *Autobiography* served both as a spiritual passport and also perhaps as an indication that his path was not that of a renunciant in the Himalayas, but one that would take him back to the US and have him try to integrate his spirituality with his life and work.

Steve Jobs's tale is by no means unique. While writing this book, I interviewed a Hollywood producer named Peter, who went all the way to Rishikesh looking for a spiritual path; it was there that he first bought a copy of the *Autobiography*. He recognized the image of Yogananda on the cover as an image he had seen in a Los Angeles newspaper when he had been a paper delivery boy many years earlier. He eventually found a Self-Realization Fellowship center just blocks away from his home in Hollywood, and that became the path to his own spiritual growth! Peter told me, 'I didn't have to go half-way around the world to the Himalayas ... it had been here the whole time!'

The Lesson

What can we learn from the young Mukunda's repeated attempts to run away to the Himalayas during his boyhood and as an impatient young man?

On the one hand, we often get visions and inklings of the path we are meant to take in life. I call these 'clues' on the 'treasure hunt' of life. We'll talk more about this idea of clues and guidance to lead us down our intended paths in life in 'Lesson #10: Getting Help and Following the Clues' and 'Lesson #11: Setbacks May Be a Part of Your Story'.

Even if we have a sense of our destiny and what we are meant to do, sometimes we have a desire to 'rush towards' it quickly (and prematurely) without being aware of (or willing to take) the small steps that will lay the foundation for our travels along this path.

Perhaps the most important lesson is that, sometimes, the thing we have been seeking might actually be somewhere near us, rather than off in some 'remote Himalayan cave'. This applies not just to the desire for a guru but to whatever path that we are meant to follow in our work and our life. While we might fantasize about going to faraway lands, it behooves us to start where we are.

For most of us, the path is not to be a monk or to go to an ashram, even if one might have an inkling (like Yogananda did) that one was a wandering monk in a previous life (or perhaps many lives). Most of us are going to live and work in the world but don't want to feel that we are neglecting our spiritual goals while we are doing so. We can find our spiritual path *while living and working in the world.*

In other words, to add some clarification to a well-known spiritual phrase: when the student is ready, the teacher will appear, wherever the student happens to be. *You don't need to go to the Himalayas!*

LESSON #2

Sometimes, the Universe Unexpectedly Gives You an Important Task

Intuition is soul guidance, appearing naturally in man during those instants where his mind is calm. Nearly everyone has had the experience of an inexplicably correct 'hunch' ...

—Yogananda[1]

... this task was appointed to you ... if you do not find a way, no one will.

—J.R.R. Tolkien[2]

This lesson may seem like one that's not explicitly mentioned in the *Autobiography*, but it is emblematic of Yogananda's entire life and mission: the task of bringing yoga and meditation to the West.

Today, Yogananda is one of the first names that come up when talking about Indian gurus who brought yogic philosophy to the West. Yet, back when he made the decision to come to America, he was a relatively unknown young swami, and there was no real indication that he would succeed so spectacularly in what might have seemed like an unassailable task.

In his book *American Veda*, which is about Indian gurus who brought yoga to America, Philip Goldberg called Yogananda the 'first modern guru'. This was partly because he emigrated and made America his home decades before the swelling interest in yoga that happened in the 1960s. Perhaps, just as importantly, Yogananda was willing to use modern methods (modern at least for the first half of the twentieth century!) to bring ancient teachings to the masses, teachings that were historically only passed on individually from guru to disciple.

It might surprise modern readers to know that some traditionalists scoffed at these moves, which included mass lectures on yoga to thousands as well as correspondence courses for those who didn't live near a guru (a group that included most of America at the time). And of course, in one of his final acts, by writing the *Autobiography* in English, he preserved many stories of Indian traditions and saints for future generations, becoming an inspiration to millions more who had never attended his lectures in person. This 'yoga for everyone' rather than 'yoga for the few' approach ruffled many traditionalists' feathers.

Yogananda's Big Assignment

But in 1920, what gave this young man who barely spoke English the impetus to believe that he could accomplish these things? Before 1920, only one major Indian guru had made an impact on the West and that was Swami Vivekananda, who arrived in the US in 1890, stayed only for a brief period and then returned to India.

In fact, you could say that Yogananda, who, although he had completed both high school (only at his father's behest) and a college degree (only at his guru's behest), was barely qualified for this task in his twenties. Moreover, as we saw in 'Lesson #1: You Don't Need to Go to the Himalayas', Yogananda's lifelong dream was to lose himself in meditation, preferably in a cave in the Himalayas, not to travel in automobiles and trains and boats across a country that valued modernization more than almost any other.

In 1917, Yogananda had established a school for boys in Ranchi (previously in Bihar, now the capital of Jharkhand) that provided education based on Vedic precepts. In Ranchi, like in Calcutta (where he only had a little room in the attic), he had only a small space, behind some dusty boxes in a storeroom, for meditation. This would be a pattern in Yogananda's life for many years—he would use whatever scrap of space he could find to meditate in—until he set up dedicated meditation ashrams in America. These small spaces, cloistered inside the din of the world, would be, as the Sleepless Saint had instructed, 'his cave, his sacred mountain'.

One day, when he was meditating in the storeroom, Yogananda had a vision in which he saw faces of people who looked like Westerners. Assuming, despite never having seen any, that they were the faces of Americans, he announced to his students that he was being 'called to go to the West'. And, sure enough, upon his return to Calcutta, he was asked to attend the International Congress of Religious Liberals in Boston as a delegate from India.

When he asked his guru, Sri Yukteswar, about whether he should undertake the long journey to the other side of the world, his master simply said, 'All doors are open for you. It is now or never.'

The young monk, still doubtful, replied, 'But master, what do I know about public speaking? Seldom have I given a lecture, and never in English.'

Yogananda's English wasn't exactly fluent, though he had learnt the language in school. Certainly a more experienced lecturer or older swami, or someone with more experience with English and/or foreign lands, would have been a better choice?

Yet, the task had clearly been assigned by destiny to Yogananda; it was his to accomplish, no matter how unqualified he felt.

The Lesson: Follow the Clues as They Come

How did the young monk know that this task had been assigned to him? Unlike most immigrants, who usually plan their emigration over many months or years, Yogananda had had his task dropped in his lap all of a sudden—'ready or not'! And you could argue that he wasn't ready—in addition to not being a fluent English speaker, he hadn't even applied for a visa and the religious conference was approaching quickly!

This is very typical of how the universe works in unexpected ways: it sends tasks our way whether we are ready for them or not. The compulsion to go in a new direction may come from an actual person, or it may emerge from a series of events that nudge us subtly (or perhaps push us not-so-subtly). In this case, there was a series of signs that made it clear to him that this was his task.

I call this process 'following the clues to find the treasure', which might seem like an insurmountable task. Just like in a good adventure film (like *Raiders of the Lost Ark*, for example), the hero or heroine doesn't have all the answers at once. It is important to be aware of the clues and then to follow them as they appear in your life.

In Yogananda's case, there were indications from his guru in the past, breadcrumbs and hints dropped by Yukteswar, that the young monk would be called to the West. In fact, part of the reason he insisted on Yogananda finishing at least an associate's college degree was that education was respected in the West. How did Yukteswar know? Supposedly, he was told by the enigmatic Babaji (we cover the story in more details in 'Lesson #14: Yoga Is For Everyone, East and West').

While we might be tempted to say that these were divine clues preceding Yogananda's task and made his eventual success inevitable, Yogananda still needed to make decisions at every step of the way. There may be breadcrumbs laid out for us to follow, but we still have to make the choice to go down a particular path.

The more direct clue came from the vision that Yogananda had while meditating, and this clue led to the next one: when he was subsequently invited to be present at the conference in Boston. Finally, when there were no seats or money available to make the trip, practical obstacles arose to his beginning the task, let alone succeeding at it. Yet, the obstacles melted away one by one, which is a different type of clue.

How do we know when a task is placed before us that it is our task *and* that it is the right time to follow through, even if we don't seem qualified? In my book *Treasure Hunt*, I lay out the rules of treasure hunting. The most important rules when following the clues are, in my opinion:

1. When a clue comes unexpectedly, it is important.
2. When a clue repeats itself, you should take it even more seriously.
3. When obstacles crop up but then melt away after you make a decision, then you know the time is right.

In fact, rule #1 may be the most important and may be the opposite of what today's self-help gurus recommend when they tell us to visualize a goal and work relentlessly towards it. When a task is presented to you without foreknowledge, that's when it might be a task that you were meant to accomplish, whether you feel ready or not; especially if you haven't put any previous thought or conscious effort to into it.

Unexpected visions are the strongest, clearest and most important clues, like the one Yogananda had while meditating. These can come to us when we are taking a walk or a shower; we might even see them in a dream.

The subject of intuition is a complex one, and sometimes we deceive ourselves into thinking that something we 'want' or 'desire' is actually an intuition. However, it is much easier to know that we possess 'true intuition' or have received a true 'clue' when the vision, intuition or invitation is completely unexpected, because we are less likely to get caught up in our conscious biases or societal expectations.

To receive these clues, we have to learn to clear our mind of our conscious biases and desires. This is why Yogananda (as well as Lahiri Mahasaya) and others emphasize that soul guidance can be accessed when one meditates and clears away the imperfections of the mind, the vrittis or mental whirlpools of energy that harden over time (which we will talk more about in 'Lesson #8: Practise Every Day, No Matter How Much Time You Have'). It is this calmness that lets us realize when an intuition is a genuine one from the Divine and not a mere expression of our delusions, desires or tendencies.

If you aren't sure whether your intuition is genuine based on the rule #1 (unexpectedness), then go to the rule #2: repetition. Wait for another clue. For Yogananda, this came in the form of the invitation to the conference, validating his internal vision with a concrete event from the physical world. This is the best kind of repetition when it comes in the form of something tangible that cannot be dismissed as 'mere subjective thinking'. A string of clues can be just as important as a single intuition, providing validation to the rational mind of the modern seeker.

Obstacles, Clues and Timing: A Trip to America

Another aspect to keep in mind about intuition and clues is that when the universe gives us a task, we may or may not think we are qualified for it. Moreover, there may be all kinds of obstacles that look like they will make the task insurmountable. This is doubly true when the clue requires us to make a big decision quickly—about moving somewhere, switching professions or committing to marriage, for instance.

Certainly, undertaking a month-long voyage to the other side of the world in 1920 was a big decision for Yogananda. Even his father feared that he would never see his son again. There seemed to be too many obstacles, given how quickly he had to make the decision: funding, the aforementioned problems with lecturing in English, getting a berth aboard *City of Sparta* (the very first ship to make the voyage from India to the US after World War I, known to Yogananda and others at the time as The Great War) and let's not forget, getting a visa and a passport in time!

When Yogananda found himself unsure of what to do or awaiting a sign of encouragement or direction, he would meditate and pray. This time was no exception. Not only did he receive confirmation in the form of a divine visitor (Babaji, a visit we will explore in more detail in 'Lesson #14: Yoga Is For Everyone, East and West') but, shortly thereafter, all the practical obstacles quickly melted away, in an almost miraculous fashion.

Yogananda's father, who at first refused to support the trip, had a change of heart and decided not only to provide the funding for the initial trip, but also to give his son enough money to stay in America for several years after the Congress. When Yogananda went to the ticket office to book a berth on the ship, he was told rather condescendingly that there were no free berths. This obstacle also disappeared, along with many others, and Yogananda found himself on his way to America.

When seemingly insurmountable obstacles start melting away, we should read it as a clue that the timing is fortuitous. To paraphrase Yukteswar, it is now or never.

Yogananda's relatively easily melting of obstacles reminds me of my own father's emigration to the US a number of decades later. While living in Lahore, my father had gotten, not just once, but twice, a visa for emigrating to America. Thinking that the universe had different plans, he decided that America was too far away and instead applied to get a PhD at The University of Paris, thinking that he could bring his wife and two very young children (my elder brother and I) along and work while attending classes. All flights had been cancelled from Lahore due to the 1971 war at the start of the school year, but he was able to get passage on the first flight out after the resumption of air services to go to Paris.

Unfortunately, the immigration policy in France, unbeknownst to him, wasn't as liberal as he expected, and he wasn't able to bring his young family to live there while he studied. The Pakistani ambassador to France, who had given my dad a part-time job at the Pakistani embassy (since it turned out he wasn't allowed to work otherwise in the country), told him that if he had gotten a visa to America, he should have gone there! This led to my father, surprising all of his colleagues (at both the embassy and at the university), walking into the US Embassy and getting a visa, yet again, to emigrate to the US. Fate, you might say, made the task much easier than it otherwise might have been!

Obstacles on the Path

However, just because fate opens a door for us, this doesn't mean that more obstacles won't crop up in our path. In Yogananda's case, multiple obstacles continued to stand in his way after he boarded the ship, including a rather hilarious first attempt at giving a talk in English while aboard (we'll discuss these in more detail in 'Lesson #10: Getting Help and Following the Clues').

Even after his initial, successful talk at the Congress in Boston, Yogananda was often jeered at on the street—a brown guy dressed in swami clothes with long hair wasn't a normal sight in 1920s America. Yet he kept going and by the time he arrived in Los Angeles several years later, he had become a well-known spiritual teacher, having given talks all across the country.

Even then the obstacles didn't stop! Some of Yogananda's biggest setbacks in the years ahead threatened to derail all the good he'd done in America and prompted him to consider returning to India, abandoning his life mission in the West. We'll talk more about these setbacks and how important they are in 'Lesson #11: Setbacks May Be A Part of Your Story'.

Sometimes we get a vision of a direction that we should go in and don't feel ready, or we feel ready but then insurmountable obstacles crop up. I call this the red light–green light syndrome. If you are truly listening to your intuition, then you will know that while the direction may be correct, it's possible the timing is off. This leads to the rule #4 of following the clues:

4. Sometimes clues indicate direction, sometimes they indicate timing. Pay attention to both.

A More Modern Example

The modern reader might think: these stories of Yogananda's big trip to the US are all well and good, but he was an ordained monk and seemed to have a direct line to the Divine. Does this lesson apply to the rest of us?

I am here to tell you unequivocally that the process of listening to our intuition, of finding and following the clues, is a universal one and is just as relevant today as it was 100 years ago. Sometimes, during this process, the universe drops a hint about a direction to go in, and if we follow that clue, we usually find a path or a task that is meant for us, whether we have foreseen it or not.

I'd like to present a couple of case studies from my own life. While the stories may not be as dramatic as Yogananda's, I believe the same process was at work in all of them: that sometimes the universe is giving us an invitation.

In 2007, after having lived in Boston for most of my career, I decided to move to Silicon Valley in California. One day, I was visiting and walking around (as many tourists do) the campus of Stanford University, one of the most beautiful campuses in country, when I suddenly had a vision of being a student there. It came unbidden; I was only there that day because I was looking for a nice place to walk. I had no concrete plans to get another degree (though I had thought about it in vague terms before). That certainly wasn't the reason I had moved to California—I had moved in order to be more involved in Silicon Valley start-ups as an entrepreneur, adviser and investor.

Note that in this first example, the clue wasn't very specific—I just saw myself there, attending classes. While I had thought about getting a master's degree, I had mostly given up on the idea by then as I was already much older than most graduate students (I was in my late thirties by then, whereas most master's students are in their twenties). This was a potential obstacle. Another was that I had been rejected by Stanford when I had applied there for my undergraduate degree while in high school almost two decades earlier. (While I was disappointed initially, it did not last long; I was thrilled to have gotten admission at MIT.)

Nonetheless, I decided that the clue was giving me a direction and that it was up to me to explore further and look for a more practical 'invitation'. When I got home, I did some research online and discovered that, in fact, there was a master's degree programme that fit me at Stanford's Graduate School of Business, one that was tailored for mid-career executives, thirty-somethings rather than twenty-somethings. This was an indication that the first clue (the vison that came unbidden) was real and not just a figment of my imagination. It was a confirmation, a validation, of the original clue.

I still wasn't entirely sure that the programme was right for me or that I was right for the programme, so I contacted the administrators. Since I had just recently moved to Silicon Valley, they invited me to meet them in person, and I found to my surprise during this meeting that they were extremely welcoming, reassuring me that if I applied I would most likely be admitted. It now felt like they were extending me a literal 'invitation'. From that point forward, *almost* everything went smoothly.

The only wrinkle that came up was that I got another invitation at the same time, to join a start-up that was doing well, as their CTO. If everything went well, going down this trajectory would of course make me extremely wealthy. I had to make a major decision—*should I join a start-up that could make me a lot of money or go back to school, which of course would cost money*? My intuition was telling me to go back to school, as I had focused on the business world for over a decade, but my conscious mind was, predictably, fixated on the money.

In the end, I chose to follow my intuition and go to Stanford to get my master's degree. I am glad I did. My time at Stanford helped me gather my bearings in Silicon Valley and fulfil my boyhood dream of going to school in California. As for the financial side, it all worked out nicely because while at Stanford I became an adviser and board member in a new start-up that produced even greater financial results. In fact, that second start-up was bought by the first one and the proceeds were more than enough to pay for my Stanford tuition!

Following the clues isn't just about logic or intuition—it's about combining both. In a sense, it's about following your heart, which is often the source of intuition and following your brain, which is about logical thinking. By following my intuition and validating the clues by looking for further clues, I was able to make what I think was the 'right' decision, in hindsight. You might say our intuition is giving us 'foresight' about the future.

Another Example: Returning to MIT

Sometimes, while we might start with a vague feeling of an invitation, there's an actual invitation waiting to be issued by someone unexpectedly.

Many years after my master's degree, I had become established in Silicon Valley and had just sold a video game company, but I wasn't sure what to do next. One day, while I was walking in a park, a little voice suggested to me that it would be nice to go back to Boston and do something at MIT, maybe even at the MIT Media Lab. It was as if the voice had come from a daydream. Once again, I had a vague sense of an invitation.

I looked around on various websites, including the MIT Media Lab website to see if there was a position or degree that I was interested in. Unlike with Stanford, where there was a degree programme that fit my needs perfectly, I found nothing specific at MIT that looked appealing.

Still, I had received the intuition, the clue, from the little voice that had told me I might want to go back to the MIT Media Lab, almost twenty-five years after completing my undergraduate research there. I decided to 'let the idea go', leaving its future up to the universe instead of pursuing it.

Miraculously, within a few weeks, an MIT professor whom I didn't know sent me an email and asked me to meet him when he was visiting California. He was in charge of the MIT Game Lab, which was physically located in the same MIT Media Lab building that I had done research in twenty-five years ago! I didn't know there even *was* a Game Lab, since it hadn't existed when I had studied at MIT. During our lunch meeting, the professor extended an actual invitation—to come and give a speech in one of their classes and perhaps to get more involved with the Game Lab. I told him about an idea I had been thinking about and we agreed to discuss it in the fall, when I was scheduled to address the class.

A few months later, I visited MIT, gave a short speech during a class and discussed my idea with them in more detail: to run a video game start-up accelerator on campus at the Game Lab during the summer. They were quite interested, but as usual, when we get a clue, it is often followed by many obstacles. Where would we get the funding? Since MIT is a non-profit institute, would it be really appropriate to invest in start-ups coming out of MIT and house them on campus?

Nevertheless, we got the whole thing set up within a few months, which was incredibly fast given the approvals that were needed. There were a number of raised eyebrows from other professors over how quickly the whole thing happened— but it was simply a case of 'the right place at the right time'. As a result of all this, I created and ran Play Labs @ MIT, an accelerator for video game start-ups, located in the Media Lab building where I had worked as an undergraduate.

There were, of course, many obstacles that I've neglected to mention. I had never run a start-up accelerator or a fund before and, to be honest, though I knew quite a bit about start-ups, I wasn't sure if I was fully qualified to run an accelerator. I needed funding quickly in order to make it happen. Eventually, these obstacles melted away and the programme was launched within a few months. The original vague intuition of 'returning to MIT, perhaps even to the MIT Media Lab' was fulfilled, starting with an actual invitation from the professor to work with them in some way.

And that's how you know that you are being assigned the 'right task at the right time', whether the invitation comes as an intuition, a vision or an actual person inviting you, as was the case with me in this particular instance.

An Unexpected Invitation

Sometimes, we plant a random seed that grows into a task completely unexpectedly.

In this day and age, invitations usually arrive in our email inboxes. I will tell you of one more task that the universe assigned to me that I felt unprepared for, but which was in fact related to my larger mission in life, and is related to your reading this book. This one occurred during the Covid-19 pandemic and reminded me of Yogananda's journey from India to America, though it didn't involve physical travel around the world (at least not yet).

As of 2020, I had written a book and some essays about meditation and career success and had written a series of articles in a few places about my affection for *Autobiography of a Yogi*. In fact, I had re-read the *Autobiography* while recovering from a medical procedure and decided to write some articles about Yogananda to pass the time. Most of my writing to date was about business or technology; my most popular book was *The Simulation Hypothesis*, which was about the idea that we live in a video game (a concept we'll talk more about in 'Lesson #7: The World is Like a Movie, a Dream, a Video Game').

In late 2020, seemingly out of the blue, I received an email from an editor at HarperCollins India, asking if I would be interested in writing a book about lessons that I learnt from *Autobiography of a Yogi* and how the book might relate to a new generation. It was one of those unusual and unexpected invitations, but one that came with a clear sense and feeling that I needed to act on it. While I had written several books before, I had never been asked by a publisher that I didn't know to write one for them, and certainly not one in India. The articles I had published about *Autobiography of a Yogi* were written on a whim; they were not part of any particular plan to write a book about Yogananda or his teachings.

Moreover, I could not say with any objectivity that I was the best person to write such a book. Books about Yogananda are usually written by devotees, renunciants/ monks, journalists or religious scholars. I was none of those things, though I was a big fan of Yogananda's book and it had had an impact on my life. Nor was I actively involved with any of his organizations in the US or India, except as a student of his teachings.

Despite these obstacles, I meditated on it and realized that it was a case of a task being 'assigned' to me. In a sense, it was pointing in the opposite direction of the much larger and more significant task that Yogananda was given, to bring his teachings from India to the US. The message had already travelled back around the world to India, and I was being called upon to add a little catalyst, for a new generation, to his message of combining the best of the East and the West. In fact, it was because I lived and worked in the modern world as a technologist and entrepreneur that the editor had felt I could provide a perspective that monks and spiritual teachers perhaps could not—an insight into how the lessons of the *Autobiography* are relevant to modern seekers in our daily lives.

You might be surprised to learn that I (briefly) considered not accepting the invitation, beset by doubts. But the more

I opened up my intuition on the matter, the more I realized it was my task to complete and, if you are reading this book now, it means I not only accepted the invitation but have also completed the task that was (rather unexpectedly) assigned to me!

So, keep this in mind when you find a task that has been set up for you, seemingly without your knowledge, by factors that seem beyond your control. The invitation is a clue that there is a treasure waiting for you.

PART II

Swami Lessons

LESSON #3

The Unexpected Lessons of the Tiger Swami

'Do you think, revered Swami, that I could ever fight tigers? ...'
'Yes ... But there are many kinds of tigers ...'
— YOGANANDA[1]

When I was writing this book, I conducted informal surveys with people who considered Yogananda's autobiography to have had a huge impact on their lives. My intention was to find out which specific stories stood out for them. For some reason, the story of the Tiger Swami was one that came up more often than I expected.

The tale of the Tiger Swami is part of a quick succession of three chapters that appear early in the *Autobiography*. Each chapter is about a different swami or saint: the Perfume Saint, the Tiger Swami and the Levitating Saint. I like to call these chapters the Swami Superpower Trilogy. Each is about an adept who had developed seemingly superhuman powers and each contains one or more lessons about life that go well beyond the superpowers themselves.

According to his various biographers, during his youth, Yogananda (then known as Mukunda) was by all accounts a 'spiritual prodigy'. This was evidenced partly by his diligence in learning many different meditation techniques (which we will speak about throughout this book), and partly by his unquenchable desire to undertake pilgrimages to holy temples and places (which we will talk more about in 'Lesson #9: Go Out of Your Way for Little and Big Pilgrimages'). It was also perhaps most evident in the way that he met and 'collected' stories of all manner of saints, mystics and holy men. This was a constant throughout his life, but particularly evident in his formative years in India, and these stories make up a big part of the initial appeal of the *Autobiography* to a Western audience.

Usually, when we find ourselves naturally attracted again and again to a particular group of people or places or themes, this reveals something to us about our karma and our mission in this life. In Yogananda's case, the fact that he had met and collected so many stories of swamis was no accident. This compulsion that he had, if we can call it that, was in fact intertwined with his life's work: to bring yoga (partly through these colourful stories) to the West.

In each of these, Yogananda usually starts by describing how he was drawn to a specific master because of their unusual abilities, like the three in the Swami Superpower Trilogy. In each of these stories, there is at least one important spiritual lesson that Yogananda wants to impart to even the most casual reader.

The interesting thing about these three tales, though, is not so much the superpower the swamis supposedly exhibit, but rather the spiritual lessons contained therein. These valuable spiritual lessons can be described as what the West calls the 'moral of the story'. Although the stories in the *Autobiography* are varied, the moral of each is usually a lesson about the futility of pursuing spiritual powers as one's goal instead of achieving spiritual awakening. It is the memorable nature of these stories that drive these lessons home.

Going over these chapters again, I found that, in addition to the obvious moral or lesson, there is usually at least one, and sometimes several, deeper, less-obvious lessons contained in them. Sometimes these lessons are laid out explicitly, but at other times, they are subtly embedded within the structure of the stories themselves. This means that they might get overlooked by the casual reader upon a first reading. I certainly hurried through these chapters quickly on my first reading, marvelling at both the superpowers and the 'moral' of the story, but not pausing long enough to ponder about each swamis' lives and karma, and what lasting effects they may have had on Yogananda's life.

I've chosen to focus on the lessons delivered by two of these three swamis to the young Yogananda (Mukunda): the Tiger Swami, whose tale is so memorable that most people recalled the main lesson easily, even years after having read the book ('Fight your inner tigers ... rather than outer tigers'), and the Levitating Saint, who in my opinion had much more of an impact on Yogananda than this one little chapter suggests. While we'll skip the Perfume Saint in this section, we'll revisit his story (and the lesson) in the next part of the book, which focuses on siddhis, or what we might call superpowers today.

Looking at these stories in the context of all of Yogananda's eye-opening and awe-inducing tales, we can see a complex collection of Eastern spiritual ideas woven into the fabric of the book, meant not only to intrigue the reader but to introduce these subtler aspects of yogic teaching to the West. In fact, I would suggest that the Tiger Swami's story is as much about karma and how it works as it is about a swami who developed an extraordinary ability to fight tigers. Today, perhaps, with the rapid modernization of the East, these stories and their lessons can do the same for modern seekers, even in Yogananda's homeland.

The Story of the Tiger Swami

The story begins with one of Mukunda's high school friends, Chandi, telling Mukunda he has discovered the location of the Tiger Swami, who had become famous for fighting tigers with his bare hands before he entered the monastic order (taking on the name of Sohong Swami upon renunciation of the ways of the world).

As was his tendency, Mukunda set out immediately with his friend on a trek to Bhowanipur, located on the outskirts of Calcutta, to see the Tiger Swami. Upon arriving, and after being kept waiting by a servant for an uncomfortable amount of time, they met the swami, who had an impressive physique (as was to be expected, given that he claimed to fight tigers). When Mukunda and Chandi asked if the robust swami really used to fight Bengal tigers with his bare hands, he demonstrated that he still had some of his former power by punching a wall with enough force to dislodge a brick.

Sohong Swami then told the boys the story of how he had come to be a tamer of tigers and how he had abandoned that life to become a swami, which led to his nickname of the Tiger Swami. Though he had been a feeble youth, he had wanted to build a strong and powerful body and fight tigers even when he was very young. He was able to do this using his willpower, becoming so strong that he was in fact able to fight Royal Bengal tigers with his bare hands, a feat that seems preposterous in modern times.

One of the missing ingredients beyond a powerful physique was mental strength and the ability to view the tigers as 'pussycats'. It was this 'compelling mental vigor', he told Mukunda and Chandi, that allowed him to have the confidence to use his strength on an actual tiger. It allowed him to convince the tiger that it was, compared to the man, really just a 'pussycat'. Anyone who has seen a Royal Bengal tiger, Yogananda says in the book, will realize that this is no small task!

The tiger fighter (who was not yet the Tiger Swami) became famous for this ability. One day, his father told him to stop fighting tigers, for if he didn't, there would be karmic consequences down the road. The arrogant young man insisted that he was not a tiger killer but a tamer of the beasts, and so he didn't think that the law of karma would cause him any problems.

Then his father told him how he had received the warning, in a manner that seems to recur often in the *Autobiography* (but seems incredible to us today). An elderly swami visited the father and conveyed to him the 'warning' that his son should stop fighting tigers, otherwise, in his next fight he would suffer deardful wounds and a 'deathly sickness' for some months, after which he would end up becoming a monk.

The young man told his father that the latter must have been the victim of yet another 'deluded fanatic'. He ignored the warning.

Soon after, the tiger fighter travelled to the province of Cooch Behar and, as usual, drew a crowd because of his fame. That evening, he received an invitation from the prince of Cooch Behar to visit his palace the next morning. When he met the prince the following day, the prince challenged him to fight his newly captured beast, Raja Begum, offering him riches if he won the fight or branding him a coward if he refused to fight the beast. The young man, blinded by his pride, quickly agreed to the various conditions laid down by the prince, including the requirement that he bind Raja Begum with a chain and exit the cage while still conscious. The prince also mysteriously didn't allow the young man to see the tiger before he accepted the conditions, perhaps worried that the fierceness of the beast would frighten him away.

Raja Begum turned out to be a bloodthirsty beast; he drew blood by cutting the swami's arm early. In a Herculean fight, perhaps his most difficult, the famed tiger tamer managed to subdue the tiger. But just he turned his back, the beast mauled him one more time. While he was able to defeat the tiger and meet the prince's conditions, he ended up losing a lot of blood. Afterward, the tiger tamer fell ill with some kind of 'deathly sickness' and was unwell for the next six months, just as the mysterious yogi had warned his father.

It was to be his last fight, for when he recovered from his illness and was able to get back to his father's home, he decided that it was time to turn his attention away from external tigers and fight his inner tigers. He sought out the swami who had given his father the message and became his disciple, which led to his entering the monastic order as Sohong Swami.

Fight Your Inner Tigers

The main lesson that the Tiger Swami imparted to the two youths was the importance of focusing on fighting 'inner tigers'. It was by focusing on these inner battles that he emerged from his sickness and had become the man they were meeting. To extend the quote from the beginning of this chapter:

> 'Yes.' He was smiling. 'But there are many kinds of tigers … some roam in the jungles of human desires.
>
> 'No spiritual benefit accrues by knocking beasts unconscious. Rather be a victor over the inner prowlers.'[2]

What are these inner tigers? These are the inner beasts of doubt, ignorance of our true nature, selfishness and other desires and fears that obscure the knowledge of our true selves. When the would-be Tiger Swami returned home after six months of being ill, he found that he had no desire to fight tigers anymore; all the fun had gone out of it. When he eventually found the swami who had given his father the warning, the swami spoke with calm assurance:

> Enough of tiger taming. Come with me; I will teach you to subdue the beasts of ignorance roaming in the jungles of the human mind. You are used to an audience: let it be a galaxy of angels, entertained by your thrilling mastery of yoga![3]

After that, Yogananda tells us, the Tiger Swami started to open his 'soul's doors, rusty and resistant with long disuse,' and he set off into the Himalayas to fight these inner tigers in earnest.

As stated earlier, this is the main point of the story and its powerful message: that our inner tigers can be harder to fight (and more worthy of our attention) than the tigers of the external world. But it is also a message that, whether in the time of Yogananda's youth or today, is very hard to take heed of and follow regularly.

In the video game industry, there is a saying that video games should be 'easy to play but hard to master'. The same could be said of this and many other spiritual lessons—easy to recite but hard to master. This is doubly true when we need to apply them to our own lives; as Freud once said about analysing one's own life, our tendency is to be satisfied too soon, with an incomplete analysis.

This can only be overcome by staying vigilant over time and sticking to whatever spiritual path we feel drawn to. It isn't just about learning meditation and meditating every day, but about learning to recognize these strange beasts that roam our minds. Little by little, as we learn more about ourselves, we learn how to start wiping away the ignorance. No single statement can do that: but some of the most important tigers to tame are the ways in which we deceive ourselves into thinking that we need certain things—material goods, success and fame—to be happy.

The Role of Our 'Karmic Tigers'

Having understood the main moral, let's now re-examine the role of tigers in the swami's life story to see if there are perhaps other interesting lessons embedded in it.

While our desires for material success are in fact some of the obstacles we face on the spiritual path, they can also be a doorway to our own karma and spiritual growth. In fact, in my opinion, our 'outer tigers', the battles that we are unconsciously drawn to fight in the physical world, can reveal something to us about ourselves and our karma, *just as meditation and introspection can.* In some cases, those outer tigers can serve as our 'on-ramp' to the spiritual path.

While we fight those outer tigers, we build our mental muscles and exercise them, learning humility and understanding what makes us unique. In short, we can build our spiritual and mental muscles while we are in the process of fighting our outer tigers, as the Tiger Swami built his physical and mental muscles.

Admittedly, fighting outer tigers is not the goal in the long run (and can get us into trouble if we do it for too long), but most of us are trying to earn a living and are, therefore, engaged in the small battles of daily life—our 'outer tigers'. The thought of abandoning our worldly ambitions and devoting ourselves full-time to fighting our inner tigers, dispelling the darkness of ignorance that all of us are caught in, can seem like a long and winding road. In fact, it can seem so far off that we assume we may never get there.

The Tiger Swami had no interest in getting on the spiritual path for many years, years that he spent achieving his childhood ambition to earn fame by fighting tigers. You might say, just as we did about Yogananda, who knew from an early age that being a 'wandering swami' was part of his life path, that tigers were part of the Tiger Swami's path in life. They were an on-ramp to his spiritual path and, had he never spent those years fighting those tigers, his story would probably be unknown today, and he may never have gotten on the spiritual path to become a swami at all!

This circuitous route was also certainly true for me. When I started my first company, I was mostly interested in learning about meditation and yoga because I thought they could help me increase my strength and willpower, which would in turn make me more successful in business. In short, I turned to meditation because I thought it would make me better at what I did—entrepreneurship, a path that I felt drawn to as if it was a script that had been written for me before this life and like a moth drawn to a flame, I couldn't help but embrace it. Of course, eventually, this path (that of being an entrepreneur and then an investor, and hoping to use spiritual principles to be more successful) led me down a second path—of integrating spirituality with work—but that didn't happen immediately.

The Tiger Swami had a strong desire to battle tigers, much like Yogananda had a lifelong desire to be a monk. In fact, the swami told Mukunda that it had been his childhood dream (strange as such a dream might seem). But how did the Tiger Swami, who had a 'feeble body', end up becoming a powerful man who could tame wild tigers with his bare hands? Sohong Swami told Mukunda and his high school friend that his belief in his ability to tame tigers and turn them into 'pussycats' had been just as important as the actual physical power that he had needed.

Building mental strength isn't the same as wishing something to be true or simply stating affirmations. You have to be able to utilize your willpower to stay on the long and hard path to worldly success. Simply saying to yourself 'I can fight tigers' isn't enough. In short, to accomplish any difficult task or dream, you need a combination of inner and outer strength, of mental willpower and external techniques.

The popular author of *Outliers*, Malcolm Gladwell, tells stories of individuals who became 'masters' in their fields by spending 10,000 hours in practice–whether they were practicing to be a pilot, a race car driver or a programmer.[4] I don't know if the Tiger Swami spent 10,000 hours practicing to fight tigers, but he certainly spent quite a bit of time physically training to master the seemingly ridiculous art of fighting large beasts.

However, I would submit that there is an important element of karma that plays into our ability to achieve certain goals, and that is based on how karmic influences create inner desire. Believe it or not, I spend a lot of time with entrepreneurs who have been told they have to just 'believe they can succeed', but by itself that isn't usually enough. You have to navigate the outer currents of the physical world and the inner currents of karma to achieve your goal.

I have a friend who is an expert at rock climbing; she and her husband would go climbing whenever they get a free weekend. I am sure that they have both spent 10,000 hours (or more) of their lives climbing. As a result, they are masters of a task that seems almost crazy to me.

However, the bigger question about the idea of mastery, the one that I have always wondered about, is: what makes one person *want* to spend 10,000 hours doing something? I can't imagine spending that many hours climbing—I have just never had the innate desire to do it. Just as with fighting tigers with my bare hands, I'm not even sure I could do it even if I wanted to, no matter how many self-help gurus might tell me that 'anything is possible'. It is physically possible for me to spend 10,000 hours climbing, but after a few hours (or a few dozen or even a hundred hours), I would get bored and stop pursuing it in lieu of something else that appealed to me.

On the other hand, when I was younger, I have certainly spent 10,000 hours programming and became an expert. No one had to give me a pep talk to convince me to do it. There was an inner motivation that came from a certainty that this was 'my thing'—in more spiritual terms, you might say it was part of my karmic script in this life.

Those things that pull us towards them in the physical world almost unconsciously are often the results of our karmic desires. To use a term that is drawn not from ancient traditions but from more modern studies of near-death experiences, we all have what is called a 'life plan'—a blueprint of the things we are meant to do.

It turns out that these things tend to coincide with the things that we are most likely to have the desire, mental strength and perseverance to accomplish. In short, these are our 'outer tigers', whatever they may be—starting a software company, writing books, singing or dancing professionally or taking care of our families and raising our children.

I mentioned that worldly desires can be obstacles on the spiritual path; having the wrong worldly desires can be even bigger obstacles. In addition to our innate desires, we also have desires that are implanted in us by society (or by our families or our classmates). Desires that are imposed on us by external factors, desires that do not arise from our own inner currents of karma, can actually be quite destructive. We end up, for example, unhappy with our work and derive no satisfaction from it, even though it is 'what we are supposed to do'.

To a certain extent, we are all susceptible to the thoughts of those around us. Our parents may want us to pursue a particular profession or even expect us to take up their profession. How do we know that the goals we obsess over are our innate desires and have not been imbibed from those around us? One way is to look at how unique a goal is to you and how you are drawn to it as your path. What are the things that you have a natural affinity for that goes well beyond those around you?

In my case, it was programming from an early age. Although my siblings also ended up in the computer industry, their routes were more circuitous (I was the only one to major in computer science, for example). In my case, I knew from the age of twelve, when I wrote my first computer program, that this was going to be a part of my professional life; you might say that it was a part of my karma, feeding on the vasanas, or tendencies, of our past (we'll talk more about the law of cause and effect throughout this book).

In this way, though the main lesson of the Tiger Swami story is that you should fight your inner tigers rather than ferocious outer beasts, I believe that fighting the literal tigers was an important part of his path. He was drawn to that path in a way that defies logic, and he wouldn't have become the person he became. Yogananda certainly wouldn't have used his story to teach us the main spiritual lesson, if he hadn't followed his initial worldly desire—to fight outer tigers!

Staying on the Worldly Path Too Long, or Getting the Message

At this point, you might be confused. Should we go ahead and fight the outer tigers of the world, as the young Tiger Swami did, or should we, as the older Tiger Swami did and advised Mukunda and his friend to do instead: to fight the beasts of our inner ignorance?

I would suggest that, in the modern world, unless you are about to hop off into monastic life, you have to do both. For this, you will need to face your outer tigers and realize they are reflective of your inner tigers. We need to spend time building our muscles (metaphorically or literally) while we pursue the fight with our outer tigers, and this will eventually prepare us for the bigger battle with our inner tigers.

For me, there is another important lesson that the Tiger Swami story offers, a lesson that is hidden in plain sight, in the structure of the story: we have different callings at different points in our lives, and the obstacles we face are sometimes the catalysts that can take us to the correct 'next step' in our path.

The law of karma, cause and effect, creates situations in the present based on the seeds of past actions. I like to think of karma as a 'questing engine' in the very complicated video game of life. Quests and achievements are the building blocks of modern video games. One rule of creating good games is, as I said earlier, that it should be easy to play but difficult to master. In order to keep a game interesting, the questing engine needs to be able to create challenges that relate to the ability and difficulty level of the player.

Sometimes, though, we stay on a path for too long, and we need something dramatic to bump us off this and path onto the 'right path'. This is what happened with Tiger Swami; once he had fought tigers and become famous, it was time for him to move on. The mysterious sadhu who had conveyed the message to him through his father had said as much. In fact, while he may have fulfilled whatever previous karma was guiding him towards fighting beasts, the prophetic sadhu told his father that the young tiger tamer was now sowing the seeds of more destructive karma.

The Tiger Swami himself said that it was as if Raja Begum was a demon that had been conjured up just for him based on his past actions. Imagine that the young Tiger Swami was playing a video game and now it was time for the boss-level battle: the toughest opponent yet, one that appeared unbeatable. It was as if the questing engine needed to put a more difficult outer tiger in front of him to convince him to stop fighting tigers!

At that point in his life, he was not about to consciously embark on a spiritual path, even though that would be where his life was headed next. We always have the ability to make decisions about what path to follow next in life; the game of Tiger Swami's life needed to give him a strong enough nudge to push him off of the path he had been on and choose a different path. It took a very serious challenge, one that left him unable to do anything for six months (though he won the battle against the tiger and claimed the worldly rewards for doing so), to knock him kicking and screaming down another path.

Embedded in the structure of this story is the lesson that while fighting outer tigers is necessary, we can end up spending too much time pursuing worldly ambitions, our outer tigers. We become stubborn and entranced by worldly rewards and we may need a very serious event to push us away from that pursuit towards our inner tigers.

Let me admit that this happened to me as well and, like the Tiger Swami, I needed a serious wake-up call. That call came not long after I had started running my start-up programme at MIT. It came in the form of a setback, not unlike the Tiger Swami's literal thrashing at the hands of Raja Begum. Though my story doesn't involve any physical tigers, my body was just as badly damaged and it took me more than six months to fully recover.

I tell the full story of this setback in 'Lesson #11: Setbacks May Be A Part of Your Story' *but* let me summarize it here.

After the initial success of the Play Labs @ MIT programme, I was gearing up to try and expand it and to create a venture capital fund. This would have sent me further down a career path that had been a key part of my life's work up until that date, but I had neglected the other part of my life's work, which was to be an author and to help bridge the gap between the materialistic world and the inner spiritual world.

As I was getting serious about creating the venture capital fund and dedicating myself to it, I had a series of health issues that made it impossible for me to continue. As a consequence of these health issues, I was literally unable to do any work that involved talking to people—I just didn't have the energy for a whole year or more. During this time, I turned my attention to an aspect of my career that I had been neglecting: my writing. And I ended up publishing two books within the next twelve months, which kickstarted both my career as a writer and my journey towards fulfilling my broader mission.

That year, each time I tried to turn my attention back to the business world, the world of money-making and venture capital, my health would get worse and I would be unable to proceed! While my physical problems were heart-related, I also found that my heart was no longer in the pursuit of money and the battles that were involved in Silicon Valley. Just like the Tiger Swami, the outer tigers I had been fighting my whole career seemed almost meaningless to me. You could say that my heart was no longer in battling outer tigers.

Of course, these kinds of 'big messages' that we cannot ignore, as in the case of the Tiger Swami (and myself), aren't *always* necessary. However, some of us might be too stubborn to pay attention to subtler clues, especially if we have achieved some level of worldly success and are hungry for more. For those of us in that position, the universe needs to kick us off the path, which it usually does with a dramatic situation that makes it difficult to ignore the message: we need to get on a different path.

So, while your outer tigers may be a key, even necessary, part of your path (your karmic script), don't spend too much time continuing to fight the same outer tigers. You may end up like the Tiger Swami or like me: needing a major (and potentially very painful) course correction!

LESSON #4

The Many Lessons of the Incomparable Levitating Saint

... The knowledge of yoga is free to all who will receive, like the ungarnishable daylight.

— BHADURI MAHASAYA[1]

I n the next part of the book, we'll turn our attention to the superpowers, or *siddhis* (as they were called by the ancient sage Patanjali) that Yogananda and others have recounted in stories of India and other traditions. We'll look at them not just in terms of Yogananda's stories, but also in terms of how we might think about these superpowers as modern men and women of science.

However, in this chapter, I want to reflect on lessons that are unrelated to siddhis, even though they are dispensed by a siddha (one who has attained one ore more siddhis), specifically the many lessons of the Levitating Saint, Bhaduri Mahasaya. This chapter in the *Autobiography* begins with Mukunda's friend telling him that he has witnessed a yogi who has attained the power of levitation. Yogananda dispenses quickly with the superpower aspect of Bhaduri Mahasaya, telling his friend that he had witnessed it already. Mukunda then goes on to describe his many varied conversations with the saint, each of which contains important lessons for young Mukunda (and for us).

You might surmise from the short length of Yogananda's chapter on the Levitating Saint that Bhaduri Mahasaya had only a minor influence on him. However, as I've gone back and re-read this chapter and other parts of the *Autobiography*, it has become clear to me that this sage made quite a distinct and lasting impression on the young man. Mukunda often undertook what he later called 'afternoon pilgrimages' to see this saint, from whom he learnt many spiritual lessons that went well beyond (and, in fact, had nothing to do with) his alleged powers of levitation.

The lessons imparted to Mukunda during these memorable sessions not only radiated outwards in his life and work as he became Swami Yogananda, but also informed the other lessons in this book. Like spiritual seeds planted and waiting to be harvested, you can call upon them in your own life when they are needed.

Bhaduri Mahasaya undoubtedly influenced Yogananda's interest in and his eventual trip to the West, and it is in a conversation with the saint that we first hear Mukunda give voice to the idea of writing a book on yoga. Even though Mukunda was suggesting that Bhaduri Mahasaya should write such a book, there is no doubt in my mind that this seed, once planted, was what germinated decades later in Yogananda's bestselling book, *Autobiography of a Yogi*.

The Lessons of the Levitating Saint

The chapter on the Levitating Saint did not make much of an impression on me when I first read the *Autobiography*, probably because it was supposed to be chapter about a levitating saint but there wasn't much levitation in it at all!

Nevertheless, the spiritual lessons of this short chapter are imparted to us, in rapid-fire style by Yogananda. In fact, this chapter may be among the densest in the *Autobiography* in terms of number of lessons per page. We will discuss them each briefly in the context of the story of the Levitating Saint, but also in the context of our own lives and spiritual search in the modern world.

Laughter Is the Best Medicine

Yogananda tells us that Bhaduri Mahasaya was often surrounded by dour and serious devotees who often tried to limit access to the saint by outsiders (including Mukunda, who was not a formal disciple of the saint). They regularly tried to deny Mukunda admittance on this ground, but the saint, perhaps with the eye of foresight of how these conversations might influence Mukunda's future as Yogananda, always intervened and told them to let 'Mukunda come when he will.'

It turns out this dynamic is as true today as it was 100 years ago. You'll find that followers of most spiritual teachers (at least those who have had organizations built around them) are often dour, joyless gatekeepers. I would go so far as to call them sourpusses. Having found the one teacher they want to follow, they become invested in demonstrating how seriously they take being a disciple on that teacher's spiritual path and how lucky they are compared to those who are not followers.

On the other hand, most saints themselves are known to possess a sense of humour. Yogananda's own reaction to the teachings of the Levitating Saint was one of joy; he often laughed raucously, the sound of which often upset the dour disciples who didn't want a kid bringing frivolity into the otherwise serious room where the Levitating Saint held court.

Mukunda told his friend Upendra that he often went to the saint and was entertained by the saint's incomparable wit. While the other, more serious disciples found it undignified when Mukunda laughed at the saint's puns and yogic jokes, this was not true of the saint himself: 'Occasionally my prolonged laughter mars the solemnity of his gatherings. The saint is not displeased, but his disciples look daggers!'[2]

'What a laugh you have!' was the saint's jolly reply to Mukunda's raucous laughter.

Yogananda's description of Bhaduri Mahasaya, written decades later, might describe not just the Levitating Saint but many advanced masters: 'An affectionate gleam came into his gaze. His own face was always serious, yet touched with an ecstatic smile. His large, lotus eyes held a hidden divine laughter.'[3]

My first meditation teacher, whom I called Ramaswami in my book, *Zen Entrepreneurship*, used to tell us that a sense of humour and enlightenment went hand-in-hand. He would say that if a spiritual teacher didn't have a sense of humour, he (or she) was probably not enlightened. He would often call me a 'serious young man', since I was always so solemn about spiritual techniques and career success, and would admonish me that I needed to 'lighten up' in the pursuit of both paths of my life.

In later years, Yogananda's contemporaries often commented on his sense of humour and his hearty laugh. I have often heard this from those who have spent a lot of time with masters—there is an unexpected humour and a twinkle in the eyes of a saint. While I can't speak about all saints in a general sense, I think there is an important connection between a sense of humour and spiritual insight.

Which is not to say that saints and masters can't be serious or stern—no doubt they often are, particularly when disciplining students or laying down rules. And there are always exceptions. Yogananda's guru, Sri Yukteswar, was known more for his sternness than his wit or humour, so there really is no general rule of thumb. My first meditation teacher, in addition to having a great sense of humour, could switch quickly to become stern when the occasion called for it.

However, it seems that when saints try to teach the rest of us about the illusory nature of the world, a sense of humour helps in conveying what is not easy to put into words. After all, life itself is a lila, a play of the gods, and you can't have fun playing if you take things too seriously! Everything we take seriously is a kind of illusion, and there's no doubt that if we saw beyond the illusion, we might also spend more time smiling and laughing than being depressed or worried or fearful.

Has it ever been the case in your own life that an activity you originally performed for fun had the fun drained out of it? If so, it's probably because, for whatever reason, you started to take it too seriously. I have had this experience many times and it usually meant that I had to back away from that activity for some time until the joy returned. Sometimes the best (and most productive) approach in life is to combine commitment with a touch of humour.

There is, according to the yogic teachings, a technical reason for this as well. When we get too serious, we constrict our energy and become so attached to a specific technique or path that we risk losing sight of the goal and missing the absurdity of everything happening around us. It is this mental clinging, this attachment that creates the vrittis, the whirlpools of thought, which not just whirl around but harden and embed themselves as samskaras in our energy fields.

The Buddha explicitly called this out, describing it as the root cause of the creation of all karma, which is what leads to suffering—our mental grasping, our attachments. Patanjali, the saint who wrote the sutras that are the basis for modern-day yoga, used similar language. We'll talk much more about this process and how it relates to yoga in 'Lesson #8: Practice Every Day, No Matter How Much Time You Have'.

On the other hand, approaching life, and even our spiritual practice, with a sense of humour can help us let go of these attachments. This lets the temporary whirlpools of our desire and attention simply whirl away, rather than solidify in the khosas (the clear sheaths that surround the body and eventually house the samskaras, according to yogic tradition).

What happens when you place heavy, solid objects in your energy field? Your energy field gets heavier and holds you down, both metaphorically (as in the case of karma) and literally as well! This also relates to the practice of levitation itself, which we'll explore in a later chapter in this book.

A wise person once said that the reason it's called spiritual practice is so that we don't take it too seriously. If you practice a sport, do you get upset every time you miss the basket or don't hit the ball? Probably not, since you are just practicing. Yet, if you miss the ball in the actual game, which we take very seriously, not only do we get upset, but so do all of our teammates and the fans watching the game.

The lesson here is that the game itself should be thought of as a form of practice. So, lighten up in your spiritual practice and your life, and don't be afraid to laugh from the belly at the absurdity of the game of life!

The Strange Behaviour of Saints

The above discussion about laughter and absurdity touches on how difficult it can be to pigeonhole saints and their behaviours. In fact, as soon as we think we know exactly what a saint's behaviour should be like, they end up surprising us.

An interesting fact that supplies context to Bhaduri's behaviour is that he had been 'secluded' indoors for twenty years when Mukunda visited him, having gone outside only for holy festivals, at which he would often be very generous to beggars.

His disciples fervently guarded his seclusion. As related earlier, one afternoon when Mukunda was visiting, the secluded saint told his gatekeeper disciples to let Mukunda stop by whenever he wanted, at which point the saint explained his choice to stay indoors.

In modern times (and even during Yogananda's time), we might think that saints secluded themselves from contact with the outside world to protect themselves. This may not be the case, Bhaduri explains to Mukunda:

My rule of seclusion is not for my own comfort, but for that of others. Worldly people do not like the candor which shatters their delusions. Saints are not only rare but disconcerting. Even in scripture, they are often found embarrassing![4]

And this gets right to the heart of the matter. In the 'physical world', we are taught, whether explicitly in the form of materialist science or implicitly through the social sciences, that everything around us is real and matters. Now, I'm not saying that things don't matter at all or that it's wrong to immerse ourselves in the world. We are here in the material world to play the game of life, so there's no reason we shouldn't do so and experience whatever our script has in store for us. However, some of us have scripts that aren't about simply 'experiencing' the material life, we find ourselves being led down a different path, to try to perceive the truth beyond the illusion: that we are in fact actors playing a part in a script.

This perspective can seem, in the words of Bhaduri Mahasaya, 'disconcerting' to others.

Many saints, going all the way back to Jesus Christ and further, were misunderstood in their own time. Their existence was considered a disturbance to the social order, which was built on assumptions about what was right and what different people's social positions should be.

Today's materialist scientists even insist that they have reality mostly figured out and that we must play by the rules given to us by science. This attitude, often imbued with arrogance is often displayed by seemingly intelligent people who instruct others, as if bragging about belonging to a superior tribe, to simply trust the science. They remain ignorant of the ways in which social assumptions and beliefs influence scientific findings, and usually end up confirming existing paradigms.

When Jesus Christ, who was a Jew, showed up on the scene, his behaviour and teachings were disconcerting to the established rabbis of the time. Similarly, if Christ were to return today, I have no doubt he would seriously upset Christian priests of the twenty-first century. The same might be true if Buddha or Krishna were to reappear (though, of course, in the Hindu and Buddhist traditions, the point of being awakened is that you don't have to return to the material world!), would they be upset by the many traditions and rituals that have obscured the true purpose of all religions? What would Patanjali think of the multi-billion-dollar yoga industry that has spread itself all over the world today? Similarly, the prophet Muhammad was seen as a reformer during his time. What would he think of today's various sects of Islam?

I make these somewhat controversial statements not because of any specific practices that these prophets and visionaries would object to, but because:

1. a lot changes in society over hundreds or thousands of years, but some things don't change,

2.   the role of a prophet or saviour in the Biblical tradition is usually to tell us what we think is important is not, in the overall scheme of things, so important at all, and

3. most of these religious figures were reformers and iconoclasts (a term literally used to refer to Muhammad and his followers after the breaking of the idols in Mecca). That they would be upset at the existing state of human affairs makes them upsetting to society in general and the people who are in power in each generation.

Bhaduri Mahasaya suggested to Mukunda what is perhaps a useful way of thinking about saints who act strangely: 'God plants his saints sometimes in unexpected soil, lest we think we may reduce Him to a rule!'[5]

This is in fact the point of the Tibetan Buddhist term, 'crazy wisdom', which means that saints engage in contradictory behaviour from that which we expect. It is meant to throw us—who follow society's rules—off. This was particularly true in India, where strange swamis have historically been tolerated and, in some cases, even venerated. But India, like the rest of the East, has modernized and, in the process, assigned greater significance to material goods and success just like the West. (Later, we'll talk about how Yogananda's relatives, including his eldest brother Ananta and his brother-in-law, looked down on him for wanting to be a swami because they believed he was being irresponsible and needed to get a 'real job'.)

In another part of the *Autobiography*, Yogananda tells the story of Trailanga Swami, an almost legendary Bengali swami who settled in Varanasi/Benares. By some accounts, Trailanga Swami reportedly lived from 1607 to 1887, which would have made him 280 years old! Some accounts even claim he was over 300 years old at the time of his death. (He was a close friend of Lahiri Mahasaya and meditated with him.)

While there are many well-documented stories of the siddhis of Trailanga Swami that were witnessed in public, he was perhaps just as famous for his 'odd' look and behaviour as for anything else. For one, he weighed approximately 300 pounds ('a pound for each year', writes Yogananda). For another, he rarely ever wore clothes. Finally, he lived in what swamis sometimes call a childlike state of ecstasy. Imagine a 300-pound nude man walking around unconcerned with the material world. This was disconcerting even to the police of the holy city of Benares (no stranger to strange saints), who attempted to put him in a jail cell. Somehow, the nude 300-pound man ended up on the roof of the jail building. The police, apparently realizing that they were dealing with a saint, gave in and let Trailanga Swami be, well, his natural, odd self.

Even without the aid of miraculous displays, anyone who questions social norms can be disconcerting to those who think they are living and thriving in a civilized modern world. Every society has rules and norms, many of which are unstated. We have these unstated rules ingrained into us from an early age and, while each culture and society may have different rules, they are perhaps becoming more uniform in the modern world than they were previously due to the ease with which information, videos, experiences, products and, now even, business and work practices can be shared.

'Divine madness' is another term used in English for those who are spiritually more advanced than the rest of us and do things we might consider uncouth. This understanding is part of the basis for the term 'avadhūta', often applied to religious teachers and adepts who behave strangely and do not follow social norms. The Sanskrit root of the word includes a term that means 'to shake'—their behaviour is, in some ways, meant to shake us, to shake things up and to catalyse the realization that our assumptions about the world are just that: assumptions!

Now, coming back to the Levitating Saint. One of his many lessons was that he stayed indoors and secluded to protect the 'public' from him and the 'shaking' that might result from avadhutic behaviour.

You might wonder: how does this affect us in our everyday lives?

That someone makes you uncomfortable doesn't disqualify them from having things to teach you. Of course, this should be taken with a pinch of salt—a thief might make you uncomfortable and teach you about your attachment to your possessions by robbing you of them, but that's not a lesson any of us want!

You should judge the value of a teacher over time, based on how they make you feel and your intuition, not just on what they say. This is true not only during your first encounter, when they might impress you with their wisdom or make you uncomfortable with their unusual behaviour. When you spend time with them, when you meditate with them and when they provide you spiritual instruction, how do you feel, both during and afterwards? Many pretenders engage in predatory behaviour, and that is all they are: predators, not saintly persons, particularly in the modern era when anyone can claim to be a guru or teacher.

We have to use our intuition to gauge whether a teacher brings us peace of mind and spiritual progress or is only a force of disturbance. Yogananda talks about the peace of mind that he got from meditating with and listening to the discourses and parables of Bhaduri Mahasaya. Yogananda's description of this is a good one to keep in mind when you are evaluating a spiritual teacher, even today, whether in person or online: 'Like a peaceful flood, he swept away the mental debris of his listeners, floating them Godward.'[6]

Women, Men and the Search for God

During one of Mukunda's visits, Bhaduri Mahasaya speaks of Mirabai, 'a medieval Rajputani princess who abandoned her court life to seek the company of sadhus.' Of course, unsurprisingly for medieval times, there were sadhus that refused to receive her because she was a woman.[7]

We will talk more in 'Lesson #8: Practice Every Day, No Matter How Much Time You Have' about how the requirements of yoga in the modern world differ from those in medieval times and even in Yogananda's time. For now, I just want to mention that Mirabai made a point that men and women were the same before God. As a result of her observation, even one particularly well-known but obstinate sadhu became aware of the error in his thinking and welcomed her; as Yogananda puts it, her response 'brought him humbly to her feet.'

Mirabai's poetry is often quoted in conjunction with that of Kabir Das, an adept who had Hindu and Muslim followers. We'll talk more about Kabir in 'Lesson #14: Yoga is For Everyone, East and West'. In the Sufi traditions, the use of the metaphor of the beloved for God is common. The ecstatic state, called 'mast' in the Indian subcontinent, is about seeking God (often expressed in the qawwali 'Mast Qalander'), and the relationship is expressed as between the lover and the beloved. In the West, this metaphor is well-known primarily due to the poetry and songs of Jalaludin al Rumi, the thirteenth-century Persian Sufi mystic.

Although Yogananda doesn't mention whether both male and female disciples were present during the Levitating Saint's discussion of Mirabai, we can see in Yogananda's life and work that Bhaduri Mahasaya's lesson about men and women being equal before God was taken seriously and like his other lessons made a lasting impression. Yogananda was one of the first Eastern yogis to come to America and not just teach but accept a large number of female followers as renunciates. This practice, along with his insistence on teaching students of all races would get Yogananda in trouble more than once with the conservative factions of America at the time (more on this later). Today, go to any yoga class in the West and you will find more female students than male, almost without exception, and this tradition may have started in Yogananda's classes as well.

Who Is Renouncing What?

Yogananda tells us that, like Mirabai, who gave up the material comforts of being a princess in order to seek God, Bhaduri Mahasaya came from a very wealthy family and gave that up at an early age to become a yogi. When a disciple exclaimed how wonderful the saint must be to have given up such wealth, Bhaduri Mahasaya responded by saying:

> 'You are reversing the case!' The saint's face held a mild rebuke. 'I have left a few paltry rupees, a few petty pleasures, for a cosmic empire of endless bliss. How then have I denied myself anything? I know the joy of sharing the treasure. Is that a sacrifice? The shortsighted worldly folk are verily the real renunciates! They relinquish an unparalleled divine possession for a poor handful of earthly toys!'[8]

Yogananda no doubt kept this response in mind when he went to the materialistic West. It is, in his words, 'a paradoxical view' of the renunciate's life—it is the person who stays in the material world, the non-renunciate, who is giving up true riches! Most of the readers of this book are probably living and working in the world (what in Yogananda's time was called a householder), so the question is: is this perspective valid or useful to us in the modern world?

I would contend it is a very valuable lesson that applies not only to a full renunciate who is giving up all of [their] princely wealth and devoting their entire life to the search for God, but also to ordinary situations in one's career and personal life. We are often faced in life with options that are materially attractive but might prove to be less fulfilling, less spiritual, less meaningful or less beneficial to us and to others than other (heart-oriented) options. In the modern world, we are constantly assaulted with images, in the media and on social media, of the things we don't have but might want. The opportunities to become attached to material wealth are infinite. Today, we are just as attached to our electronic tools and our extended social media tribes. We post images of things and become attached to the gratification that comes from 'friends' (whether we have met them in real life or if they are just online connections) liking and re-sharing our posts.

There will be points in our life when we are called upon to make decisions that involve a financial trade-off—like taking time off from work to pursue your own interests, which might be artistic or spiritual or philanthropic, things that make you feel alive but may have limited potential for 'success' by the standards of the material world we all inhabit.

I mentioned in 'Lesson #2: Sometimes, the Universe Unexpectedly Gives You an Important Task', how I turned down an opportunity for potential financial gain and followed my heart to go back to school at Stanford. I felt like this was the right thing to do, despite the fact that it would cost me money, but it turned out to be the right decision in the end.

After I graduated from Stanford and became a successful entrepreneur and venture capitalist in Silicon Valley, I was only writing as a hobby when I had the time. Even at this stage, I found it difficult to internalize this important lesson, surrounded as I was by people and a culture that value 'success'. Many of my peers from MIT, for example, had started companies and some of my closest friends had gone on to enter the upper echelons of Silicon Valley, with companies that were valued at hundreds of millions and even billions of dollars (these companies are called 'unicorns' in Silicon Valley, a term that was coined by a classmate of mine from MIT who became a famous venture capitalist).

Yet, at a point that was perhaps the zenith of my entrepreneurial prowess and influence, when I could have raised a new VC fund or joined one of my former business partners' companies, I ended up with what can be called a karmic choice. I have referenced this story in many other chapters, including the previous chapter about the Tiger Swami. Let's just say that, at that point in my life, I decided to focus on my writing, which was much more meaningful to me than trying to make another million dollars (or to become a billionaire, a level that several of my classmates have now achieved, at least on paper).

Yet, despite initially listening to my calling, as my health returned, I found myself slipping back into the trap of 'material success'—how well has this book sold, how well has this investment done, etc. This temptation wasn't just about money—it was a habit that had to do with being in a position of influence and authority in my career and amongst my peers. It is about both our inner attachments and about social influences which dictate what 'success' is all about.

But by adopting Bhaduri Mahasaya's paradoxical view, we don't need to be the ones 'giving up' something by making heart-and-spirit-centred choices. Rather, those toiling primarily for outward material success are the ones sacrificing a more spiritual, fulfilling and, perhaps even, healthier life. As Yogananda speculates, Bhaduri Mahasaya's view 'puts the cap of Croesus on any saintly beggar, whilst transforming all proud millionaires into unconscious martyrs.'

We will revisit this lesson throughout the book, but for now let us move on while mulling over some more of Bhaduri's Mahasaya's words on the matter. These words, which were about him giving up a life of luxury, are best remembered whenever we have to face a decision that make us choose between following our heart and financial gain: *'The divine order arranges our future more wisely than any insurance company.'*[9]

Taking Yoga to a Distant Land

If you think we haven't extracted enough lessons from this one richly packed but extremely short chapter in the *Autobiography*, worry not—there are more. A few short paragraphs in the chapter show us that Yogananda's destiny seemed to have been either perceived, or at least hinted at, during Mukunda's afternoon pilgrimages to see the Levitating Saint.

One day, after school, Mukunda had arrived early, prior to the evening lecture and meditation session, before Bhaduri Mahasaya's other disciples. Bhaduri Mahasaya showed Mukunda some thick envelopes and said: 'Those letters come from far-off America.'

He told Mukunda with a glint in his eye that the societies he corresponded with in America were interested in yoga and added humorously that they were '... discovering India anew with a better sense of direction than Columbus!'

Christopher Columbus was, of course, funded by the monarchs of Spain to find a seafaring path to India by going West rather than East from Europe; until his dying day, he insisted that the islands he had found in the Caribbean were actually India, and the name he gave to the natives of those islands was 'Indians'. Native Americans are still called Indians for this reason. Yogananda was to later write that this odd chapter in history may have created a strange karmic relationship between these two countries, so emblematic of the East and the West.

Then the saint said something that caught Mukunda's attention, and he quoted it decades later when he was writing the *Autobiography*. Aside from saying that yoga should be '... free to all who will receive, like the ungarnishable daylight', Bhaduri told Mukunda. 'What rishis perceived as essential for human salvation need not be diluted for the West. Alike in soul though diverse in outer experience, neither West nor East will flourish if some form of disciplinary yoga be not practised.'[10]

Yogananda himself says it was 'veiled prophetic guidance' and that he didn't appreciate the full meaning of these casual intimations: that he himself would someday '... carry India's teachings to America.'

Yet, at some level, the seed was planted, and not just for Swami Yogananda's future immigration to live in America. The next line in the chapter has Mukunda saying to the sage, 'Maharishi, I wish you would write a book on yoga for the benefit of the world.'

Bhaduri refuses, saying that he is training disciples, which is of course how the knowledge was passed on until someone like Yogananda appeared and became 'the first modern guru' in the West, teaching large numbers of people through correspondence courses, public talks and, of course, his book. Today this is common practice, with apps, YouTube, online articles and Zoom calls serving as the primary methods of disseminating spiritual wisdom far and wide.

We'll explore the idea that Yogananda was, in fact, a bridge between the East and the West, at least between India and America, further in 'Lesson #14: Yoga is For Everyone, East and West'. Bridges, as we know, go in both directions, and so in that chapter we'll also explore the return of Yogananda's wisdom, from the West to the East.

The significance of the Levitating Saint's conversations with young Mukunda cannot be underestimated. It's no accident that, as a mature man, Swami Yogananda referred to these sessions as 'afternoon pilgrimages' (see 'Lesson #9: Go Out of Your Way for Little and Big Pilgrimages'). The seeds planted in these sessions may have been essential factors in Yogananda's everlasting legacy.

As I have implied in many of the other chapters, each of us may have a destiny, a script that is written for us (or, depending on what you believe, by us or by others), for the gameplay session we call life. This destiny need not be anywhere near as dramatic as that of Yogananda, who bridged several continents and great civilizations. It may involve just touching the lives of a few individuals, but those few individuals will carry whatever seeds we plant to new and interesting shores.

To illustrate the importance of these seeds, shortly after Mukunda, now ordained Swami Yogananda, decided to go to the West, he went back to visit Bhaduri Mahasaya and ask for his blessing. This, for me, was always one of the more poignant scenes in the *Autobiography*, because it became not only one of the major themes of the book but also one of the themes of Yogananda's life.

Since Yogananda passed away more than seventy years ago, many have extended that legacy. In my own small way, writing mostly for the West, I have strived to add a little bit to that legacy with my books, bringing Eastern spiritual ideas to places that would normally be devoid of such thinking, namely the worlds of science, technology, business and entrepreneurship.

Bhaduri Mahasaya's last words to Yogananda were like water imbued with spiritual life force, telling the seeds that had been planted years earlier that it was time for them to grow and sprout. These words also gave Yogananda some of the courage to embark on his daunting mission to bring yoga to the West.

Whenever you are about to embark on a difficult task that feels like it could be overwhelming, particularly when it involves people that you have never met or places you have never been to, remember these words of the Levitating Saint. Imagine them being spoken not to a young Yogananda by the Levitating Saint, but to you, and modify them so they relate to whatever difficult journey or task lays ahead of you:

> Son, go to America. Take the dignity of hoary India for your shield. Victory is written on your brow; the noble distant people will well receive you.[11]

PART III

Superpowers, Karma and Illusion

'Are we living in the material age, or are we dreaming?'

– KEDAR NATH BABU*

---

* Yogananda, *Autobiography of a Yogi*, 'The Saint with Two Bodies', p. 29.

LESSON #5

The Ancient Arts of Bilocation, Levitation and Telepathy

I saw a yogi remain in the air, several feet above the ground, last night at a group meeting ...

— YOGANANDA[1]

In the *Autobiography*, there are numerous instances of a saint appearing in more than one place at the same time and of saints levitating in the air. There are also stories of telepathic messages being sent from master to disciple, with or without the physical materialization of the master—more than 100 years before text messaging and instant messaging had been invented!

What are we, as modern readers, to make of these stories, which are among the most colourful, memorable and perhaps incredible stories in all of the *Autobiography*? The way Yogananda tells us these stories leads us to believe that such incidents were perhaps not so extraordinary as they might seem to us today. That they seemed to occur regularly is attested to by the fact that Yogananda himself saw each of these phenomena (levitation, bilocation, telepathy) at work multiple times when he was young. If you add to these the stories he'd heard about but wasn't present for, the sum is a mountain of potential evidence for things that modern science tells us *cannot* happen. And that's just from one source (the *Autobiography*); there are many other accounts of such abilities (from India and elsewhere) that have survived to this day.

Siddhis in the *Autobiography*

These stories are examples of siddhis that were catalogued by Patanjali in his classic work, *The Yoga Sutra*. Although Patanjali lays out eight specific siddhis, which I like to refer to as superpowers in modern parlance (owing to the popularity of comic books and superheroes like Superman and Spider-Man), there is nothing inherent in this particular classification. Siddhis can be (and have been) classified in many different ways, and there is no agreement amongst saints or traditions of the number of different abilities that can manifest.

Some of the siddhis described in the *Autobiography* are more believable to modern readers than others. For example, we have all had the experience of thinking about someone and suddenly getting a call from that person, or the opposite, calling someone and being told that they were just about to get in touch with us. By itself, this ability perhaps isn't as dramatic as it seems at first glance. The term 'synchronicity', coined by Carl Jung to capture this phenomenon, when an outer event coincides with an inner event, has become quite popular. Jung defined it as an 'acausal connection' between two events. There is some kind of connection, but the mechanism is invisible to us and we are likely to write it off as mere 'coincidence'. Thus, it is 'acasual' only from a scientific perspective; scientists can't say whether one caused or influenced the other, so we are left with a 'meaningful coincidence', the more popular definition of synchronicity.

Perhaps because it involves mostly unseen connections and a series of coincidences, synchronicity is one of the more believable examples of supernatural phenomena to modern readers. It is also a highly subjective experience because it involves an inner event that only the subject knows about, so it can't be proved; as scientists like to say, it is non-falsifiable because there is no way (via modern science) to verify or falsify your statement that you were just thinking about something or someone.

Jung actually used the term 'synchronicity' to refer to a broad class of paranormal phenomena. The instances of telepathy in the *Autobiography* (of which there are many) could also be classified as a kind of synchronicity. It is a combination of a subjective event (one that occurs in the mind of the receiver) and an objective one (the message sent by the sender). What's objective about it is that, when the sender or receiver shares the message with a third party, the other person can confirm the veracity of the message. Alternatively, it could be a message about an event at a remote location that the recipient didn't know about, but which can be verified later.

One reason modern scientists don't believe in telepathy is that we don't know the mechanism behind it and it seems difficult to reproduce in the laboratory. In fact, the 'unseen' connection between the sender and receiver is a key part of the definition of telepathy. The messages Yogananda mentions in the *Autobiography* are quite specific; they resemble text messages we would send from our phones today (e.g., 'Meet me on the 9:00 a.m. train'). This takes them outside the purview of pure synchronicity, which might involve vaguely 'thinking about someone' and into the realm of telepathy.

The way these telepathic messages are presented in the *Autobiography* is much more dramatic. They often involve the receiver seeing the sender in the room (or on the ground outside in some cases), as if the latter has actually, physically appeared to send a message. The receiver often describes what the sender was wearing in Yogananda's telling. Does this mean that these are verifiable instances of siddhis (or, to use a vernacular phrase, 'siddha' powers or superpowers)?

It isn't so simple. It's unclear whether Yogananda was using the material appearance of the person as a plot device to make the telepathic messages seem more believable. Would a person standing next to the receiver have also 'seen' the sender, who is usually an accomplished yogic practitioner like Lahiri Mahasaya or Sri Yukteswar, or would they have said there was nothing there? This would tip the siddhi into the subjective or objective sides of the axis of believability.

On the one hand, Yogananda clearly tells us, even as Patanjali did, that siddhis can be obstacles on the path to self-realization. The example of the story of Yogananda's encounter with Gandha Baba (the Perfume Saint) is a case in point. This particular adept had spent years perfecting the ability to make any scent waft up from your hand, one of many secret abilities he had learnt from a 'master in Tibet' who was said to be over 1,000 years old; other such talents included the ability to materialize objects like food items. We'll talk more about this particular siddhi, the power to materialize real things, in the next chapter.

The scent 'materialized' by the Perfume Saint was real, as Yogananda's sister verified. Yogananda had asked the saint for the scent of jasmine and, when Yogananda encountered his sister Roma, she immediately remarked on the fragrance. However, Yogananda made it clear in this chapter that he was less than impressed with this particular superpower. It seemed to him almost a trivialization of God's power to use yoga to create everyday scents.

Siddhis can be, says Patanjali, signposts of a yogic adept; they can also be obstacles along the path to self-realization if we become too attached to them. Yogananda (and most of the genuine spiritual masters) often hammer this message in—that as impressive as they are, superpowers can hinder rather than aid the quest.

Even so, these particular instances of bilocation, levitation and telepathy that Yogananda tells us about are presented more like the achievements of great saints than hindrances. This may be, in part, because of Yogananda's life-long fascination with collecting stories of mystics who had achieved certain incredible abilities. In some ways, once you get beyond the wonder, the abilities are presented as tools that accomplished yogis can use at will, just as we can send messages using a mobile phone today.

The Art of Bilocation

Some believe that the siddhis are fantastical elements of the *Autobiography* that Yogananda probably made up to make his book more exciting. Whether they were made up or not, we can assume that the reason for the inclusion of so many stories of superpowers by him is that they are meant to expand our minds: to remind us that modern science doesn't know everything.

In this line of thinking, when Yogananda came to the West, during the early years of the radio and the telephone, he no doubt needed to add pizzazz to his stories of yogis and sadhus from ancient India. Since television hadn't yet been invented, a story about the actual appearance of a saint who was known to be far away could be counted on to provide a dramatic departure from the mundane, demonstrating the power of yoga and inspiring curiosity in Westerners about the yogic path.

To a certain extent, it worked—the tales of superpowers, inserted causally into a story about his life history and chock-full of spiritual lessons, certainly intrigued millions and brought them to the yogic path.

Should we truly dismiss these abilities so quickly, as many modern readers do, despite knowing that the yogic tradition has existed since time immemorial, since well before Patanjali first made reference to the siddhis?

Let's start with bilocation—the ability to appear in more than one place at a time, clearly visible to others. Usually, a story of bilocation involves a saint appearing before a disciple somewhere, while others testify that the yogi was in another location (perhaps many miles away) the whole time.

To the true believer, the stories are meant to reinforce the exalted spiritual levels of those who have travelled before us and to provide Yogananda's first-hand evidence that the siddhis do in fact exist and are something we can all aspire to. They are also meant to demonstrate how our understanding of the material world, which is what science and technology have made us masters of, is still incomplete.

Yet, it is not reasonable to assume that Yogananda made these abilities up, when they are referenced in many places and are not even unique to the yogic tradition of India. Bilocation, the art of appearing in more than one place at time, though rare in many parts of the world, is not unheard of in other traditions. This includes the Catholic traditions of Europe, the native traditions of the Americas and the Islamic traditions of the Middle East to name just a few.

The real message of these siddhis may be that they challenge our understanding of the world; they make us wonder what it is real and what is not. We will expand on this subject significantly in 'Lesson #7: The World is Like a Movie, a Dream, a Video Game'.

The Saint with Two Bodies

The first time Yogananda mentions this siddhi in the *Autobiography* is when, as a boy, he was sent on an errand to Benares by his father. Since Mukunda's father, Bhagabati Ghosh, was an executive at one of the major railroads in India, it was not uncommon for him to send his sons to various places in northern India with first-class train tickets to deliver messages or for some other purpose.

As mentioned previously, Yogananda's father was a disciple of Lahiri Mahasaya, the saint from Benares who, though Yogananda never met him (he passed away in 1895), plays a huge role in the *Autobiography*. Lahiri was the householder yogi who was instructed to start the modern tradition of kriya yoga that Yogananda was a part of. (We'll explore Lahiri's incredible stories in 'Lesson #12: Lessons from Babaji and the Great Engine of Karma'.) By virtue of his relationship with Lahiri, Yogananda's father was a brother disciple of Sri

Yukteswar, and of a certain Swami Pranabananda, whom Yogananda nicknames 'The Saint with Two Bodies' in one of the many miraculous tales of siddhis and superpowers in the *Autobiography*.

In this particular story, Mukunda, only twelve years old at the time, asked his father if he could go on a sightseeing trip to Benares. Bhagabati allowed him to go and gave him a first-class ticket, on the condition that he deliver a letter from his father to a certain Kedar Nath Babu in Benares. However, not knowing exactly where Kedar Nath Babu was to be found in that ancient city, Bhagabati instructed his son to first seek out Swami Pranabananda.

Upon arriving in Benares, Mukunda found Swami Pranabananda at his residence, clad in a loin cloth and sitting in the lotus posture on a small dais. The swami cheerfully welcomed the boy and inquired if he was, in fact, 'Bhagabati's son'. This confused the youth since he hadn't had time to introduce himself or deliver his father's letter of introduction. After reading the letter, the swami told Mukunda to sit down while he located Kedar Nath Babu.

But, instead of getting up from the dais, the swami went into meditation, entering what seemed to be a state of clairvoyance to locate the whereabouts of Babu. While the swami was meditating, Mukunda, uncharacteristically for the spiritual prodigy, became impatient and wondered how the swami would find his father's friend sitting there. Looking around the room restlessly, he spotted a set of wooden sandals.

Sensing Mukunda's concern, the saint assured him, 'Little sir (chotto mahasaya), don't get worried. The man you wish to see will be with you in half an hour.' The swami, still sitting on the dais, then mysteriously retreated into a meditative silence.

A half-hour later, the swami announced that the man was nearing the door. To Mukunda's surprise, when he looked outside a man appeared and asked him if he was Bhagabati's son. When Mukunda asked him how he knew he was waiting at the swami's home, the man looked puzzled and related the first (but not the last) of the many miraculous stories in the *Autobiography*.

Babu told the boy that Swami Pranabananda had appeared to him, wearing wooden sandals, in another part of the city, not more than half an hour away, and told him that Bhagabati's son was waiting for him at the swami's residence. Kedar Nath Babu had agreed to come and followed the swami, who had other errands to run and quickly disappeared into the crowd.

Mukunda told his father's friend that the swami had not left his sight and had been sitting in the lotus posture in that very place for the past hour. This amazed both of them and prompted Kedar Nath Babu to exclaim, rather memorably:

Are we living in this material world or are we dreaming? I never expected to witness such a miracle in my life! I thought this swami was just an ordinary man, and now I find he can materialize in an extra body and work through it![2]

They entered the saint's room and found him sitting there just as he had been for the last hour, dressed exactly as Kedar Nath Babu had seen him, except that the swami had been wearing the wooden sandals that were now placed in the corner.

The swami was nonplussed at the pair's amazement, telling them:

Why are you stupefied at all this? The subtle unity of
the phenomenal world is not hidden from true yogis. I
instantly see and converse with my disciples in distant
Calcutta. They can similarly transcend at will every
obstacle of gross matter.[3]

In this instance, it wasn't Mukunda who saw the swami appear
in two places, it was his father's friend, Kedar Nath Babu. Still,
the way the tale is told, there is no doubt that Yogananda wants
us to believe (and that he himself believed) that the swami
had in fact appeared in more than one place at the same time.
While we don't know whether the swami's doppelganger was
only seen by Kedar Nath Babu or could be seen by everyone
else on the street, there is meant to be no doubt about the fact
that Babu got the message. In Western mystical traditions,
this second body is often called the 'etheric double', and there
are other examples in the *Autobiography* itself of a master
appearing in more than one place (often in places hundreds of
miles from each other) at the same time.

My Master, in Calcutta, Appears in Serampore

Before we analyse this story further, let's go to a second story,
in which Yogananda claims to have seen the materialized body
of a saint himself. Again, in this instance, Yogananda received a
very specific message just like Babu did, and once again, we see
the twin superpowers of bilocation and telepathy interlinked
to the point where it's hard to separate them from one another.
It's also again unclear whether the double was seen by others,
since Yogananda was alone when he received the message.

Many years after this story in Benares, when he had become
a disciple of his own guru, Sri Yukteswar, Mukunda was

attending college in Serampore. He lived in a boarding house near the school (the same one where Sri Yukteswar told him he had seen the magic of the fakir, Afzal Khan, from 'Lesson #4: The Many Lessons of the Incomparable Levitating Saint'), and made a daily pilgrimage to Yukteswar's ashram.

Yogananda had, as he seemed to do with all of his friends during his youthful years, convinced his roommate in the boarding school, Dijen Babu, to become a student of the spiritual path under the tutelage of Sri Yukteswar as well. The pair often walked to the ashram together for their daily lessons. One day, they found out that Sri Yukteswar wasn't there; he had travelled to Calcutta on urgent business. The master also sent them a note informing them that he would be arriving the next morning by the 9 a.m. train and instructed both of them to meet him at Serampore station.

At 8.30 a.m., half an hour before they were to meet Yukteswar at the station, Mukunda received a 'telepathic message' that flashed instantly in his mind: 'I am delayed; don't meet the nine o'clock train.' This frustrated Dijen, who had received no such message and preferred to put his faith in the note they had received from their teacher. You could say that Dijen was a modern materialist. Trusting the physical object of the note, Dijen left for the 9 a.m. train as instructed.

Until this point, we have only heard about Yogananda's intuition, but then the story takes an interesting turn. After Dijen left for the station, Mukunda, to his astonishment, noticed the 'clearly materialized figure of Sri Yukteswar' in the sunlight streaming into the room! Yogananda emphasizes that this wasn't an apparition, as he felt his master's robe, touched his shoes as was customary at the time and, to quell his own doubting mind, even touched Yukteswar's toes to make sure they were real 'flesh and blood' and that he wasn't hallucinating.

Yukteswar said he was pleased that Mukunda had got his message and told Mukunda that he would be on the 10 a.m. train. He even told him that he would be preceded by a boy with a silver cup. His master finished by placing his hand on Mukunda's head and then, Yogananda tells us, vanished bit by bit as if he were a 'scroll being rolled up'.

Immediately after, Dijen returned from the station, dejected that he hadn't found their teacher on the designated train, at which point Mukunda matter-of-factly told his roommate that their master would be on the next train at 10 a.m. At the appointed time, Mukunda dragged his roommate back to the station, where they saw their teacher following a boy with a silver cup, just as the master's apparition had told Mukunda!

The Message and the Lesson

Dijen was of course first amazed, and then angry that Mukunda got the message but didn't share it with him, feeling he had been deceived by his friend. Sri Yukteswar patiently explained that he had sent the message to both of them, but Dijen didn't get it because his mind was too restless.

Clearly, the point the guru was trying to make was that if you are able to meditate and rest your mind, it will assume the state of a clear pond without any ripples on its surface. This pond of the mind can reflect not just sunlight but also the kind of light that transmits messages telepathically. Dijen then apologized to Mukunda for not believing him.

Is this story really about telepathic messages sent from one person to another, or about bilocation? It sounds like the story of the Saint with the Two Bodies—too incredible to have been true, at least the part that has to do with the physical manifestation and Mukunda being able to 'feel' his master's robe, toes, etc.

Once again, we find Yogananda telling us stories about experiences from decades earlier that may have had some immediate practical purpose (delivering a practical message when mobile phones hadn't been invented) but were really meant to serve him in his lifelong mission to inspire and educate a modern audience about yoga and the spiritual path.

I would suggest that these stories of bilocation are themselves messages, not just from Sri Yukteswar to his disciple or from Swami Pranabananda to Bhagabati's friend. They are, rather, messages from Yogananda (or *through* Yogananda) to us, the public, that is interested in these spiritual powers.

Perhaps anticipating that Yogananda would one day tell this story to a distrustful world, Sri Yukteswar, during the short encounter when he appeared before Mukunda in the boarding house, told him something that should be noted, a sentence that is meant as much for you and me, the readers of the *Autobiography*, as it was for Mukunda his student: 'As I still stared mutely, Sri Yukteswar went on, "This is not an apparition, but my flesh and blood form. I have been divinely commanded to give you this experience, rare to achieve on earth."'4

The real lesson of this story, though, is different from the lessons that can be gleaned from the stories of other siddhis and superpowers. In the cases of the Tiger Swami, the Levitating Saint, the Perfume Saint and the Mohammedan wonder-worker (in the next chapter), the lesson is that superpowers aren't the real goal and can be a distraction from and obstacle to our spiritual growth.

In this case, the real lesson is that there are benefits to clearing the mind and that meditation is a worthy goal that will take you, the student, to a higher level of consciousness, where you can perceive both telepathic messages and (possibly) materialized forms of individuals who aren't there. At another level, the story is also meant to convince a sceptical, modern Western audience that the events described actually took place, even though they seem fantastical to modern ears.

However, unlike in other cases where Yogananda presents superpowers as something that many saints had, in this case he explicitly makes the point that this experience was 'rare to achieve on earth.' This leads me to believe that his raison d'etre for including this story was as much to impress upon readers the importance of a clear mind as to try to convince us that his master really appeared before him in Serampore.

In short, the mundane message about the arrival of a train wasn't meant to travel only from Calcutta to Serampore; it was meant to travel ahead in time, as it has—here we are, discussing the message over 100 years after it was delivered! We will talk further about the importance of a clear mind as the goal of all yogic practices in 'Lesson #8: Practice Every Day, No Matter How Much Time You Have.'

Bilocation in Other Traditions

Serious devotees of kriya yoga might be upset that I seem to be dismissing the question of whether the bilocation *actually* happened, at least in this second case. I am not dismissing it at all, but am simply pointing out that there was a subjective aspect to the bilocation (since it was only seen by one person and couldn't be verified) as well as an objective one (the message that was carried could be verified). This was the case in other stories in the *Autobiography*, too; for example, Babaji appeared in a room that Yukteswar and Lahiri Mahasaya were both in, but Yukteswar was not able to perceive the master while Lahiri could see him clearly. The master told Yukteswar that his gaze 'was not yet faultless'; again, that his mind (and thus his gaze) wasn't yet clear. The really important lesson is that of having a clear mind, one that can perceive without disturbances (ripples on the surface of a pond) and clearly reflect what is happening. This is perhaps more important than the bilocation or telepathy itself.

While I initially dismissed this tale as perhaps exaggerated by Yogananda to make his point, I decided to ask someone I respected what she thought about these tales in Yogananda's *Autobiography*. Diana Pasulka is a professor of religion and philosophy at the University of North Carolina and a respected scholar of the Catholic faith. I knew that she had spoken about these types of tales and superpowers in the context of the tradition she was an expert in, making her an ideal source for some perspective.

I suspected that she, a modern scholar of religion from a respected educational institution, would say these were likely made-up stories meant to teach lessons, not to be taken literally. And sure enough, she said that most modern scholars tended to treat religious texts as metaphors, not as events to be interpreted literally.

However, Dr Pasulka clarified her remarks and went on to suggest that this point of view was part of the goal of modern educational systems to indoctrinate scholars into today's materialistic view of the world, according to which miracles and siddhis were not only impossible but worth studying as purely sociological phenomena, meant to aid in the spread of the religion and to get people to believe.

Then, to my surprise, Pasulka told me that she had come to believe that tales like these should not be summarily discounted. She had first read Yogananda's book when she was a child in San Francisco; having grown up in a Catholic tradition, she did not find stories of saints performing miracles unusual. Still, she said that her introduction to the world of the fantastic and miraculous was Yogananda's book, which her parents had on the bookshelf and which she devoured at a young age.

When she became a scholar of religion, she was indoctrinated, as most scholars are, into believing that these stories weren't real and should be treated as metaphors. As she progressed in her career and continued researching Catholic traditions (including in the private archives of the Vatican), she discovered manuscripts that described similar miracles witnessed by large numbers of people, making them difficult to dismiss so quickly.

In fact, at the Vatican, she found an old private manuscript that included the testimony of the 'Devil's advocate' in the investigation into the miracles of Joseph of Cupertino, a saint who was said to have levitated in the presence of not just a few. There were almost 1,000 signatures from people who claimed to have witnessed this levitation.[5] In the Catholic tradition, the Church responds to reports of a miracle by assigning an agent, called the Devil's advocate, to be sceptical of the stories. In the case of Joseph of Cupertino, the Devil's advocate assigned by the church was a supporter of science, a 'big-time rationalist' (according to Pasulka) who thought he could easily disprove the reported levitation of Cupertino. Yet he came to believe, on the strength of the volume and veracity of the testimony, that it had actually happened!

Pasulka also told me the story of Maria of Agreda, a nun at a monastery in Spain who said that while meditating, she would 'travel on the wings of angels' to a strange new world. At the same time (the 1600s), Native American population in New Mexico (a state in southwestern USA) had claimed to see a nun matching the description of Maria. There are no other records of a Catholic nun being sent to that part of the world in that era.

In the Catholic tradition, stories of saints levitating and bilocating seem to be intertwined. Maria of Agreda was said to have done both. Admittedly, those stories are from so long ago that they may stretch modern credibility; they are older than Yogananda's stories by far. But Dr Pasulka also told me that she had looked seriously into the story of Padre Pio, who was also documented to have bilocated and levitated much more recently ... in the 1940s!

Dr Pasulka said that not only shouldn't these stories be discounted, but the very question of whether they are 'real' or 'not' may be beside the point. These stories, she said, could be hinting at a different way of understanding other dimensions and/or realities which are real, but don't fit into our theories as we have articulated them at the moment.

Dr Pasulka came to believe these stories shouldn't be dismissed because, as a result of her intensive research, she recognized that it was the job of the Devil's advocate to produce evidence against the miracles being investigated. Well-documented stories of miraculous events within the Catholic tradition that had been subjected to scrutiny restored Pasulka's faith in the possibility that such events could be 'real', a faith that the modern educational system had tried to stamp out.

Pasulka now says she believes that Yogananda's stories could be records of actual events that have been reported in

India, and that they are similar to events reported all over the world.

More About Levitation

Yogananda describes the levitation phenomenon in his chapter on the Levitating Saint (the ones whose lesson we examined in 'Lesson #4: The Many Lessons of the Incomparable Levitating Saint'). When his friend Upendra tried to impress Mukunda by telling him he had discovered the location of a levitating saint, Mukunda told him that he had met the Levitating Saint many times and was familiar with him. It seems that Mukunda developed a reputation early for knowing about yogis and siddhis and so, of course, his friend asked him how it all worked.

> A yogi's body loses its grossness after use of certain pranayamas. Then it will levitate or hop about like a leaping frog. Even saints who do not practice a formal yoga have been known to levitate during a state of intense devotion to God.[6]

Yogananda reminds us in this chapter of what Pasulka reminded me of: that levitating saints are not uncommon in other religious traditions. Yogananda tells us that St Theresa of Avila and other Christian saints were often observed in this state of levitation.

Different traditions suggest that there are different ways of becoming light enough to levitate. In the case of yogis, this is mostly achieved through pranayama and other yogic exercises, and sometimes by hopping around rather than 'floating motionless'. With the Christin saints, it seems to have been possible because of devotion to God and prayer, and not because of any particular techniques. In both cases, there is a lightness of the physical body that allows for either the hopping or the levitation—or, in in even more esoteric cases, flight.

St Theresa would often float spontaneously, while not engaged in any kind of exercise or meditation, which became inconvenient because she had duties at the monastery! She would just 'float up'. There is no doubt that the significant amount of time spent on and the level of sincerity in their devotion leads to this accomplishment; Yogananda and other saints have attested to this. Just as pranayama and yoga affect the subtle body, so too does practicing devotion to God.

Though these kinds of siddhis appear all over the world, no other part of the ancient world has catalogued and explored the different paths to God as comprehensively as the Indian subcontinent. Bhakti, or devotion, is just one of the paths towards God that was catalogued by the ancient rishis.

Some yogis are said to have adopted levitation as a practical method of travelling, which doesn't seem to be the case with most Western saints or with Bhaduri Mahasaya. In the Tibetan traditions, there are many saints which were said to levitate and, in some cases, actually fly. The best-known of them today is the eleventh-century yogi Milarepa, who is regarded as Tibet's most famous yogi and stories about him flying in the air are commonplace in that tradition. Since Tibet is one of the highest altitude places on Earth, surrounded by the Himalayas, flying would a most useful skill to get where you are going quickly!

Though Milarepa had manifested occult powers even before meeting his guru and accumulated bad karma from them, it was his master, Marpa, who instructed him in the ways of the yogic path, which eventually led to his self-realization. Marpa is called the 'translator' because he travelled from Tibet, known as the Land of Snows, across the Himalayas to Kashmir where he met Naropa, who taught him the 'six yogas' of Naropa.

Levitation is not explicitly one of the six yogas (nor are there stories of Marpa flying like his disciple). The six yogas, instead, are focused on enabling the realization of the illusive and dream-like nature of the body, the energy body and of physical reality itself. As we will explore in 'Lesson #7: The World is Like a Movie, a Dream, a Video Game', once the dream-like nature of physical reality has been understood, manipulating the dream-world is not so hard to do and nor is flying in it.

The way to do this is to first recognize the dream-like nature of reality. One approach, which is one of the Six Yogas of Naropa called Dream Yoga, is akin to what we call lucid dreaming today: to realize in the middle of a dream that you are, in fact, dreaming (and your physical body is asleep.) My personal lucidity test, which tells me that I'm dreaming, is my ability to fly—something I (unlike Milarepa) am unable to do in the physical world. Flying in the dream world, once you have become aware of it, is not hard to do because you are already in your energy body.

However, there are times when I cannot fly as well as I could at other times. Sometimes I float up and, at other times, I barely get off the ground. There is a heaviness that is contained in the energy body and it regulates how easy it is to fly in the dream-world. It is analogous to what Yogananda says about the 'grossness' of the physical body, which is related to the grossness or heaviness of the energy body, which in turn is related to how many things we are holding on to, mentally and emotionally (also known as samskaras).

How do we lighten our load? That is, in fact, the process of spiritual practice and brings us to what this section of the book is really about. If a modern, rational professor like Dr Pasulka can come to believe that these kinds of superpowers—bilocation, telepathy, levitation—not only exist but that Yogananda likely really witnessed them, one must wonder what the nature of the material world is after all.

For a modern reader like me, an engineer and scientist by training, my conversation with Pasulka and others about the *Autobiography* left me wondering: if these stories are to be taken literally, in addition to their spiritual lessons, how does it all work? That is a subject we will take up after another detour. Like the stories discussed in this chapter, the next story made me wonder about the question that Kedar Nath Babu asked Mukunda over a century ago in Benares: are we dreaming or living in a material world?

LESSON #6

A Karmic Lesson Embedded in a Story About a Jinn

Years ago, right in this very room you now occupy, a Mohammedan wonder-worker performed four miracles before me!

— SRI YUKTESWAR TO YOGANANDA[1]

In one of the most memorable tales in the entire *Autobiography*, Yogananda tells us about 'a Mohammedan wonder-worker', a fakir (or Muslim holy man or mystic) who is able to perform incredible tasks, such as producing objects out of thin air and then causing them to vanish. This is accomplished through control of an invisible entity named 'Hazrat', who is responsible for grabbing material objects and transporting them to another place or making them disappear (these objects, especially the valuable ones, usually ended up sometime later in the possession of the somewhat selfish fakir).

My first thought on reading this tale was that Hazrat was a jinn, like those depicted in the fictional tales of the Alif Layla, or *One Thousand and One Nights* (also known in English as the *Arabian Nights*). I wasn't the only one to think so—some have accused Yogananda's *Autobiography* of being as fictional as the *Arabian Nights*, right down to this tale of a fakir and jinn. This was probably one of the tales that stayed in my memory since first reading the book in the 1990s. It invoked both incredulity ('This didn't really happen, did it?') and curiosity (specifically regarding the jinn of whom I had heard much about when I was a little boy living in a small village near Lahore).

At the surface level, the tale is constructed like that of a parable for youngsters presenting an obvious moral—that you shouldn't use siddhis for material gain, and that this will slow down your spiritual progress. When I read the tale again recently though, I realized that as in many of Yogananda's tales, there is more than one lesson embedded within the story. Its implications may go beyond this surface-level admonition to reveal subtler truths about our tendencies across lives, our desires and inclinations, as well as how our karma creates interesting situations for us.

Finally, it offers a new perspective on the relationship between the material and the unseen worlds, and the role of the spiritual entities that inhabit these worlds, notably the jinn. It also raises important questions about Yogananda's tales and how they were collected, constructed and then released to the public. Was he just relaying what he had heard or was he embellishing the tales in order to make his points easier to digest (and remember)?

The Tale of Hazrat and the Fakir

In this incredible chapter of the *Autobiography*, Yogananda is
told the tale by someone he considers unimpeachable, implying
that we, the readers can assume the tale is 100 per cent true.
It was narrated to him by Sri Yukteswar, while Yogananda
was attending classes at Serampore College. He had taken
up residence in a small building not far from the college and
Yukteswar's ashram.

In fact, it was a visit by Yukteswar to Mukunda's dormitory,
an old building that Yogananda tells us fronted the Ganges, that
prompted the tale. His guru claimed to have witnessed several
miracles in that very same building. Telling Mukunda a story
about miracles was like offering candy to a child, so Yukteswar
was assured a captive audience. Not only did Mukunda always
want to know all of the details of these types of miraculous
stories, he recalled these details many decades later while
writing the *Autobiography*.

Yukteswar told him of a fakir named Afzal Khan. When
Afzal was young, he helped an old Hindu yogi by fetching him
some water in a small village in eastern Bengal. Presumably, this
happened at a time when social relations between Muslims and
Hindus were strained, because the old yogi was very impressed
that the boy hadn't succumbed to 'ungodly sectarianism' that
others in the region had. The yogi was so impressed that he
decided to reward young Afzal: 'I am going to teach you a
certain yoga method which will give you command over one of
the invisible realms. The great powers that will be yours should
be exercised for worthy ends; never employ them selfishly.'[2]

The yogi also told Afzal that he would do this because Afzal
had brought good karma from past lives. However, he warned

that Afzal also carried selfish tendencies from past lives, and that selfishness would be particularly risky for the young man and soon-to-be fakir.

Afzal, by way of this yogic technique, was able to gain control of an invisible entity called Hazrat, who could procure for Afzal any object he desired. All he had to do was touch the object or otherwise indicate his desire to Hazrat, and the obedient jinn would snatch up the item, making it disappear from the physical world. Later, the object would appear in Afzal's possession or wherever the fakir told Hazrat to put it.

It didn't take long for Afzal to cultivate a dubious reputation, as valuable objects started to disappear when he was around. The purloined objects ranged from gold to money to train tickets, and soon a small band of followers grew around Afzal, hoping to learn his technique. Soon, his dubious reputation preceded him and people became very cautious when Afzal visited their towns. Yukteswar told Yogananda that Afzal managed to avoid getting into trouble with the authorities because in some cases, the objects didn't disappear until he was gone, and didn't reappear in his possession until much later. Moreover, it was Hazrat who took them, not Afzal, which made it difficult to prove theft or press charges in any case.

At this point, the story took a personal turn for Yukteswar, who met Afzal while visiting the building that Mukunda had a room in. He witnessed a number of miracles involving different objects. One of these objects was a valuable watch that belonged to Yukteswar's friend, Babu. Afzal told Babu, who was quite distressed about the disappearance of the watch, that if he wanted it back, he would have to go home and get the Rs 500 he had stored in a safe. Babu did so and Hazrat dutifully returned the watch.

Of particular interest in this story is the following detail: Afzal instructed a young Yukteswar to write something on a stone and to toss the stone into the river from a place near the building. Afzal then told Yukteswar to fill a pot with water from the river and bring it to him. The fakir instructed Hazrat to retrieve the stone and deposit it in the pot with the water. Yukteswar verified that it was the same object; it had his handwriting on it.

The coup de grace of Afzal's miracles involved his summoning a banquet for a party of twenty, on plates that were lined with gold. The vast quantity of food and the plates materialized out of thin air for the assembled group. Hungry and thrilled, they ate their fill; whatever requests they made for food or drink were fulfilled almost instantaneously by the indefatigable Hazrat, and this seemed ample reward for the rupees that Babu had given up.

What Happened to Afzal Khan

Years later, the same friend (Babu) showed Yukteswar a newspaper article that revealed what had happened to Afzal Khan. The article was a mea culpa of sorts by the fakir, stating that he had been misusing his yogic powers. One day, years after the encounter with Yukteswar, the fakir had come across a limp old man on the road who asked Afzal to heal his limp and showed him his only material possession, a ball of gold.

True to character, Afzal simply touched the object and walked away. Suddenly, the gold was gone, causing the old man to raise an outcry. But it was Afzal who was in for the real surprise. It turned out this old man, who was not crippled after all, was the same yogi who had taught Afzal the yogic technique many years earlier. The yogi had come in disguise to check up on him after hearing rumours of his dishonest behaviour.

Afzal claimed that the old yogi took away his ability to command Hazrat, but, upon his repentance and recognition of what he had done wrong (and based on his goodwill from previous lives), agreed to let him continue to command Hazrat to bring him food and clothing whenever he was in need of them. Afzal then became a man of God and devoted himself to spiritual practice rather than material gains.

Superpowers and the Yogic Path

Many people are drawn to the yogic path because they think it will help them in the physical world—whether through improved physical health (physical yoga poses or asanas) or through better concentration (meditation) or relaxation and stress relief (mindfulness). These things can, in turn, lead to more material success. In my opinion, these kinds of benefits serve to draw people (particularly the young) to yoga initially rather than aid the quest for spiritual enlightenment. There is also the hint, implicit in *Autobiography of a Yogi* and countless other books, that yogic techniques will empower one to perform superhuman feats, essentially gaining superpowers.

Any genuine spiritual teacher like Yogananda will warn us about this line of thinking. The siddhis may be signposts along the path, but they are not the purpose of yoga and, in fact, can cause the seeker's progress to plateau. To keep moving along the spiritual path, we have to leave behind thoughts of gain in the physical world.

Does that mean it's wrong to start on the yogic path for health-related or material benefits (or even superpowers)? I don't think so. In fact, it is what often places those of us who also grow up with a strong desire for material success on the yogic path in the first place. Once we are on the path, we begin to appreciate the complex interplay of karmic forces that leads to situations being created for us in the material world.

In *Zen Entrepreneurship*, I readily admitted that I started meditating and practicing breathing exercises (pranayama) because I thought they would help me increase my ability to concentrate and consequently be more successful in the wild world of start-ups. The promise of 'superpowers' was always lurking at the back of my mind. In fact, years before I had encountered the *Autobiography*, I read a book called *Super-Learning*, based on research that was undertaken in the former Soviet Union and in other places, which promised that the use of certain music and breathing techniques would improve one's ability to effortlessly memorize up to thousands of words.

Though I was never successful at using these techniques to memorize thousands of words (I was only in high school and didn't quite have the patience), the rhythmic breathing exercises have stayed with me to this day. In fact, pranayama is based on the same principles.

Perhaps my interest in seeking out those who have 'superpowers' and reading about them is why this specific tale from the *Autobiography* got lodged in my mind. We know that Yogananda as a youth sought out any yogis or stories of yogis who had any kind of superpower. Of course, in the case of the story of Afzal Khan, Yogananda's lesson has less to do with the superpowers themselves than with the matter of what one intends to use them for and the possibility of misusing yogic abilities for personal gain.

The Lesson of Afzal Khan (and Spider-Man too)

This story has a clear-cut lesson: do not misuse spiritual techniques (and the potential superpowers that might manifest because of them) for personal material gain, particularly at the expense of others. The superpowers are to be used to help others (which is implied when the yogi teaches young Afzal the technique whereby he can control Hazrat).

Afzal Khan enriched himself by getting Hazrat to take objects of value from others, ranging from jewellery to expensive clothes. But he also sometimes used Hazrat to produce meals fit for a palace, like the one he conjured up for Yukteswar and his friends. The old yogi explicitly asks Afzal at the end of the chapter to cure his limp—giving Afzal the ability to use his superpower for good.

The funny thing is that this is also the lesson of many modern superhero stories. The Spider-Man franchise has popularized a quote that could just as easily have come from the old yogi who mentored Afzal: 'With great power comes great responsibility.'

What's Karma Got to Do with It?

While this is the obvious lesson of the story, I believe there is an interesting and deeper lesson about karma. The story is not just about reaping what we sow but about how the situations created for us in the world are often unique to our personal karma. In fact, the old yogi implies that the karma from Afzal's past lives was part of the reason the boy was granted the powers in the first place. The granting of these powers came with an explicit warning to 'not misuse' them.

You might have assumed that Afzal Khan's initial encounter with his future guru (when the old man asked him to fetch water and Afzal did so) was a chance meeting. This assumption would be incorrect. There are the obvious aspects of karma at work here: part of the reason the yogi teaches him the technique is the 'good karma' from Afzal's previous lives. Part of the reason the guru decides, after releasing Hazrat from Afzal Khan's control, to allow him to continue to call on the spirit for food and clothing, is again his good karma from previous lives.

Clearly, Afzal was drawn to the spiritual path and followed yogic techniques for years before he achieved full control over Hazrat. You might say that Afzal had an inclination for the spiritual path. This is, of course, the easiest way for us to learn about our karma: our karma is what we are drawn to. So ask yourself: what are you drawn to, which others around you are not even remotely interested in pursuing?

In my own life, I was the only one of four siblings, born and raised in a Muslim family, to have even the remotest interest in yoga and the Vedas. We were all, however, drawn to the technology industry. Competence with computers was true for all of us; however, I had a particular affinity for computer programming, and this led me to study computer science at MIT and make it my profession, which led me to become an entrepreneur. When I took up programming, it was far from the kind of thing that most people did—either in the United States or in the subcontinent, which has, of course, become one of the centres of software computing talent in the world over ensuing decades.

So, one aspect of karma is that we are drawn towards specific professions; we also have specific tendencies, which are referred to as vasanas in the yogic traditions. We'll save a bigger discussion about affinities for another lesson, but as I said, the deeper lesson here is about karma, and I don't just mean good karma or bad karma, but the complexities of karma.

Afzal Khan's guru, the one who taught him to summon and control Hazrat also warned him of the potential for disaster:

> I am going to teach you a certain yoga method which will give you command over one of the invisible realms. The great powers that will be yours should be exercised for worthy ends; never employ them selfishly! I perceive, alas! that you have brought over from the past some seeds of destructive tendencies. Do not allow them to sprout by watering them with fresh evil actions. The complexity of your previous karma is such that you must use this life to reconcile your yogic accomplishments with the highest humanitarian goals.[3]

You will notice that Yogananda masterfully gives us a story in which a situation is manifested to perfectly provide a person with a test that gives him the ability to either resolve or to prolong his karma (the 'past seeds of destructive tendencies'). We will explore this idea further in future lessons as we discuss karma and its central role in creating challenges and setbacks for us.

However, if Afzal Khan were a character in a video game and one of the major tests he had to pass concerned whether he was inclined to help others or help himself, how would we create the right challenge for him? One obvious way would be to have a yogi teach him a magical technique that granted him a superpower and then let him choose what to do with it.

While karma is often thought of as recompense for previous actions, the real meaning of karma is to be found in the nature of the seeds: how they are planted and how they sprout to create further karmic situations. These new situations, the saplings that are produced by the engine of karma, in turn allow us to resolve the karmic seed, or plant new seeds for the future and prolong the cycle.

This is how the universe or, as it is referred to metaphorically sometimes, the Lords of Karma, are testing you: by manifesting just the right situation to help you deal with the issues left over from previous incarnations. The tests that you face will be different from the tests that I face, because of our different tendencies, but you can bet that they will be perfectly tailored to what each of us needs in this life.

So, while the first lesson from Yogananda's story is that we shouldn't abuse superpowers or yogic techniques for material gain, the deeper lesson is that our karma will manifest just the right situation for us to either resolve or prolong specific tendencies that we have carried into this material universe. These personalized situations are like personalized quests or challenges. How does this work? We'll talk more about it in 'Lesson #7: The World is Like a Movie, a Dream, a Video Game.'

Side Discussion: Where Did Aladdin's Jinn and Yogananda's Hazrat Come From?

I would hate to end this chapter about the story of Afzal Khan and Hazrat without talking a little bit about the veracity of the story and the powers of the legendary jinn.

In the West, we're familiar with tales of jinn through the well-known tale of Aladdin, perhaps the most famous of the tales in the *Arabian Nights*. The tale has in recent decades been introduced to a new generation through the 2019 Disney movie (and the 1992 animated film before that). Now when I think of a jinn, I think of Robin Williams or Will Smith singing a song to Aladdin explaining his powers and insisting to Aladdin that he never had 'a friend like me'. Of course, Afzal Khan never had a friend like Hazrat, either!

In *Aladdin*, the 'genie' (anglicized version of jinn) appears when he is summoned by rubbing a magic lamp, and offers the holder of the lamp three wishes. It turns out that, in the original tale of 'Aladdin and the Wonderful Lamp', there was no limit on the number of wishes and there were actually two jinn, one that was attached to a magic ring and one, more powerful, that was attached to the famous lamp. They were referred to as the 'slave of the lamp' and the 'servant of the ring'.

Where did these tales come from? And how do they relate to Yogananda's inclusion of this tale in the *Autobiography*?

My father told me that he'd read the Alif Layla in Urdu when he was a kid, and I had naturally assumed that it and other well-known tales like 'Ali Baba and the Forty Thieves' had made their way from Arabic to Urdu, just like they had made their way from Arabic to English. However, the origin of the Aladdin story is actually quite murky. While the story was included in translations of the Alif Layla, scholars tell us that it wasn't a part of the original Arabic renditions of the Alif Layla; it was added when the collection was translated into French by Anthony Galland, the first Western translation of the folk tales. The stories of Aladdin and Ali Baba don't exist in any of the original Arabic manuscripts that pre-dated Galland's French translation, published around 1709. Galland learnt of the stories from a Syrian traveller, Hana Dayib, who happened to be living in France.

Yet, there are many other tales in the *Arabian Nights* that were part of the 'original collection' and feature jinn playing central roles. It turns out that there is no agreement on what constitutes the 'original collection'; the tales were told orally for many years before they were written down. That the Arabic tales had some origin in Persian lore is generally agreed upon; some even think that a few of the tales made their way into the Islamic world from ancient India.[4]

The similarity of Yogananda's story to the kinds of tales that are now commonly associated with the *Arabian Nights* has led many commentators to suggest that Yogananda simply made up this story in order to reach a lesson about misusing spiritual powers, knowing that his audience, Americans initially, were interested in the material benefits that might come from yoga. Also, the Aladdin tale was well-known throughout the West and in India by the time Yogananda wrote his book.

This, however, ignores the lengths to which Yogananda went to make the incredible tale sound credible. For one thing, he said it was told to him by Sri Yukteswar, in whom Yogananda had full faith. Then there is the matter of Yukteswar having narrated the tale to Yogananda in the dormitory where he claimed to have witnessed Afzal Khan's miracles, the same building in which Yogananda was staying then.

Additionally, given that Yogananda's father was a prominent member of a railroad company, we cannot ignore that Yogananda makes it a point to emphasize that Afzal Khan became well-known among railroad employees as someone who was able to procure tickets without paying for them. Both railroad employees and jewellers were wary of him, calling him the Terror of Bengal during those years. And finally, Yogananda tells us that Yukteswar came across Afzal Khan's very public apology in a newspaper that was widely read in Bengal, though he doesn't tell us which newspaper. One might presume that it is possible to track down this newspaper account.

It is true that these facts don't guarantee any kind of veracity, especially since Yogananda never claimed to have seen these miracles himself. We could scour other yogic traditions for similar tales and look for more recent tales or tales that are easier to verify. We could also look to other spiritual traditions, including the Islamic ones, for tales in which a jinn makes objects appear or disappear.

Swami Rama, who was once Shankaracharya before he relocated to the West to found the Himalayan Institute and is thought by some to have been associated with a lineage that was similar to Babaji's and Lahiri Mahasaya's, tells a similar tale in his autobiographical book. It is about a man who could magically transport objects from far away to wherever he happened to be. In one instance, he made objects from a restaurant at the Savoy, a well-known hotel in London, appear instantly in India. The lesson of Swami Rama's story is similar to that of Yogananda's tale: miracles by themselves are not equivalent to spiritual progress. And perhaps this story appeared in Swami Rama's autobiography for the same reason that Yogananda chose his story: because the underlying lesson was something he struggled with when he was younger.

Notwithstanding the above, spiritual lessons about superpowers and karma are hard to ignore because of how memorable they are. They serve as a great hook for readers, encouraging them to imagine a material world that isn't what we think it is, an idea we will revisit many times in this book.

Regardless of whether this tale unfolded exactly the way that Yogananda said it did, like many of the other stories in the *Autobiography*, you don't have to believe it to learn the lessons embedded within it!

LESSON #7

The World is Like a Movie, a Dream, a Video Game

From science, then, if it must be let so, man learn the philosophic truth that there is no material universe; its warp and woof is maya, illusion. Its mirages of reality all break down under analysis.

— YOGANANDA[1]

Know all things to be like this:
A mirage, a cloud castle, a dream, an apparition,
without essence, but with qualities that can be seen.

— BUDDHA, THE DIAMOND SUTRA

One of the central messages of Yogananda's *Autobiography* is that there is a world beyond that which we see. This is expressed in the ancient teaching that everything we see around us in everyday life is a result of not being able to see beyond the veil of maya, or illusion. This is one of the central lessons of this book too.

This worldview underlies not only the nature of the suffering that we see around us (the 'warp and woof' of the material universe that Yogananda referred to) but also provides the modern mind with a framework within which many of the miracles described in the *Autobiography* seem possible. Science is increasingly confirming the non-existence of a physical, material world.

The goal of spiritual practices, according to Yogananda and mystics through the ages, ranging from the rishis who authored the Vedas and the Buddha to the more mystical side of the Judeo-Christian religions, including the Sufi Imams, Christian Gnostics and the Jewish Kabbalists, is to pierce the veil and commune with God.

In English, the word most often used for this is 'enlightenment' (or 'liberation'). We'll have more to say about this in 'Lesson #13: Lifting the Veil: The Everlasting Beyond the Illusion'.

For now, we must understand, as Yogananda did, that this process, which is meant to reveal the 'ultimate nature of reality', is not something that we can describe in words. And yet, it is important to use the language of this world to make it accessible to ordinary folk like you and me. One of the most powerful ways to do this is to use metaphors, which bypass our logical minds and can be understood at a deeper level by the part of the brain that is used for creativity. Metaphors can produce an instant understanding of even very complex concepts.

Throughout the centuries, mystics of all religions have effectively utilized very similar metaphors to convey the idea that the physical world around us is not the real world.

Their goal in doing this is to try to detach us from our 'over-attachment' to the triumphs and tragedies that we experience on a daily basis. These metaphors compare physical reality to a dream, a stage play and, starting in the twentieth century, a film (via Yogananda).

I have tried to pick up the same thread in my recent books, using an updated metaphor that might seem like a departure from what the mystics of yore have said, but really isn't. This is the metaphor of the world being like an interactive multiplayer video game, a computer simulation. To truly understand this metaphor and why I think it may be the most powerful one yet, we have to understand the nuances of the metaphors that have been used to date. Yogananda himself upgraded the metaphors of his predecessors by incorporating references to the latest twentieth-century technologies to make them appropriate and accessible for modern men and women. In this book, I'd like to do the same thing in the twenty-first century.

The World Is a Dream

When we dream, we think that the dream-world *is* the real world. Think about the recent dreams you have had. Have you had a dream that involved less-than-ideal circumstances and woken up breathing a sigh of relief, thinking, 'Wow, I'm glad that was *just* a dream!'?

The dream metaphor is one that has been used for thousands of years. Yogananda himself used it to describe not only the illusory nature of the world but also the doors of entry into and out of this incarnation. 'Birth and death are doors through which you pass from one dream to another.'[2]

Many sects of Buddhism consider the dream metaphor central to their philosophical positioning. When a woman asked the erstwhile prince Siddhartha, shortly after his enlightenment, what he was, he used a term drawn from his native language, Pali: 'Buddha'. Though this is often translated today as 'enlightened', the literal meaning of the word is 'awakened', based on the Sanskrit root word 'budh', which means 'to be awake' or 'to become aware'.

Common sense tells us that if someone can 'awaken', then they (and the rest of us) must be asleep. The metaphor of dreams has been a staple of the Buddhist worldview since the very beginning of the religion. There is even a branch of Buddhist yoga called dream yoga, which was pioneered by the mysterious Indian mystic Lawapa a millennium ago (in the tenth century) and eventually reached the Kashmiri pandit, Naropa. It then travelled a treacherous journey over the Himalayas to reach Tibet, carried and translated by Marpa the Translator. The lessons were then preserved in Tibet for almost a thousand years, only to end up back in India after the Chinese occupation of Tibet. Dream yoga is one of the surviving teachings of the six yogas of Naropa.[3]

Naropa, who is better known in the Buddhist traditions than in the Hindu ones, is an interesting case study for the modern educated mystic. He was a scholar at Nalanda University and could argue about the finer points of enlightenment. However, he eventually realized that he didn't really know what it was like to 'awaken from the dream'. This realization arrived in a form that seems to have been quite common in these ancient tales: a strange visitor, in this case a woman who looked like an old hag.

Naropa embarked on a new journey of apprenticeship, replete with miracles like with ones in Yogananda's autobiography. Unlike Yogananda's book, which deals with a time with historical records, Naropa's tales go back a thousand years and much of what survives is only colourful metaphor. What is important for us in this chapter is that Naropa, like other educated individuals, was predisposed through his learning against the actual experience of 'waking up' and had to overcome his 'intellectual knowledge' before reaching the ultimate realization.

The point of dream yoga is to learn to awaken your waking conscious mind while dreaming, to 'become aware' in the middle of a dream that what you are seeing is just a dream without physically waking up. In the modern world, this process (stripped of its spiritual significance) is called 'lucid dreaming', and there have been studies of it at places like Stanford University's Sleep Lab. While the specifics of dream yoga aren't important here (some of its techniques are a little too specific to Tibetan culture and there are now numerous Western books on techniques that might be more attuned to the modern world), the important point is the metaphor of the world as a dream.

The point of dream yoga is that once you can recognize that the dream-world around you is not 'the real world' and that there is another you whose memory has been temporarily blocked, you can use the same kind of technique to 'wake up' while in the 'physical world' as well. According to these traditions, the physical world around you is not the real world either; it's like a dream, and there is a bigger aspect of you that you cannot ordinarily perceive, whose memory has been temporarily blocked, while you experience this illusory world.

Why can't we ordinarily perceive this larger aspect of ourselves? This takes us back to the heart of the word 'maya', which I (and others) have been translating as 'illusion'. However, the original meaning in Sanskrit is closer to 'a carefully crafted illusion', like something a magician might do on a stage. A sleight of hand for which we willingly suspend disbelief, so as to 'experience' the magic show and to ooh and ahh at the illusion, which we perceive to be real.

This means that when we incarnate, we pass through the veil of maya, entering the stage play. The Greeks used another metaphor to characterize incarnation, of crossing the River of Forgetfulness, which is why we can't remember the other self that is asleep. Similarly, in China, the Goddess Meng Po brews the 'tea of forgetfulness', which we take before incarnating; after we die, we cross back to the 'other side' and drink from Meng Po's brew again first to forget our troubles from the previous life and then to remember the larger part of ourselves.

The dream metaphor is universal, primarily because everyone dreams, according to scientists, whether we remember our dreams or not. It is also a very powerful reminder that things may not be what they seem to be and an easy way to understand what it means is not remember the real truth.

The World is Like a Stage Play

Another metaphor that is often used when talking about the illusory nature of the world around us is that of a stage play. Let's look at this slightly more closely. I used that specific term, 'stage play', in place of a more generic 'theatre' metaphor for a reason: it has two elements, that of the stage on which a show is presented and that of the activity of 'play', which we think of as being for children. Both are important in understanding how this relates to the ultimate reality that the sages tell us about. In the times of Shakespeare, the actors were called 'players'.

One of the professors I worked with at the MIT Game Lab was fond of saying that 'play' is one of the oldest human social activities. Almost every ancient civilization has left marks of its culture, and these invariably include traces of how they played. Even today, playing games is one of the ways that, as kids, we learn to interact with others based on various rules—whether we play cards or chess or cricket or soccer/football. 'Play' is not only fun but also, when it is governed by predefined rules, a way to instruct and to experience life.

Another human activity that is almost as ancient as play is that of storytelling. We could refer in this connection to the so-called primitive humans who gathered around a campfire and told stories, the bards who memorized Homer's epic tales, the refined storytelling traditions of the Arabic world at the height of the Islamic empires in places like the coffee shops of Aleppo or epics like the Mahabharata and Ramayana from India's distant past. The art of storytelling was not just preserved in these cultures; some of them took it to new levels, performing stories for audiences in such a way that the audiences could lose themselves in the performance.

This is the tradition to which the movie theatre and streaming series of today belong. At the cinema today, the screen is so big that we lose ourselves in the make-believe world that seems larger than life. With our tablets and computers we now binge watch episodes of shows and lose ourselves in the story at home too, only to emerge at the end of a season or series, wondering what will happen next.

At some point, the stories transformed into acts with scripts and multiple actors. The Greek civilization transformed the theatre, with multiple actors on a stage performing for the audience, into high art. You can think of a stage play as being a special kind of 'production' that is designed to persuade both the 'players' (i.e., the actors) and the audience to lose awareness of their surroundings and become immersed in the trials and travails of the characters in the play. The skill of a 'player' comes down to how well they can forget their previous life and inhabit the role they are playing on stage.

Perhaps then it's not so surprising that the Vedas, written by the rishis, who are thought to have lived some 3,000+ years ago, use a term whose meaning contains the conceptual germ of the stage play: 'lila'. The lila is thought to be the play of the gods, an elaborate state of play that the gods orchestrate to amuse themselves and us. Looking up the definition of 'lila' in the Encyclopedia Britannica, we see a range of meanings that are all close to each other: 'play', 'sport', 'spontaneity', or 'drama'. In yoga, 'lila' is often referred to as the 'divine play'.

This metaphor of the world around us being a 'divine play' in which we are all players has more recent currency as well. Some 500 years ago, Shakespeare penned something similar in a now-classic line from *Hamlet*: 'All the world's a stage and the men and women merely players.'

The next line from the play even contains hints of an understanding of maya: 'They have their exits and their entrances; And one man in his time plays many parts.'

This describes very well the idea that the world around us isn't the real world; it is a kind of scripted drama, in which we are all players *and* the audience. The more we forget who we are, the more engrossed and immersed we become in playing of our assigned roles and taking the events with the utmost of seriousness.

Even the Quran hints at this idea that the physical world is only a distraction, a pastime, an amusement, and in various translations, a kind of game: 'This life of the world is but a pastime and a game. Lo! the home of the Hereafter—that is Life, if they but knew.'[4]

The Suffering of the World and Motion Pictures

The stage play metaphor is one that has persisted for thousands of years, but as technology and media interacted more and more with traditional forms of storytelling and theatre, the metaphor has been updated. In the twentieth century, our advanced understanding of light and motion made it possible to tell stories in a new, engrossing, realistic way: the art of motion pictures.

An illusion is defined as something that looks real but is not. The ideas of light and vision, of what we can and cannot see, are intrinsically linked to the concept of the illusion, particularly a carefully crafted illusion (maya) that is put on for us to lose ourselves in.

Yogananda himself used this updated 'modern' metaphor of the physical world being like a motion picture. Unfortunately, this metaphor wasn't available during Shakespeare's era or in the time of the Vedas, or they might have used it too!

The metaphor came to Yogananda through a rather disturbing and interesting vision. In 1915, shortly after being ordained 'Swami Yogananda' by his guru, he had a peculiar but illuminating vision while meditating. That was a bloody year in Europe, with the Great War that had erupted the previous year still going strong. The scale of suffering caused by that war had never been seen before, partly because our technological capacity for destruction had reached new levels, with the advent of machine guns and automated artillery that could gun down many men in a short period of time.

In Yogananda's engrossing vision, he was in the middle of a naval battle when his ship was blown up, and he jumped into the sea to save himself. He was then struck by a bullet in his chest and it seemed to him that he was in the process of dying. Suddenly, he found himself back in India, meditating in the middle of a room in Calcutta, in hysterical tears after his vision of the near-death experience. He wondered: was he dead or alive?

> A dazzling play of light filled the whole horizon. A soft rumbling vibration formed itself into words:
>
> 'What has life or death to do with Light? In the image of My light I have made you. The relativities of life and death belong to the cosmic dream. Behold your dreamless being! Awake, my child, awake!'[5]

Later, he entered a cinema to see newsreels of World War I and, upon seeing the horrific devastation, asked, 'Lord ... why dost Thou permit such suffering?' The answer not only gave him a new way of looking at the world but also a new understanding of the concept of maya, which he had read about but now intuitively understood:

> To my intense surprise, an instant answer came in the form of a vision of the actual European battlefields. The horror of the struggle, filled with the dead and dying, far surpassed in ferocity any representation of the newsreel.
>
> 'Look intently!' A gentle voice spoke to my inner consciousness. 'You will see that these scenes now being enacted in France are nothing but a play of chiaroscuro. They are the cosmic motion picture, as real and as unreal

as the theater newsreel you have just seen, a play within a play.'[6]

The voice in Yogananda's vision went on to tell him: 'Creation is light and shadow both, else no picture is possible.' The voice went on to make the point that, in a motion picture, pain and tragedy seem real, but that a man or woman no more dies than an actor who portrays death in a movie scene is actually dead. Ceaseless joy, Yogananda writes, is not the state of this world.

Yogananda and the Law of Miracles

This interplay of light and vision, scenes and acting, the 'real and the unreal',[7] is at the heart of the lessons Yogananda learnt from his vision and subsequent insight into the nature of maya and suffering. While living in America, he would often make this point when others asked why suffering was permitted in this world: the world is made of light, like a motion picture being projected, and we are merely playing parts—parts that have been prescribed for us, though we may have more say in what happens than actors generally do.

This idea of the world being light is also the explanation Yogananda gives for the many miracles that he describes in his book. If the world is insubstantial and made of light, any miracle can be projected onto the screen of reality, and the script can be changed by someone who has mastered the knowledge of maya. This is how the masters can do things that seem incomprehensible to those of us who are readily caught up in the illusion:

The motion picture art can portray any miracle. From the impressive visual standpoint, no marvel is barred to trick photography. A man's transparent astral body can be seen rising from his gross physical form, he can walk on the water, resurrect the dead, reverse the natural sequence of developments, and play havoc with time and space. Assembling the light images as he pleases, the photographer achieves optical wonders which a true master produces with actual light rays.[8]

Yogananda goes further and explains how the master's powers of will and of visualization can project onto reality any phenomenon, raising questions about what constitutes a miracle if everything we see is illusion:

Through a master's divine knowledge of light phenomena, he can instantly project into perceptible manifestation the ubiquitous light atoms. The actual form of the projection, whether it be a tree, a medicine, a human body, is in conformance with a yogi's powers of will and of visualization.[9]

Yogananda further tells us, combining both metaphors of dream and film, that our nightly dreams are like little movies that are put on for us to watch every night. They are types of illusions. We are the directors and scriptwriters and projectors of our nightly motion pictures:

In man's dream-consciousness, where he has loosened in sleep his clutch on the egoistic limitations that daily hem him round, the omnipotence of his mind has a nightly demonstration. Lo! there in the dream stand the long-dead friends, the remotest continents, the resurrected scenes of his childhood. With that free and unconditioned consciousness, known to all men in the phenomena of dreams, the God-tuned master has forged a never-severed link.[10]

The Ultimate Metaphor: The World Is Like a Video Game

The dream, the stage play and the motion picture are useful metaphors, but none of them can serve as the ultimate metaphor for the nature of reality, because they lack one element that the masters tell us we have: the element of free will, the agency to change the script!

I believe that if Yogananda or the rishis or even Shakespeare were alive today, they would use a more up-to-date metaphor while preserving the basic underlying concept of the world as maya. I can imagine what they might say, struggling with previous metaphors:

> The world is like a dream, but also like a motion picture, but also like a play, but one that is interactive, where the players, though they each come in with a script, have some agency to choose their actions and affect the outcome and re-write the script, and they can even become aware that they are in the middle of a play or dream or movie.

The metaphor that makes the most sense today is that of an interactive video game. In role-playing video games, like World of Warcraft or Fortnite or Roblox, we as players exist independently outside of the game. However, we descend or enter into the video game to play a specific character, with whom we identify, and then we are able to only perceive the world through the eyes of that character, which is coincidentally called an avatar. The word 'avatar' comes from an old Sanskrit root that means 'to descend'.

To have a video game that perfectly replicated our experience of the world would require much more sophisticated rendering and projection capabilities than are available in video games today. But in my previous book, *The Simulation Hypothesis*, I laid out a course for technology development that would allow us to build simulated virtual reality environments that would be indistinguishable from physical reality. Assuming we develop some of those technologies, which are the crux of what's now called the Metaverse, it's likely we will also develop a 'full immersion' mode for ourselves within a few decades.

In the same way that video games today are much more sophisticated than the video games of the 1980s like Pac Man and Space Invaders (classic games that I played as a kid); the ultimate video games will be able to convince us that we are in 'reality' when in fact we are in an illusory world. Everything that happens in this world would be, as Buddha suggests, 'reflections on a very clear mirror, devoid of inherent existence.'

When we play a video game, from the character's point of view, it appears that everything is real and well-ordered, complete with physical rules that prevent us from, say, walking through walls. Moreover, today, unlike with the video games of the past, we have millions of players who are simultaneously engaged in a lila of their own, a grand play in a world that is sustained as 'real' by the immersion of the players whose characters are denizens of that world. A multiplayer game is in fact the 'play' of many individuals at the same time who agree to inhabit and play roles in a shared illusory world.

The Simulation Hypothesis and My Story

If you think this sounds like the science fiction scenario depicted in the Matrix franchise, you are right. The idea that we might be inside a video game was once considered pure science fiction—until as recently as 1999, when the first Matrix movie starring Keanu Reeves as Neo and Laurence Fishbourne as Morpheus was released. But since then, many scientists, philosophers and technologists have started to take the idea much more seriously. Moreover, it has turned out to be an effective way to bridge the ever-widening gap between science and religion and their competing views of the world.

Yogananda was extremely interested in the parallels between what science has learnt about the nature of the universe and what the mystics have been telling us for ages, and I believe he would willingly take to this metaphor of the video game. Having researched not only the *Autobiography* but also Yogananda's life, I have sincerely come to believe that he would consider the findings of quantum mechanics, which are so baffling (a phenomenon called the observer effect), to be similar to how we render in video games. I will talk more about Yogananda's interest in modern technologies and metaphors in 'Lesson #14: Yoga is For Everyone, East and West'.

I first became keenly interested in this topic in 2016 when I visited a technology start-up that was designing a virtual ping pong game. The virtual reality headsets of the time were much bigger and clunkier than the ones we have now, and they required wires. By the time you read this, virtual reality headsets will have got even smaller and will have better graphics, I'm sure.

Anyway, I became so engrossed with the table tennis game that, for a moment, I forgot I was in virtual reality! My body instinctively tried to put the 'paddle' down on the 'table' and I tried to lean against the table, just as I might after a real game of ping pong. Of course, there was no table. The controller in my hand fell to the floor and I almost fell over.

That's when I realized that virtual reality technology was approaching what I like to call the Simulation Point, a theoretical point at which our virtual environments, as depicted in our video games, will become indistinguishable from physical reality.

This idea, that we might live inside an ultra-sophisticated video game, known today as the Simulation Hypothesis, was always thought to be science fiction, more suitable for movies like *The Matrix* and *The Thirteenth Floor* than for serious discussions of science and technology. As I began to explore it, I found the work of Oxford philosopher Nick Bostrom, who argued that if any civilization anywhere in the universe ever reached the Simulation Point, it was likely that we were, in fact, already inside a computer simulation.[11]

The specifics of the argument involve calculations of the number of simulated worlds and simulated beings and the likelihood of being in a simulated world vs. the likelihood of being in a real physical world (called a 'base reality'). Once a technological civilization like ours reaches the Simulation Point, we could easily create many simulations—in Bostrom's work, these are called ancestor simulations—in the same way that we can simulate ancient India or Rome within a video game like Civilization. The incremental computing power needed to create a new simulated world, which might have billions of simulated beings, is almost trivial once you have reached the simulation point.

While Bostrom's simulation argument has led many academics to get serious about the idea that the physical world isn't the real world, the idea, as we have seen, has been around in many forms within the world's religions and philosophical traditions. Plato wrote more than 2,000 years ago about the allegory of the cave in which the residents are chained to one wall and can only see the wall opposite the cave's opening. These residents only see the shadows thrown on the wall when 'real people' in the 'real world' pass by the cave. It may look like shadow puppet theatre to those of us outside the cave, but the ones chained inside take the shadows to be 'reality' because they have no idea what the 'real world' is like.

More recently, French philosopher and mathematician Rene Descartes added another link to the chain of philosophical concepts that are predecessors to the modern-day idea of reality as a video game or simulation. Descartes conceived came up with a thought experiment about an evil demon of 'utmost power and cunning [that] has employed all his energies in order to deceive me.' The nature of the deceit that Descartes was concerned with sounds a lot like the idea of maya or illusion. Descartes continued: 'I shall think that the sky, the air, the earth, colours, shapes, sounds and all external things are merely the delusions of dreams which he has devised to ensnare my judgement. I shall consider myself as not having hands or eyes, or flesh, or blood or senses, but as falsely believing that I have all these things.'

In the end, Descartes concluded that he couldn't be sure the world was real, and the only thing he could be convinced was real was his consciousness, leading to his famous statement: 'I think, therefore I am.'

NPC Versions vs. RPG Versions of Video Games

This simulation hypothesis, which uses video games as the latest metaphor for reality, has many implications. For one thing, this metaphor could potentially achieve something that would be close to Yogananda's heart: it could bring the worlds of science and religion together. Both of these worlds of thought and practice are about the search for truth, even if that truth is pursued in completely different spheres and with completely different methods.

Today, there are many committed atheists who would dismiss most religious arguments and mystical experiences (not to mention many of the miraculous events reported by Yogananda in his autobiography) as nonsense. However, when presented with a technological or scientific argument about being in a simulation, they are more than open to the possibility that the beings outside the simulation might seem 'supernatural' to those of us who are locked into a simulation.

Moreover, video games are played by players at different levels and with different abilities. As you build your skill set (through quests and achievements), your character levels up and can suddenly see objects that others can't see and perform actions and cast spells that others are incapable of. Something similar may be going on with masters and adepts who master the siddhis.

There is another aspect of simulation theory that scares people in the religious realm, which I think should be addressed. I like to think of it as a conflict between the NPC (non-player character) and RPG (role-playing game) versions of simulation. In the NPC version, we are all 'non-player characters', like AI (artificial intelligence) characters inside video games that you interact with as part of the gameplay. If everyone was an NPC, this would imply that we don't have souls; we are just lines of code and data.

However, there is another version of the simulation hypothesis in which we are all players of the video game, which I call the RPG (role-playing game) version. In this version, we exist outside of the computer-generated reality, but we choose to download ourselves into our character, our avatar.

This version allows us to store information on the server about our current life, past lives and, more importantly, the quests and achievements (the karma) that we have yet to fulfil. This version of the simulation hypothesis fits the understanding that the physical world *seems* real and that we have agency in this seemingly real world. We can make choices that guide the gameplay session (otherwise known as life), but there may also be certain karmic scripts that our characters are meant to follow.[12]

Let's Play the Game

It is this version of the simulation hypothesis that most fits the metaphor of the material world being an illusion, maya, and of us being participants in the lila, the play of the gods. We might even say that it is our lila too—it is our form of 'play' and much more interactive and immersive than a stage play. We are the players!

The interactive, multiplayer video game can be thought of as the latest, most accurate and most useful metaphor for the nature of our reality. This offers a better perspective on several issues: not just why there is suffering and why it's important but also why we shouldn't take it too seriously. It also provides explanations for how the magic and miracles

Yogananda described in his autobiography can be explained while satisfying the modern, scientific need to respect the rules of the physical world.

In a video game anything is possible, characters can float up, some can regenerate arms and legs, come back to life, show up in multiple places at once and objects can be rendered in front of our eyes out of nothingness.

Keep this metaphor in mind as you face challenges and obstacles in the material world, which is inevitable. Changing perspective can help us deal with the most difficult situations in life. Think how the metaphor of the motion picture, and the realization that everything that is physical is actually made of light, changed Yogananda's view of the world and suffering the world. Similarly, adopting the metaphor of the video game, consisting of a player (the real you) and a character (in the game) can change your perspective: 'One's values are profoundly changed when he is finally convinced that creation is only a vast motion picture, and that not in it, but beyond it, lies his own reality.'[13]

And the next time anyone asks you about the nature of reality, ask them if they have ever played a video game!

PART IV

Walking the Worldly and Spiritual Paths

Intuition is soul guidance, appearing naturally in man during those instants when his mind is calm.

— YOGANANDA*

---

* Yogananda, *Autobiography of a Yogi*, 'The Cauliflower Robbery', p. 177.

LESSON #8

Practise Every Day, No Matter How Much Time You Have

Yoga is a method for restraining the natural turbulence of thoughts, which otherwise impartially prevent all men, of all lands, from glimpsing their true nature of Spirit.

— YOGANANDA[1]

Most would agree that progress on the spiritual path comes from spiritual practice. But what does 'practice' mean exactly? It usually refers to some form of meditation, yoga, prayer or devotion prescribed by the spiritual school you have chosen or belong to, which will likely have its own spiritual beliefs and techniques.

Yogananda's autobiography mentions the practice of kriya yoga, but in general it doesn't get into details of specific techniques. The purpose of the book was to inspire readers to take up the yogic path by opening of their minds to spiritual possibilities. All the mentions of kriya yoga by Yogananda are meant to inspire the reader to seek out and learn about that form of spiritual practice. And, given the large number of people that have read the book, we can conclude that many have been inspired to start some form of yogic practice, although not necessarily the specific techniques taught by Yogananda.

The traditional route (if you were to enter a monastic order during the time that Yogananda grew up, for instance) was to find a guru and spend most of your time engaged in the practices prescribed by that guru. Yet, if you look at his early life, you will realize that he spent much time getting inspiration from stories about swamis and visits to pilgrimage sites. His advice even after he began teaching in the West to most people was to integrate spiritual practice into your daily life, not to make spiritual practice your life!

The traditional approach—joining a monastic order—isn't practical for most modern seekers anyway. We have jobs, families to support and other interests that are part of our karmic path. In fact, Yogananda was called the 'first modern guru' because he, like Lahiri Mahasaya, taught techniques to those who lived and worked in the world, to those referred to as the 'householders' in his time. Today, somewhere between five minutes and an hour a day is the most that the majority of us can dedicate to formal spiritual practice (and for most of us it's closer to the smaller number).

Yet, there are forms of spiritual practice that involve mindfulness and remembering God and the Divine in the course of our daily lives. When my first meditation teacher told me that I could mediate eight hours a day, I looked at him incredulously. He explained that it was only possible if I used my work to practice mindfulness throughout the day.

In this chapter and in 'Lesson #14: Yoga is For Everyone, East and West', I want to emphasize the universality of yoga. Most people who have read Yogananda's autobiography never take up the specific practices he taught; rather the stories inspire them to find their own path. In my research on the impact of the *Autobiography*, I came across a number of people belonging to many different religions—Jewish, Christian, Islamic, Buddhist and others—who ranked the book highly as a source of inspiration to live a more spiritual, compassionate life.

For this reason, the real lesson I want to emphasize in this chapter is not that you need to find a Yogananda-approved organization and practice a specific technique (though you may end up doing that, which I would encourage—there is a list of those in the appendix). The real lesson in this chapter is that you should practice whatever yogic exercises you have been drawn to, from whatever lineage appeals to you and inspires you. It might be a type of meditation linked to a Hindu lineage like Yogananda's, an Islamic Sufi practice, a Buddhist meditation technique, a Kabbalistic path or an entirely different type of devotional practice or prayer.

The key lesson is that you need to practice yoga of some kind every single day—it doesn't even matter how long you spend at it, as long as you spend some time each day renewing your connection with the Divine.

A Bit About Yogananda's Lineage and the River of Yoga

Yogananda spends a lot of time in the *Autobiography* describing the lineage of his particular brand of yogic practice, which he calls kriya yoga. Kriya yoga was passed down from the seemingly immortal Mahavatar Babaji, who lives in the

Himalayas, through Lahiri Mahasaya of Benares, who taught Yogananda's guru, Sri Yukteswar. We'll talk more about Babaji, perhaps the most awe-inspiring figure in a book filled with awe-inspiring figures, in 'Lesson #12: Lessons from Babaji and the Great Engine of Karma'.

The lineage doesn't stop with Yogananda. He started an organization in India (the Yogoda Satsanga a Society of India [YSS]) and one in the West (the Self-Realization Fellowship [SRF]). While these two organizations are the formal keepers of Yogananda's teachings, they in turn spawned many additional traditions that trace their respective lineages directly to Yogananda, often started by his students. For example, Ananda was founded by Yogananda's direct disciple, Swami Kriyananda, and another of Yogananda's disciples, Roy Eugene Davis, helped found several organizations in the US, such as the Center for Spiritual Awareness in San Jose. And this is not to mention the many other traditions that trace their lineages back to Lahiri Mahasaya and the even larger number whose trails lead to Babaji and perhaps even further back.

Anyone who studies the history of yoga realizes that it is like a giant river, with many tributaries flowing off of bigger and smaller branches. It is a river that is constantly branching and merging, a process which continues today.

Interest in the particular lineages of yoga sourced to Babaji have ballooned in large part because of Yogananda's autobiography. Lahiri Mahasaya, the primary disciple of Babaji in the nineteenth century, said that his life will be known about because of a book published fifty years after his death, which will foster '... a deep interest in yoga which the West will manifest. The yogic message will encircle the globe ...' Sure enough, Yogananda's autobiography was finished in 1945, fifty years after the death of Lahiri Mahasaya in 1895, and published in America the next year.

Authentic Lineages and the Pizza Effect

Many yogic teachers (including Yogananda) are very careful to lay out the authenticity of their lineage. One question that arises in the mind of the modern reader is: does the lineage really matter? This is a complex question, especially today when lineages and techniques are often mixed up in ways that might not have been the case hundreds of years ago, when the techniques were exclusively passed down from guru to disciple.

If you are learning from someone who claims a direct lineage, can you assume you are getting the original unfiltered teachings? Yes and no. When we read biographies of Yogananda, for instance, while we can be sure of his lineage, it's hard to decipher exactly what has been adapted to a Western audience and what comes straight from the Himalayan master Babaji down to the present.

For one thing, in the West, Yogananda needed to emphasize that the teachings of yoga were in harmony with the teachings of Christ—and so there is a lot of Biblical theology in the *Autobiography*. This baffled me when I first read the book, since yoga is a much older branch of spirituality than Christianity (or Judaism), and you really don't need to learn anything about Christ to learn about yoga. However, it makes sense when you put it in context—Yogananda's life task was to convince a sceptical Western audience that the teachings of an eccentric (by Western standards, at least) yogi from India were aligned with and not opposed to the dominant religion in the West. Today, that appetite has changed in the West. The reason many in the West turn to Eastern traditions is not because they want to reaffirm the tenets of the religion they grew up with but because they are looking for a more personal experience of the Divine and believe that yoga can provide that.

Even so, the question of 'authentic' vs. 'inauthentic' traditions, while easy to ask, has no easy answers. All religions are like rivers, with tributaries branching off at several points. They adapt themselves to different regions within the same country and evolve even further as they travel from country to country and continent to continent.

Anya Foxen, a professor of religious studies at California Polytechnic State University, wrote her doctoral thesis on Yogananda's yogic practices, which ultimately took the form of her book, *Biography of a Yogi.* Though the book is more scholarly than spiritual, meant for an academic audience, she traces the roots of some of the practices we call 'authentic yoga', and even ancillary practices like Yogananda's energization exercises. When I spoke to Dr Foxen, she made the point that, with so much shared history and information exchange between the East and the West, it is very difficult to define 'authentic yoga' techniques because at some point in the past they have all been adapted in ways that gave them their present form and some have even travelled back to India.

I also spoke to several other scholars, including Philip Goldberg, who wrote perhaps the best-known biography of Yogananda in the West, and Jeffrey Kripal, a professor of religion at Rice University who has studied many Indian teachers who came to the West to disseminate yoga. One point made by all of these scholars is that Yogananda's techniques were not only adapted to Western sensibilities but, having become popular in the West, made their way back across the oceans to Asia. Yogananda himself wasn't very well-known when he left India in 1920, but today his teachings are more popular than ever in his homeland.

Scholars call this constant adaptation, change and travel the pizza effect. This is because the original pizza, which hailed from a small region in Italy, bears very little resemblance to what we think of as pizza today. The version of pizza eaten around the world today was popularized in America and then made its way back to Italy. Now you can get American-style pizza almost anywhere in the world, adapted to local preferences.

The same is true of yoga, says Dr Foxen; the further back you go to find 'authentic' yogic practices, the more you realize that so many lineages and practices have cross-pollinated, even within a country like India with its many subcultures, and definitely as yoga has travelled, that the question of authenticity may be meaningless.

The key is to focus on the practice that works best for you in the present, since all great spiritual teachers, including Yogananda, will adapt their teachings to their students and the milieu in which they are teaching.

Yogananda has stressed that, no matter where you are on the river of yoga, you don't need to espouse an allegiance to any particular lineage to practice it (though, as I've said, his lineage has been preserved in many places). He wrote: 'Yoga requires no formal allegiance. Because the yogic science satisfies a universal need, it has a natural universal appeal.'[2]

The Body and Limbs of Yoga

Let's now talk a bit more about what yoga is and what it means to 'practice it'. Today, yoga is known around the world because millions of men and women practice the physical postures, or asanas, known as hatha yoga. This popularity is in no small part because of Yogananda himself, as the *Los Angeles Times* stated in a headline recently: 'If you practice yoga, thank this man who came to the U.S. 100 years ago.'[3]

In truth, Yogananda didn't emphasize hatha yoga or the postures known as asanas in his book or his life, though he did teach them to some of his students. Yogananda was quick to point out that asanas constituted only one of the eight limbs of yoga, as defined by the sage Patanjali in his *Yoga Sutra*.

While Yogananda advocated physical exercises and some hatha yoga, the truth is that yoga as Yogananda popularized it was much more about what we might call meditation today than about asana. In the *Autobiography*, Yogananda takes great pains to return us to Patanjali's original definition of yoga and its eight limbs.

It is not known when precisely Patanjali wrote the *Yoga Sutra*, which is considered the authoritative ancient text on yoga. Most estimates range from 200 BCE to 200 CE—a span of 400 years! What we do know is that this sutra was written much later than the Vedas, and even later than Buddha's lifetime; therefore, all of these former teachings were familiar to Patanjali and likely to be incorporated into his seminal work.

So how does Patanjali define Yoga? The original Sanskrit says:

Yogas chitta vritti nirodhah

There are many English translations of this phrase and, though they all kind of agree about what it's saying, they use slightly different words in translation, giving each definition a slightly different shade of meaning. Yogananda himself defines yoga by translating this famous phrase to mean both 'neutralization of the alternating waves in consciousness' and 'cessation of the modifications of the mind stuff.'

Yogananda's disciple, Swami Kriyananda, who helped Yogananda prepare commentaries on the ancient texts for modern Western audiences in English, asks us to take the words individually in his book, *Demystifying Patanjali*. The correct translation for vrittis, he reminds us, is not exactly 'waves of consciousness', but rather 'vortices' or 'whirlpools', a translation that agrees with how many scholars define vrittis.

The more difficult term to get right in English is perhaps 'chitta', which Yogananda (and many others) translate as 'mind stuff', but I think this is rooted in a misconception that is common in English translations of ancient Indian texts of both Hinduism and Buddhism (and their many, many subsects). Most of these translations use the concepts of 'thought' and the 'mind', which in the West and in English are distinguished from the feelings or emotions or sensations of the body. I don't believe, after looking at what many modern scholars and swamis have to say on the subject, that yogic concepts were meant to have this distinction.

'Mind stuff', or chitta, Yogananda reminds us in a footnote in the *Autobiography*, is 'a comprehensive term for the thinking principle, which includes the pranic life forces, manas (mind or sense consciousness), ahamkara (egoity), and buddhi (intuitive intelligence)'. You can see that this is a much more comprehensive definition than one that focuses on just thoughts or just feelings or just energy—it needs to include all of them.

For those who are not used to Sanskrit terms, bringing all of these concepts under one umbrella can cause the eyes to glaze over. A better definition, one that doesn't skimp but also doesn't overwhelm, is needed. Swami Kriyananda, who was born J. Donald Walters, a native English speaker who in fact didn't speak Sanskrit, chose an interpretation based on what Yogananda had taught him. Swami Kriyananda's translation of Patanjali's famous definition is as follows:

Yoga is the neutralization of the vortices of feelings.[4]

His translation hints at the important idea that when we feel emotions for something, we get attached to that thing. It is this attachment, the feeling of emotion, that is the problem—not just the thought (though I think the two terms are indistinguishable in the original formulation). In the yogic system, this means that a thought or a feeling is a whirlpool that then hardens and eventually turns into a samskara, an imperfection in the envelopes of energy and consciousness (called 'khosas' in Sanskrit). These samskaras, once hardened, become part of our karma and must be dealt with at some point in our journey through the wheel of samsara—the cycle of births and rebirths.

It's worth examining the possible alternative definitions of the terms in Patanjali's definition to see if we can come up with a more appropriate translation of it:

Chitta = mind stuff or feelings or comprehensive consciousness
Vrittis = vortices or whirlpools
Nirodhah = stopping, cessation, neutralization

Taking all this into account, I'm going to offer a slightly revised rendition of the definition of yoga that I think will help modern seekers get to the heart of the matter. It should incorporate all of the definitions of the individual words, but should also pay heed to an implied underlying concept that most existing translations hint at. This concept is implied through the use of the terms 'waves' and 'whirlpools'. You can't have waves or whirlpools without a substrate in which they form—a river, an ocean.[5]

'Yoga is about the cessation of the whirlpools of thought and feeling in the river of consciousness.'[6]

This is longer than most translations, but a true translation needs to do more than just translate words; it needs to convey the essence of idiomatic expressions and assumptions that are built into those words in one language by doing the same in the other language.

Translation and Snow Globes

One of my mentors that taught me about dreaming traditions, Robert Moss, referred to himself as a practitioner of shamanic dreamwork rather than a yogi. Often, Robert, who is originally from Australia, translated ancient Native American and Australian Aboriginal concepts and practices of dreaming for modern practitioners. This process went well beyond translating languages. He offered an interesting explanation of what he did based on an older idea of translation. He told me once that when he was speaking with modern-day members of the Iroquois (a collection of tribes of indigenous people who lived in the north-eastern region of what is now the USA) about introducing the modern world to some of their dream-related traditions, they said that he was performing a very specific type of 'translation'. This term literally meant to take a plant out of one type of soil and plant it in another type of soil with care.

Going by this definition of 'translation', I think my longer translation works not because it a simple literary translation, but because it helps to plant the essential idea of Patanjali's definition of yoga into the modern soil of English in the twenty-first century.

Although many Indians generally know of Patanjali's definition of yoga, those who practice yoga in the US and in other countries are often surprised to learn that yoga is not simply, nor even primarily, defined by the yoga poses that they have learnt in their local classes.

Nevertheless, most modern casual practitioners of hatha yoga recognize that it 'stills something' in the body, which helps with stress release, well-being and health. So, upon a little reflection, it usually isn't hard for a Westerner to make the connection between this definition and the practices they have learnt. They know that at the end of their yoga sessions, particularly when they lie on the yoga mat and perform the sivasana pose (translated as either 'corpse pose' or, a term I like better even though it's not a strict translation, 'peaceful pose'), they feel like something has been 'calmed'.

For Westerners, I like to use the image of a snow globe when describing this calming effect. A snow globe is a semi-circular glass dome with a scene built inside it, usually a winter scene from some northern land. The globe is generally filled with water or some other transparent liquid and the 'snow' is actually some substance like glitter or confetti that can move around in the liquid. When the globe is shaken, the 'snow' is disturbed and this makes it seem like a snowstorm has been unleashed upon the scene. It takes a while for the snow to settle down after a shaking. During that time, you cannot see the actual scene—your view is obscured. Then, once the snow eventually settles down, you see cleary what the imaginary snowstorm was hiding, but was there all along!

This is a powerful metaphor for the practice of yoga, irrespective of technique or limb or method, that I think Yogananda would agree with. The vrittis rage like a snowstorm and yoga can help calm them down so that light can flow freely into the globe of the consciousness. Yoga, then, is any practice, from any of the eight limbs, or even practices from other traditions like prayer, that accomplishes this 'stilling' of the vrittis, the whirlpools of thought and feeling.

The Eight Limbs of Yoga

Having generally defined yoga, Patanjali goes into very specific details of the practices of yoga, defining the eight limbs of yoga (which Yogananda also discusses in his autobiography). These limbs are:

1.　Yama (moral conduct). These are generally the 'don'ts' of the code of yoga. These 'include noninjury to others, truthfulness, non-stealing, continence and non-covetousness.'[7]

2.　Niyama (religious observances). These are the 'dos' of the code of yoga. They prescribe 'purity of body and mind, contentment in all circumstances, self-discipline, self-study (contemplation) and devotion to God and guru.'[8]

3.　Asana (right posture). Though Patanjali meant this to refer to the posture assumed during meditation (i.e., a

specific asana, sitting with the spinal column straight),
the word asana refers to all kinds of postures now.

4. Pranayama (control of prana). 'Prana' is defined as the
    subtle currents of energy or life force, and pranayama is
    well-known today as the name for breathing exercises
    that help to regulate the flow of prana in the body.

5. Pratyahara (withdrawal of the senses from their
    perception of external objects). According to
    Kriyananda, Yogananda said that true meditation is
    achieved when one focuses so much during meditation
    that one loses awareness of the senses.

6. Dharana (concentration). Dharana is the actual process
    of focusing or concentrating on an object.

7. Dhyana (meditation). Kriyananda in his commentary
    admits that this one is very difficult to translate but has
    to do with meditating on 'higher aspects of reality' or,
    more simply, meditating on God or the divine. This is
    not necessarily what modern meditation is about. We'll
    go over the various techniques as they are practised
    today in the next section.

8. Samadhi (superconscious experience). Finally, the
    goal of all the eight limbs is to help reach samadhi, the
    experience of the superconscious. This last limb and
    the word 'samadhi', as used by Yogananda, have to do
    with love and merging with God and experiencing that
    which is beyond maya, beyond the veil of illusion. We
    will talk more about this in 'Lesson #13: Lifting the Veil:
    The Everlasting Beyond the Illusion'.

As you can see, each of these is either a technique or practice
for the purpose of stilling the vrittis, the whirlpools of emotion/

feeling/thought, so as not to create attachments on a daily basis that make it into our karma.

The Four Classes of Modern Techniques

The modern practitioner of yoga may find the eight limbs a little overwhelming. While the difference between asana and pranayama is generally clear, the differences between pratyahara, dharana and dhyana are subtler and rely on slightly different techniques, which have been created in order to achieve the aims of these specific limbs.

While the eight limbs of yoga are still well-known, I've found that most modern schools have boiled down the techniques to a few categories. These techniques, though they rely on the eight limbs, are often combined together into a specific kind of meditation or yoga practice. For the purposes of completeness, you can include a bit of each of these in your practice every day, though again that isn't always practical for modern seekers.

The categories of practice you are likely to encounter today (or perhaps have already encountered) can be summarized as follows:

1. Physical techniques: hatha yoga postures (asana), energization exercises, and others

2. Meditation techniques: watching the breath, being present, mantras, concentrating on a single thing

3. Pranayama: specific breathing techniques, sometimes combined with asanas and meditation to control the breath and thereby the flow of prana

4. Energy techniques: concentrating on energy centres or chakras using visualization and, potentially, physical manipulation

You'll notice that these categories are not mutually exclusive. For example, the meditation technique that I first learnt about involved meditating on chakras, moving energy up the spine, and also watching the breath, so it spanned all four categories.

Yogananda taught energization exercises (details of which can be found online if that's something you want to add to your practice). He also taught hatha yoga, but because of the times, he only taught those postures to his male students. His female students practised the energization exercises and the other techniques, which is ironic, because today, at least in the West, the majority of hatha yoga practitioners in any class tend to be women.

Since *Autobiography of a Yogi* was meant to inspire and not instruct, the details of these techniques were not available in the book itself. Yogananda did however advocate a daily routine that combined several types of practices and this is still taught by the SRF in the West and YSS in India. It includes the Hong-Sau technique (a type of breath meditation) and the Om technique (which was less about chanting a mantra or 'Om' than about listening for the divine sound), combined with pranayama and kriya yoga, as revealed by Babaji. Kriya yoga is a type of energy technique that moves the 'kundalini' energy up the spine. You can learn more about it through these organizations or even read about the techniques online.

The rivers of yoga, which originated in India, have now spread to many parts of the globe and there are inevitably many other techniques that I haven't mentioned or may not even be aware of, but which could be categorized into or across one or more of these four basic categories. When I was in college, I took a yoga class as my physical exercise option each quarter.

Sometimes it was a hatha yoga class, which was all about asanas and physical postures, and sometimes it was a kundalini yoga class, which was often about holding an asana and practicing the breath of fire. Both had different kinds of effects: one left me feeling calmer while the other left me energized. Both had value.

While traditionalists will say adapting yoga to other traditions is not really yoga, if you use Patanjali's definition, then any practice that helps to smooth out the whirlpools in the river of consciousness is a type of yoga. And there is no greater authority than that ancient sage. Yogananda himself wrote: 'Anyone who practices a scientific technique for divine realization is a yogi.'[9]

A Word on the Spread of These Techniques

In ancient times, most yoga techniques were passed down from guru to disciple as they wandered about or within ashrams and monasteries. Today, many spiritual seekers learn about a specific tradition over the internet, on social media or from reading books, after which they seek to learn more. Indeed, you can find discussions of most of these techniques (including Lahiri's kriya yoga, as it's often called, though it was revealed by Babaji to Lahiri Mahasaya) online.

In the past, including during Yogananda's time, the main details of kriya yoga were kept secret and passed down only when a student who had been practising the basic techniques was 'initiated' into kriya yoga. Is the online availability of techniques today a good thing or a bad thing? The answer, of course, depends on your perspective.

I asked Ryan Kurczak, a teacher of kriya yoga who was a disciple of Roy Davis, who in turn was one of Paramhansa

Yogananda's direct disciples and started his own spiritual organization to teach these techniques. Ryan now shares the techniques of kriya yoga online in videos on YouTube (and in a series of books). While this might upset some traditionalists, Ryan made the point that this was a continuation of the process that started with Lahiri Mahasaya.

When Lahiri learnt the techniques from Babaji during their meeting in the Himalayas near Ranikhet, kriya yoga techniques were meant only for those who were renunciates, a small group that wandered the Himalayas with their gurus. Ryan reminded me that it was Lahiri who petitioned Babaji to lift these restrictions and make it permissible to share the techniques with householders, i.e., those who were married, had kids and led otherwise 'normal lives'—what I call modern seekers.

Lahiri Mahasaya was in a unique position to ask this because he himself was a householder. He had been married and had had kids before his encounter with Babaji. He even had a day job that had sent him to an office in Ranikhet (which turned out to be a 'clerical error' since there really wasn't much for him to do in that office, so he took to wandering the mountains where he encountered Babaji). The actual dialogue between Lahiri and the deathless Babaji is instructive:

Angelic Guru, as you have already favored mankind by resurrecting the lost Kriya art, will you not increase that benefit by relaxing the strict requirements for discipleship? ... I pray that you let me communicate Kriya to all sincere seekers, even though at first they may not be able to vow themselves to complete inner renunciation. The tortured men and women of the world, pursued by the threefold suffering, need special encouragement.[10]

Babaji accepted the request, allowing Lahiri to share kriya with all sincere seekers. In fact, Babaji told Lahiri that there was a reason he had waited until Lahiri was older and was firmly established as a householder, before contacting him and initiating him. Babaji also allowed some of Lahiri's students to teach the kriya techniques to others, gradually loosening restrictions around the practice.

It is known that Babaji told Sri Yukteswar of his interest in the West and that he would send him a disciple who would take yoga to the West—that disciple turned out to be Yogananda (we'll talk more about this in 'Lesson #14: Yoga is For Everyone, East and West'). Yogananda actually angered many traditionalists back in India by using 'modern methods' to disseminate his teachings to large gatherings in the US. He also used correspondence courses and mass initiations, which horrified some traditionalists who thought that Yogananda was going too far from ancient traditions.

Ryan told me, when I interviewed him, that he understands this to be a continuous process, whereby what was once esoteric knowledge went from being completely cordoned-off to being taught to householders, to being taught in the West, and so making the lessons available online is a continuation of the same process today.

In fact, Ryan suggests (and I agree) that techniques for moving energy up and down the spine are hardly secret anymore. I learned a very similar technique for meditating on the chakras to move the energy up the spine many years before I learned of the techniques of kriya yoga. There are many traditions that teach the energization of the spine through pranayama and visualization.

This is not meant to imply that there aren't good reasons for keeping some techniques secret, or only teach to qualified students. In one case, some techniques they can be dangerous for those who have not engaged with the preliminary practices. An example of such a practice can be found in the Tibetan traditions. I have mentioned the six yogas of Naropa, which are meant to prepare a disciple for life leaving the body through recognition of the illusory nature of the world and the body. These include 'phowa', or consciousness transference, which is a method for transferring your consciousness at death to a particular location in the intermediate stage, known as bardo in Tibetan. There is a seventh, secret technique, related to phowa, called 'forceful projection' (or 'drong-juk'), which involves learning to project your consciousness out of your body into another living thing or a recently deceased body while you are still alive. This is somewhat creepy and perhaps there is a good reason to keep it under wraps only for advanced practitioners.[11]

Again, as Ryan reminded me, simply knowing the ABCs of a technique doesn't mean you know all the whys and wherefores or that you will practice it regularly. So, while most techniques are now public, you may still need instruction on the right way to practice the technique to ensure that you make progress. This is the logic of many organizations, including SRF who will only offer kriya initiation after the student has studied and practised Yogananda's other techniques for some time.

Which Technique Do You Need Now?

Many traditions claim that their techniques (in some cases, there is only one technique, but in other cases there are many different sub-techniques that fall into the four categories), if practised properly, are sufficient for self-realization or liberation. This may be true, but one of the (many) benefits of having a teacher present to teach you is that you are pointed towards the right technique at the right time.

While I am a big fan of the fact that the methods of teaching these spiritual techniques have opened up and become accessible to the many rather than the few, learning online makes it difficult to identify the technique that will help you the most given your state of development and experience.

An in-person teacher, a guru, can assess your progress and select the techniques you need at any given point in time. In the modern world, the need to address stress or health issues may be as important as the desire for spiritual evolution. The word 'kriya' itself means 'technique', although Yogananda refers to kriya yoga as a specific technique. Many others from the river of kriya yoga that was started by Babaji make the point that there are many kriyas.

As with anything else, I encourage modern seekers to use their intuition. Sometimes, a modern seeker who has tried different techniques will receive indications that a technique is or is not appropriate, or about the next step in their growth. In my own case, these have come in the form of 'clues', a term that I use for synchronicity, feelings of déjà vu, intuition, messages from the external world that come at the right time, dreams and coincidences. We talked about these clues in 'Lesson #2: Sometimes, the Universe Unexpectedly Gives You an Important Task' and will learn more about them in 'Lesson #10: Getting Help and Following the Clues'.

The types of techniques that are ideal for you will vary depending on your health, circumstances and inclinations. If you tend more towards the mental plane, like me and many engineers, computer programmers and academics, then the 'mental' techniques of meditation, concentration and visualization might come most naturally to you. However, you may also need to balance the meditation and visualization with techniques that involve the body—pranayama, energization exercises, asanas and hatha yoga, which go beyond simply meditating on your breath and thoughts. And if you find these physical techniques effective, don't assume you don't need the more mental techniques anymore. Remember that yoga is about the cessation of the vrittis, the whirlpools, of thoughts *and* feelings. If you spend all your time in the mental plane, then you have plenty of vrittis, whirling about here and there— vrittis everywhere!

When I was first learning to meditate, I had a friend tell me that she found it much easier to meditate after a hatha yoga session. Practicing hatha yoga made it seem like she was halfway there already, whereas if she just sat down to meditate, she found herself dealing with so many thoughts that it was difficult for her to stay focused; she sometimes even got headaches.

In some ways, this echoes the principle that the limbs of yoga reinforce one another. They are not meant to be mutually exclusive. Before you think about moving the kundalini up the shushumna (the central energy channel), one of the core practices in kriya, you have to prepare the body and the channels for the experience, which is why Yogananda recommended doing other exercises first.

Similarly, you may need specific techniques to address the state of your mind and your body at a particular point in time. In the modern world, we often have to deal with health issues that result from bad diets, lack of exercise and the ways in which we repress our thoughts and energies on an everyday basis, and sometimes the interventions performed by modern medicine leave us with *more* problems and side effects. At such times, we need yoga more than ever before to get our bodies back on the right track, yet we can't always practice as much or as vigorously as we might like, and many yoga poses may be difficult to do with our specific ailments.

In my own case, when I was on a long road to recovery from heart surgery, I could no longer perform the hatha yoga techniques that I used to because of aches and pains in my chest and shoulder (when you have been through a heart crisis, you take all aches and pains in that area quite seriously).

It was suggested to me by a practitioner of functional medicine that I might want to try a particular pranayama, alternate nostril breathing, to build back my breathing abilities and, though she didn't state this, to balance the energy flowing through the left and right sides of my body. This helped quite a bit—I slowly worked my way back to being able to do more. It was what I needed at the time.

A few months later, a monk from the SRF told me that it could be beneficial for me to do Yogananda's energization exercises several times a day before moving onto kriya yoga exercises.

In both cases, I was familiar with the suggested techniques already, having dabbled in them in the past. I had even recommended alternate nostril breathing as a good warm-up before meditation because it affects our mind–body state, making it easier to transition from the external world to the internal one. Modern medicine has found that breathing out for longer periods than you inhale can activate the parasympathetic nervous system, which helps us heal and digest and recover.

But, despite my familiarity, it was only when I received these messages from others that I realized these were the techniques I needed to focus on at that point in time. I started to do the energization exercises twice a day and continue to do so till now. Soon, I was able to resume some of my hatha yoga poses. In a different era, I would have had a single teacher tell me this. The modern seeker often relies on clues from the outside world—often from different sources, as in my case—and then using their intuition to guide them to the right technique at the right time.

How do you know if a clue is guiding you towards a specific technique? Well, for one, you have to try it out, and then trust your intuition and your body. More recently, as I started to do some of the hatha yoga techniques, they aggravated an old knee injury, making it difficult to continue those particular poses. That's the kind of obvious clue that comes from your body and you should treat it quite seriously that a certain technique is not for you at the current time!

Conclusion: Even a Little Practice Goes a Long Way

Patanjali also spelt out the paths of yoga, each of which now has many tributaries. Many of these tributaries have merged with other tributaries. Some have died out, but there are still new ones being formed using ancient techniques that have been modified to fit a more modern audience with a more modern lifestyle.

Lahiri Mahasaya also instructed his disciples to add yogic practices to whatever religious tradition they were a part of.

'A Moslem should perform his namaz worship five times daily,' the master pointed out. 'Several times daily a

Hindu should sit in meditation. A Christian should down
on his knees several times daily, praying to God and then
reading the Bible.'[12]

Moreover, in figuring out which techniques are right for
you, you have to take into account your natural tendencies.
Yogananda tells us that Lahiri Mahasaya, far from preaching
a specific path of yoga, simply advocated adding the kriya
technique to whatever path was most appropriate for a
particular disciple.

> With wise discernment, the guru guided his followers
> into the paths of Bhakti (devotion), Karma (action), Jnana
> (wisdom), or Raja (royal or complete) Yoga, according to
> each man's natural tendencies.[13]

I would like to end this chapter with a translated passage from
the Bhagavad Gita. This verse was quoted by Babaji in his
reply to Lahiri Mahasaya when the latter suggested that yogic
techniques could and should be practised by every sincere
seeker, not just renunciates: '*Swalpamapyasya dharmasya
trayate mahato bhayat*'[14] (Even a little practice of this dharma
will save you from great fear—the colossal sufferings inherent
in the repeated cycles of birth and death.[15])

So, find the technique that works for you at this time,
whether it's because it was suggested by a specific teacher or
you were led to it by clues brought to you by the tumultuous
waves of maya in the physical world.

More importantly, remember the definition of yoga—
we are all full of vrittis that need to be calmed! Any practice
that achieves this is yoga, according to the ultimate authority,

Patanjali. More important perhaps than the technique itself is that you practice every single day, even if it is for a small amount of time. Even a little practice of this dharma, as the Gita and Babaji tell us, will have great benefits.

So, in conclusion: practice yoga every day, no matter which technique you are drawn to, no matter how much time you have in your busy schedule.

LESSON #9

Go Out of Your Way for Little and Big Pilgrimages

There is great value in visiting places where saints have lived. Such places are forever permeated with the vibrations left there by the divine souls who walked those grounds.

— YOGANANDA[1]

Wandering day after day in the Holy Land, I was more than ever convinced of the value of pilgrimage.

— YOGANANDA[2]

One of the aspects of Yogananda's life that has always stood out for me was his propensity to go out of his way to visit a person or place that he thought would be intriguing or helpful to him on his spiritual path. He displayed this kind of wanderlust even when he was young. He would often travel to the outskirts of the great city of Calcutta to find a particular swami or visit a particular temple dedicated to a goddess. The *Autobiography* and his various biographers confirm the vast number of miles that he covered during his life on trains, boats and, of course, on his feet, in both his homeland and the United States.

We have already talked in other chapters about his having visited specific saints, so in this lesson we will focus on the importance of visiting spiritual places. I like to call these 'places of power', places that have a sacred energy and can help us in our spiritual quest, as they helped Yogananda a century ago.

There are generally two kinds of places of power that we can visit on a little or a big pilgrimage: natural power spots and man-made power spots. Some spots are considered divine because of the presence of a god or gods (like Mt Kailash, where Lord Shiva resides and), so they might form a third category. However, our recognition of the Divine at a particular spot is usually brought about by its interaction with humans who were there or by its descent into corporeal form at that location.

Natural power spots are usually places of beauty that inspire certain feelings and put us in certain states of mind. The Himalayan range as a whole is considered a hub of natural power spots because it is, for the most part, uninhabited (though some portions of it have more people than others). The rule of thumb generally seems to be: the less the people around, the easier it is to meditate.

Yogananda and many other teachers compared thoughts to radio frequencies (he also explained the telepathy of advanced yogis using this metaphor). What this means is: the more the people around and the more the thought-radio-waves being broadcast, the harder it will be to pick up the natural energy of a place. The real reason for this goes back to the vrittis that all of us are creating all the time. The more the people around, the more likely are we to create vrittis or to pick up on the individual thought dramas of others. And the more likely it is that we will get caught up in the 'warp and woof' of samsara.

Going to a pristine place that has a scarcity of thought-radio-waves puts you in a serene state of mind. It is easier to forget about the cares of the world. If you sit down to meditate in a place like this, you are already halfway there!

Man-made power spots are usually built on natural power spots, but have acquired a kind of specialness because of certain events that occurred or activities that happened there. In a sense, it is the reverse of being distracted by the vrittis of current people—it is the use of the thought-radio-waves not only of current residents but also past residents who we were engaged in a certain kind of activity. The level and clarity of the event or activity leaves a residue, and it is possible to tap into this residue.

One way this happens is through the collective thought waves that seem to imbue the place with an energy—positive or negative—that makes certain activities easier to perform. I remember once visiting MIT, years after I had graduated and become an entrepreneur, and running into one of my business mentors there. I asked him why he was working at MIT when he clearly wasn't a student or an alumnus. He said he found it very easy to sit down and write computer programs there. The collective energy of the thoughts of scientists and engineers, students and teachers who dwell on a campus just makes certain things easier. This is why ashrams can be powerful and it is easier to meditate in an ashram than it might be at home or in a supermarket for example.

Perhaps the more interesting method (to Yogananda at least) of imbuing a place with a certain sacredness is for a saint or advanced adept to spend a lot of time there. I have come to believe that their spirit ends up being connected with that place—the energy of that adept becomes linked with that place. For example, the cave where Lahiri Mahasaya first met Babaji near Ranikhet is now considered a place of power, not just because it is a cave in a (relatively) secluded spot in the mountains but also because it is possible there to tune into the energies of Lahiri Mahasaya and his teacher, Babaji.

It's as if the cave can give you multiple doses of spiritual power or energy—natural, man-made and (depending on your view of Babaji) possibly divine. This cave has been preserved and is now a tourist attraction/pilgrimage site. You can even see videos of it online now.

Throughout the Indian subcontinent, there are places like this; caves that a particular yogi or followers of a particular tradition frequented or places where a saint dwelled or a supernatural event occurred. Many of the caves in the Himalayas, though not nearly as well-known as Babaji's cave, have names. Temples and mosques are often set up at spots where saints meditated or prayed or where a miracle occurred.

When I visited Pakistan in 2008, we went to a place called Kallar Kahar in the Great Salt Range of Punjab. This town was near the ancient site of Katas, which was once home to temples and universities associated with three of the world's great religions (Hinduism, Buddhism and Islam), though today it is mostly a religious pilgrimage site and tourist attraction. The ruins of the Hindu temple surround a small pond, which, it is said in the Puranas, was created from the teardrops of Lord Shiva. The temple also appears in the Mahabharata.

Just next door are the ruins of several Buddhist stupas that once served as a monastery. The difference in architecture is striking—the Buddhist structures are quite plain compared to the more ancient Hindu temples. This site also once hosted an important centre of learning during the Islamic period: the university at Katas was responsible for a number of important astronomical observations.

In downtown Kallar Kahar, we noticed a small mosque built around the tomb of a particular saint. I also noticed peacocks all around it and was told that these peacocks visited the tomb of the saint, who was called the Peacock Saint. He had undertaken solitary meditation for forty days and forty nights in that spot (known as a 'chilla' in the Sufi tradition). There is now a mosque next to the tomb.

I found this site, which is still important to locals, as intriguing a modern pilgrimage site as the ancient neighbouring site of Katas. As is the case with all religions and spiritual traditions when they travel across cultures, Islam has been adopted into various local desi forms, which incorporate the subcontinental penchant for paying attention to saints and giving them importance. This process is ongoing and it is the result of the Divine mixing with the human. It happened to Christianity, for example, as it travelled across Europe and Buddhism as it travelled across Asia—and to yoga in its journey from India to the West (and back to the Indian subcontinent).

Yogananda almost always took time out during a trip to visit sites of natural beauty, i.e., natural power spots or places and temples where saints dwelled or were still dwelling. When Yogananda visited Europe on his trip back to India in 1935, he took plenty of time to roam around the continent and visit sites

of natural beauty. He even visited a Catholic saint, Therese
Neumann, who had exhibited the stigmata while in Germany.

Little Pilgrimages vs Big Pilgrimages

When I was young, I lived in Saudi Arabia and we drove across
the desert on the Riyadh-Mecca highway to visit the holy city
of Mecca. The centrepiece of Mecca is of course the largest
mosque in the world, Masjid al-Haram, which houses the
Kaaba, the spot towards which all Muslims around the world
direct their prayers every day. The cornerstone of the Kaaba,
called the Black Rock, is thought to be a meteor that fell from
the sky. The religious mythology is that the stone was given to
Adam when he fell from heaven.[3]

Mecca is filled with the kind of energy that I have discussed
above, making it a double- or triple-strength place of power.
It was not only supposedly the spot where Adam and Eve fell
from Paradise but also the spot where Abraham was instructed
by God and where God ushered a fountain out of the ground
for Abraham's thirsty family. This spring, which still runs today,
is considered the holy spring of Abe Zam Zam. Moreover, the
sheer number of people who have visited and continue to visit
Mecca each year imbues it with an energy. It was already a
pilgrimage site in the desert well before the modern-day religion
of Islam was born in the early part of the seventh century CE.

Places like Katas or Mecca, which housed centres of
learning and piety associated with multiple religions for
thousands of years, can be considered very strong pilgrimage
sites and attract lots of visitors. Another would be the Dome
of the Rock in Jerusalem, also known as the Wailing Wall, a
pilgrimage destination in the Holy Land for Christians, Jews

and Muslims. The holy city of Benares, or Varanasi, located on the banks of the Ganges, is considered the spiritual capital of India, with some 2,000 temples, and draws countless Hindu pilgrims every year.

While growing up, I was told that all Muslims should try to perform the Hajj (undertake a pilgrimage to Mecca) at least once in their lives. This was quite a trek in ancient times and, despite the ubiquity of airplanes and motor vehicles, can be quite an ordeal even today due to the heat and remoteness of the holy city. Thus, my impression was always that a pilgrimage was a long journey and one that you only undertook once in your life! This is what I call a *big pilgrimage* today, one that people may undertake rarely because of the travel and effort involved.

But a pilgrimage doesn't always have to be so closely tied to a religious centre. In the 1960s, many Americans undertook a kind of pilgrimage to Kathmandu, as part of an ever-increasing interest in Eastern religions. This had almost become a 'coming of age' rite for an entire generation.

In Yogananda's book, we see that small pilgrimages don't have to involve extensive travel. A pilgrimage could be as simple as going out of your way on vacation to visit a sacred temple or taking a bus to a site on the outskirts of the city you live in. This could be a small pilgrimage that you undertake once or a place that you go to semi-regularly as a spiritual tradition of your own.

This is a lesson that I can attribute for myself partly to the *Autobiography*—that, in addition to big pilgrimages every so often, we should undertake *little pilgrimages* as often as we can. The key to the value of such a small pilgrimage can be found in the words of Ram Das, an American professor at Harvard who travelled to India and returned to America a spiritual teacher, who tells us in one of his books that the secret to any act, whether it is motherhood or social protest, is in the attitude of the performer.

As we saw in 'Lesson #8: Practice Every Day, No Matter How Much Time You Have', yoga is all about calming the whirlpools of mental and emotional activity. While this is primarily an inner and personal practice, going to a sacred place or a place of natural wonder, fills your mind and emotions with a different quality of experience. This naturally helps you calm the vrittis and connect with the Divine. It also gets you out of your habitual thoughts and emotions, which again makes it easier to perceive the Divine without the normal storm of whirlpools blocking your access.

In my own case, when I lived in Silicon Valley, there was a park near San Francisco Bay, just outside of Google's corporate headquarters, that easily took me away from the hustle and bustle of the Valley and the mental activity that is inescapable in such a concentrated place. This park, called Shoreline, gave me a view of the mountains and the bay, and the breeze (sometimes colder than I liked) had a way of calming the disturbances of the mind that had built up during the day, making it an ideal sunset spot. I felt as if I had gone hundreds of miles away from the mental activity of Silicon Valley—even though it was just down the road from where I lived. In essence, it was a little pilgrimage that I could undertake every few days and come back from refreshed.

Some Examples from the *Autobiography*

It is the importance of these little pilgrimages that I really want to emphasize in this lesson.

As has been noted, Yogananda often wanted to visit incredible mountainous regions to observe the wonders of nature and temples of particular saints in out-of-the-way places, where he seemed to naturally connect with the Divine.

There are a number of instances in the *Autobiography* of a significant event occurring during a trip to a temple. We have already noted that Yogananda always made it a point to meditate and pray at temples, usually to the icon at the centre of the temple. One such visit was a trip to a temple in Srinagar, just after he had finally made the trip to the Himalayas that he had been seeking for so long.

The Srinagar temple was dedicated to Adi Shankara, perhaps one of the few well-known swamis of old whose wanderlust rivalled that of Yogananda, though Shankara primarily travelled within India on foot and did not have railroads to assist him. Also known as Adi Shankaracharya, Shankara the wandering monk, who lived in the eighth century CE was a reformer. He helped reorganize the swami order (of which Yogananda and other ordained swamis were members) and clarify and strengthen the doctrine of Advaita Vedanta.

This particular temple, which Yogananda called a 'mountain-peak hermitage', was a hybrid place of power, with both natural and man-made sources of energy. It seems that the power was not lost on Yogananda, as he immediately fell into a trance that was to prove prophetic:

As I gazed upon the mountain-peak hermitage, standing bold against the sky, I fell into an ecstatic trance. A vision appeared of a hilltop mansion in a distant land. The lofty Shankara ashram before me was transformed into the structure where, years later, I established the Self-Realization Fellowship headquarters in America. When I first visited Los Angeles, and saw the large building on the crest of Mount Washington, I recognized it at once from my long-past visions in Kashmir and elsewhere.[4]

And this perhaps dramatically demonstrates the benefit of going to temples or other sacred places that are in areas of natural beauty—they naturally draw us into a receptive state in which we can have intuitions and visions. There is no reason not to believe his account of this vision, as it was the kind of vision he claimed to have had multiple times about several buildings that would later show up in America.

The significance of a hermitage on a mountain in a place of natural beauty (Kashmir) is directly relevant to his vision as well as the building he would acquire for the SRF headquarters many years later, which was located on a mountain in a natural place of beauty overlooking Los Angeles, California. It was as if that resonance made it easier to see the similarities across time.

But it is, I believe, also significant that this vision first appeared to Yogananda in a temple dedicated to Adi Shankaracharya. Yogananda often referred to his tireless crisscrossing of North America, where he logged so many miles that he would definitely have been in the top tier of modern frequent flier programmes, as a 'spiritual campaign'.[5] The parallels with Shankaracharya's own spiritual campaign to reform the swami order and to spread the ancient wisdom of the Vedas and yoga across India is clear.

As I've said, visiting a place, particularly one that is imbued with the energy of or dedicated to a particularly well-known person (or saint or god or goddess) puts us in alignment with the energy and thought process of that person or divine entity. The ease with which Yogananda went into the trance and saw the vision of a mountaintop headquarters is indicative of this.

During the trip to Kashmir, he was accompanied by his guru, Sri Yukteswar; perhaps it was natural that a teacher travelling with his students would want to stop at one or more temples during his trip. But in general, this was also a habit that was ingrained in Yogananda, who usually went out of his way on trips not just to visit sacred sites but also to meditate at those sites, if possible. This usually ended up conferring some unintended benefit or having an unexpected effect on whatever the purpose of his journey was.

Another story (which is also discussed in 'Lesson #10: Getting Help and Following the Clues'), Yogananda tells us in this connection has to do with his sister, Roma, who was concerned about her materialistic husband Satish. Satish was of a worldly sort and didn't believe in wasting time on spirituality. Yogananda agreed that if she could get Satish to accompany them on a short pilgrimage to the temple of Kali in Dakshineswar, they would perhaps be able to find a way to orient him towards the spiritual life.

Satish instructed Yogananda—whom he thought of as a foolish 'little monk' for admiring dirty sadhus in the modern age—to make sure he provided for their lunch, which had to be arranged beforehand as the temple closed for the noon hour.[6] Yogananda instead spent his time meditating on the Goddess Kali (of whom there is a statue in the temple); he had an ecstatic vision, after which he prayed to the Goddess to turn the heart of his brother-in-law towards a more spiritual direction.

When the temple closed at noon, Satish admonished the young monk, calling him a 'little fool' because he thought they wouldn't be able to have any lunch, to which Yogananda's reply was simple: 'Divine Mother will provide.'

Satish, who might represent all of the sceptics in the modern world, said emphatically, 'I would like to see your Divine Mother giving us food here without proper arrangements!'[7]

Just then, seemingly miraculously, they were approached by a monk who had seen Yogananda meditating, taken it upon himself to arrange food for the party and made an exception to the temple's policy, which forbade arranging food for visitors who did not make arrangements beforehand. Amazed at this turn of events, Satish's heart was indeed turned away from the material towards the spiritual.

This is one of many examples of a prayer being answered both literally (in this case, with food) and also metaphorically, in that the real prayer wasn't so much about the food as about turning a 'doubting Thomas', as Yogananda likes to call them, into a believer. This was possible because Satish was shocked that in fact, through Yogananda, provisions were delivered when he had given up hope of a lunch meal. We'll talk more about asking for help in the context of this and other stories from the *Autobiography* in 'Lesson #10: Getting Help and Following the Clues'.

While these two examples (and others) are related to Hindu temples, the idea is actually quite universal. Visiting a sacred place that was at some point inhabited by a saint of any religion or a spot once used for sacred ceremonies and untainted by the radio waves of ordinary everyday activity that infect our cities brings benefits of its own. Praying or meditating in such a place is usually much more effective than doing so elsewhere. This is partly because the energy that has accumulated there on account of the holy presence makes it easier, just like programming was easier at MIT because of the collective energy and visualizing a future spiritual centre in the mountains was easier at a temple dedicated to Adi Shankaracharya in the mountains in Kashmir.

Sauntering—To the Holy Place in the Mountains

Yogananda's descriptions of Kashmir serve as prominent examples of the swami expounding on the natural beauty of the places that he was able to visit in his life. Obviously, as we saw in 'Lesson #1: You Don't Need to Go to the Himalayas', Yogananda had been trying to visit the sacred mountains since he was twelve years old (and perhaps since the vision he had when he was eight years old), so his trip to Kashmir had a particular significance for him.

> Joyous anticipations filled our hearts as we neared central Kashmir, paradise land of lotus lakes, floating gardens, gaily canopied houseboats, the many-bridged Jhelum River, and flower-strewn pastures, all ringed round by the Himalayan majesty ...[8]

> For the first time in this life, I gazed in all directions at sublime snow-capped Himalayas, lying tier upon tier like silhouettes of huge polar bears. My eyes feasted exultingly on endless reaches of icy mountains against sunny blue skies.[9]

> In this storied vale one finds an epitome of all the earth's beauties. The Lady of Kashmir is mountain-crowned, lake-garlanded, and flower-shod. In later years,

after I had toured many distant lands, I understood why
Kashmir is often called the world's most scenic spot.[10]

In fact, for anyone who is the on the yogic path, a visit to the
mountains in the northern parts of the subcontinent can be
just as full of meaning as a visit to a specific holy temple or
city. The same is true of other parts of the world. Yogananda
compared the beauty of Kashmir to the Swiss Alps, Pike's Peak
near Denver, Colorado, the Highlands and Lochs of Scotland
and Yellowstone National Park in the US.

This trip to Kashmir stands out because of his connection
with the Himalayas and their meaning in his life. A place of
power thus derives its power from its natural beauty, but
also from the state of mind that it puts us in when we visit it.
Communing with nature is in a sense a communion with the
Divine that created the world, maya though it may be, and the
sense of wonder and awe that imbues these spots can help to
take us beyond our everyday limitations and open our minds
and spirits to that divine creative energy. It's not that this
kind of energy doesn't exist in the cities or centres of human
activity—it's just harder for us to tap into it while caught in our
storm of vrittis.

I find that walking in places from where mountains are
visible is almost always like taking a little pilgrimage. At the
time of writing this book, I was in Arizona, a desert landscape
that is rife with large mountains and small buttes that are awe-
inspiring. There is a park called Papago Park, where a breath-
taking light show is orchestrated by nature every night at sunset,
each show different, yet each one serene. These mountains are
much smaller than the Himalayas, and not necessarily filled
with saints, though they have an ancient energy going back to

the Native American tribes that lived on this land for hundreds (or perhaps thousands) of years before modernity arrived.

In California, naturalist John Muir (after whom the famous Muir Woods of redwood trees north of San Francisco was named) was a big fan of the connection between pilgrimage and nature. It is because of him that many aspects of California's wilderness were preserved, including the giant redwood trees in the patch of northern California that bears his name.

Too often today, we see modern people possessed with the urge to finish tasks, particularly for the purpose of physical exercise. The terms 'do the mountain', 'run the trail' and 'hike the trail' are common. However, taking it more slowly and appreciating the natural beauty and the state it can put us in is perhaps more important than getting vigorous exercise by 'attacking the mountain'. Near Stanford University, which is located in a particularly picturesque part of Silicon Valley in California, there are some hills that are referred to by the structure that was built on top of them, the Stanford Dish, a radar telescope that sits high overlooking the valley. The dish is surrounded by beautiful scenery and a trail that, while a little steep, offers vistas and an energy that can automatically put you in a state receptive to the Divine.

I remember ambitious modern students of Stanford and employees of the big tech companies that litter the area, dressed in their workout attire, zooming through the scenery as quickly as possible to 'get the hike done', rather than enjoying the beauty around them. They would often be in pairs and spend more time talking than appreciating the landscape or feeling the energy; they were there to 'hike', not commune.

Muir in particular didn't like the term hiking—he preferred to 'saunter' in the mountains:

Do you know the origin of that word 'saunter?' It's a beautiful word.

Away back in the Middle Ages, people used to go on pilgrimages to the Holy Land, and when people in the villages through which they passed asked where they were going, they would reply 'A la sante terre', 'To the Holy Land'.

And so they became known as sainte-terre-ers or saunterers.

Now these mountains are our Holy Land, and we ought to saunter through them reverently, not 'hike' through them.[11]

So, when you take time out to either go to the mountains (or like me, just go for walks in places from where the mountains are visible), try to remember the connection. Try to saunter and appreciate the beauty of the mountains and, just as importantly, the state they put you in. Don't just hike!

A Pilgrimage to Yogananda's Hermitage by the Sea

As already mentioned, a pilgrimage site where a particular holy person resided for a long time that preserves some aspects of their presence and also contains natural beauty is like a double power spot and can automatically put you in a meditative state. I've mentioned mountains, but pilgrimages to the ocean can be equally powerful, as the sound of the waves can help to reduce our inner dialogue and wash away some of our vrittis and samskaras, if we let it.

I'd like to end this chapter with a story of a personal pilgrimage I undertook while writing this book. The Mt Washington headquarters of the SRF has naturally become a pilgrimage destination for those who study Yogananda's writings and want to walk the paths that he laid out. But in another vision, one he had at his school in Ranchi, he saw several sites that would one day manifest in California, including the Lake Shrine (which is located in Santa Monica) and the hermitage at Encinitas. Each site is unique and has a different energy. The hermitage in Encinitas is located on the edge of the ocean, overlooking it from cliffs that wind down to a beach where Yogananda often walked. He spent so much time on the beach that its formal name now is Swami's Beach.

Yogananda spent much of the last decade or so of his life in the Encinitas Hermitage, working on the *Autobiography*. The years 1941–1945 were spent by him almost exclusively living in this beautiful place and working on the book day and night. The hermitage is still preserved by the SRF and is sometimes open to visitors for tours, with a beautiful garden that is generally easier to visit than the hermitage itself.

Since Yogananda wrote most of the *Autobiography* in his study in this building, which has windows and a patio that opens up to cliffs overlooking the beach and the majestic (and warm, I might add) Pacific Ocean, I thought this would be a great destination for me, a place where I could get the proper inspiration for finishing this book. I wanted to undertake a kind of pilgrimage to tap into his spiritual energy and the mental activity that took place there while he wrote his classic, and in so doing, perhaps even receive his psychic blessing for my book.

There was only one problem. The hermitage was closed and they were not accepting visitors due to the COVID-19 pandemic. San Diego (the biggest city near Encinitas) was just far enough away that I didn't want to drive or fly there without an assurance that I would be able to visit the site.

I almost gave up on the idea, but after I contacted some folks at SRF, they told me they would be able to set up a special visit for me, just weeks before I was to move out of California, which would have made it even more difficult for me to visit. I have to give special thanks the individual monks and nuns who reside there and the administration of SRF for setting up the special visit for me.

I was able to tour the beautiful gardens, which are designed to make it easy to meditate (with the sounds of the ocean audible nearby). I also was given a special tour that included his study, which has been preserved just as it was. The position of the desk was the same as it had been when he wrote out much of the *Autobiography* by hand at it. I was able to go in and spend as much time as I wanted, examining some of the artefacts that were there and, more importantly, communing with the energy that lives there. Although I wasn't alone, I was able to close my eyes and, thanks to the serene surroundings and the sounds of waves rising and falling, I naturally fell into a meditative state to absorb the energy in this place of power.

It was while I was standing next to Yogananda's writing desk and naturally falling into a trance that I sensed the swami's presence and energy in a concrete way that I had never experienced before. It was like I was gazing at the version of him from the time when he had written the *Autobiography*—and in my vision, he too sensed I was there. He stood up, opened the patio doors and showed me some of his papers. He pointed to me and then to his papers. He picked up the papers and, in a move that at first horrified me, he tossed the pile out towards the ocean and they scattered in the ocean's breeze.

But suddenly, each of the scattered papers turned into a small white bird and flew off in different directions. I understood.

The papers were his messengers to the rest of the world. Now I understood why he was able to devote so much energy for such a long period of time to the culmination of his lifelong task, his karma, of leaving behind the pages, the little birds that would touch the lives of millions.

In this vision, the version of Yogananda I saw seemed to be sending me messages that were tailored for me specifically. His spirit (or at least my version of it in my vision) seemed to recognize that I was a writer and that it was important for me to keep this image in mind, of our pages being the messengers that we leave behind in our books.

It's one thing to know this intellectually, and another to have a strong vision imbued with feeling of the pages becoming little birds and carrying the message to different parts of the Earth. From that point on, whenever I ran into the usual stumbling blocks while writing this book, I would simply call up the image from my mini-pilgrimage to Encinitas, and it would not just change my state but give me both the inspiration and spiritual energy to complete my task!

While my scientifically minded friends would tell me that this was 'just my imagination', when I mentioned it to the small group that was showing me around, they smiled knowingly. They often had experiences in which they could feel the energy of Yogananda's presence, usually in the study or his small bedroom, which was just across the hallway. Sometimes, they told me, it would occur in a particular spot in the hallway, between the two rooms where he spent so much time and concentrated so much of his mental effort and energy. This was the perfect example of a natural place of power that was also a man-made place of power created by the presence of a master, an adept, and the activities that he had performed there.

Unlike many of my modern colleagues, I have no problem ascribing *both* a subjectivity and an objectivity to this experience and others like it. It was a subjective experience, tailored to me, an author who was writing about Yogananda, emanating from the spirit of the man himself. And yet there was clearly an objective aspect of prana or energy that I felt in my body and others had also felt. The subjective nature of visions doesn't diminish their power; in fact, I would say that is part of what makes them so powerful!

The Lesson: Go Out of Your Way with Little Pilgrimages to Spiritual Places

And that is perhaps the real lesson—that we should go out of our way to undertake little pilgrimages to sacred places, places of power. These might be man-made or natural or, in the most potent cases, they are a combination of these with a touch of the divine.

In all types of sacred places, try to connect with the aspects of those places that are holy or meaningful to you. In a natural place, try not to 'hike' or 'exercise', but rather to saunter, to wander around slowly and aimlessly, soaking in the energy and letting your natural thoughts slowly quieten down.

Pay attention to your energy in both types of holy places. In a man-made place, a temple, hermitage or other site that has meaning, you may not need to sit down and formally meditate or pray as Yogananda often did when visiting temples. You may, as was the case with him in Srinagar and, to a lesser extent, with me in Encinitas, just close your eyes, soak it in and suddenly find yourself having a vision, or you may just feel a presence or an energy. The more your thoughts calm down, the easier it will be to pick up on this energy or presence or feeling or divine guidance.

You can do this with or without an intention. The key is to let go, to not hold on too tightly to whatever your intention is (if any) and to let the place of power answer you naturally. Treat the intention like one of those little birds: send it off to fly and see what message comes back. After that, trust your intuition and feelings. Don't question yourself too much. Take whatever experience you get, even if it is just an experience of calm.

You never know what you are going to find!

LESSON #10

Getting Help and Following the Clues

Attune yourself to the active inner Guidance; the Divine Voice has the answer to every life dilemma. Though man's ingenuity for getting himself into trouble appears to be endless, the Infinite Succour is no less resourceful.

— LAHIRI MAHASAYA[1]

Whenever anyone utters with reverence the name of Babaji ... that devotee attracts an instant spiritual blessing.

— LAHIRI MAHASAYA[2]

Setbacks, Challenges and Help

One of the lessons that comes through in the *Autobiography* is that Yogananda often asked for help from individuals or entities that technically weren't present in the physical world with him. This included asking for help from his guru, Sri Yukteswar, from his paramguru, Lahiri Mahasaya, from Lahiri's guru, Babaji, as well as from the Divine Mother or from an aspect of divinity, a goddess. At least in the *Autobiography*, it seems like Yogananda almost always got the help he was asking for!

Sometimes this took only a moment or two of praying and at other times it took hours of praying. Sometimes it was to help with something profound, like converting his brother-in-law, Satish, an avowed sceptic (see 'Lesson #9: Go Out of Your Way for Little and Big Pilgrimages'), and sometimes for seemingly frivolous causes like showing off to his sister by asking the Divine Mother for two kites that were flying near them (both came).

Is it really so easy to get help from beyond? Yes and no.

When we encounter challenges and setbacks, it's only natural to ask for divine or human help. The Divine seems to be responsive to the rest of us when we desperately need help, unlike with Yogananda, who was seemingly able to seek help whenever he wanted to. The questions of challenges and setbacks and asking for guidance or help are all related, and we'll cover them in this and the next chapter. In this chapter, we'll look at the stories about asking for help and see what they can teach us, and in the next chapter we'll see how setbacks can be part of our karma and our storyline in this life.

Yogananda's First Speech in English

Let's start with a few examples that will show us that, in the words of Professor Dumbledore to Harry Potter, 'Help is always available.' Though Yogananda wasn't alive when Harry Potter novels or the movies were released, I think it's a sentiment he would have agreed with.

The first example I'd like to explore is from the time when Yogananda was aboard the *City of Sparta*, the first ship to leave India for America after World War I, sailing for the Congress of Religions in Boston in 1920.

You might say this was the real beginning of Yogananda's big mission in this life—to bring yoga to the West. Well before he got to the convocation in Boston, where he gave a significant speech, he ran into his first challenge on the ship. I have already mentioned that Yogananda may not have been the most qualified representative of the swami order to attend this gathering in America. Yet, as we explored in 'Lesson #2: Sometimes, the Universe Unexpectedly Gives You an Important Task', it was likely in his karma to go.

During the voyage (which took two months), he was asked by another passenger to give a lecture: 'Please favor the passengers with a lecture next Thursday night. I think we would all benefit by a talk on "The Battle of Life and How to Fight It."'[3]

Though Yogananda had studied English at school, he had never given a lecture in English and was pretty far from what you would call fluent. Preparing for this onboard lecture threw him into a tailspin:

> Alas! I had to fight the battle of my own life, I discovered on Wednesday. Desperately trying to organize my ideas into a lecture in English, I finally abandoned all preparations; my thoughts, like a wild colt eyeing a saddle, refused any cooperation with the laws of English grammar.[4]

Yet, 'fully trusting in Master's past assurances', he went ahead and showed up for the lecture ... but was unable to say anything:

'No eloquence rose to my lips; speechlessly I stood before the assemblage. After an endurance contest lasting ten minutes, the audience realized my predicament and began to laugh.'[5]

As he usually did, Yogananda a sent silent prayer to Sri Yukteswar, asking for help. Suddenly, he heard his guru's voice in his head: 'You can! Speak!'

Yogananda started to speak and successfully completed the lecture, speaking for forty-five minutes in English, which surprised no one more than the young swami himself! Afterwards, Yogananda couldn't recall a single word that he'd spoken, but some discreet inquiries revealed that the audience had enjoyed the lecture.

I'm sure this story has drawn a smile from multiple readers who have experienced issues with public speaking in the past or, as in my own case (though I never had issues with speaking per se), have shown up to give a talk without being fully prepared.

In this case, Sri Yukteswar, among others (see 'Lesson #14: Yoga is For Everyone, East and West'), had assured Yogananda that it was his task to go to America, so it's no surprise that when he found himself in a jam, he issued a silent prayer to his guru. While it may seem to us that not all of our prayers are answered, I have come to believe that there is a subtler karmic element to the help that we do get: perhaps prayers are answered only when it serves a purpose. In this case, the prayer was for a purpose related to Yogananda's mission, his task in this life and his karma, and thus help was granted.

A Bit of Heresy: Whom to Pray To?

Before we get deeper into aspects of answered and unanswered prayers, let's talk a little bit about an act that has been going on for as long as there have been humans: praying to the Divine to get us out of a jam (usually one of our own making!). This brings up a related and important question: if you are going to ask for help in a prayer (silent or verbal), whom should you pray to? Should it be a living person, someone who has passed away or a divine entity?

Though Yogananda in this story was praying to his guru, who was still corporeal (i.e., still in his body), most prayers are addressed to gurus and saints who have passed on, or to divinity in the form of gods or goddesses. My advice is: if you need to ask for help, you should feel comfortable asking any divine entity that is familiar to you and that you feel will help you in that situation. These two criteria (familiarity and likelihood of receiving help) are like axes along which you can direct your thoughts to the right recipient of the prayer.

You could, for example, issue a prayer to any guru of Yogananda's lineage (Sri Yukteswar, Lahiri Mahasaya or Babaji), as long as you have silently connected with them in meditation prior to the moment of prayer. You could pray to a goddess or god (they are after all aspects of divinity after all) or to an archetype.

In the Islamic tradition, people are taught not to pray to any specific person or idol but to pray to Allah, to go directly to the source itself. In the Christian tradition, prayers are often directed to Jesus; the evangelical subsects are even more explicit that 'Jesus has a plan for you'. Some Catholics pray to specific saints (or to Mary mother of Jesus). In the Indian subcontinent, it's not uncommon to ask for help from a specific saint in whose name a temple has been set up, or even a mosque; the saint serves as a conduit to divinity. Even in the Buddhist tradition, even though the Buddha was very circumspect about gods and goddesses and explicitly told his followers not to worship his visage, it is not unheard of to pray to Shakyamuni Buddha and to the Bodhisattvas, though this prayer is generally directed for the liberation of 'all sentient beings'.

At the risk of sounding heretical to a number of religious traditions, I would suggest that it almost doesn't matter who or what you pray to, as long as you connect it with a feeling of divinity. If you give it a specific form and you are sincerely trying to connect with that (departed or corporeal) person or entity or aspect of divinity, then your prayer becomes more focused. If you are part of a tradition where you have connected with that entity or aspect of divinity before, you are more likely to get help. The closer you are to that divine energy—whether it emanates from a guru, a prophet, a long-dead saint, a departed relative or an aspect of divinity (i.e., a god or goddess) or God himself (or herself)—the more likely it is to come through for you when you need it.

Even Romans and Greeks prayed to their gods. Yet each of the gods had a specific purpose, and there was a reason or season to pray to each one, which would be much like praying to a specific aspect of divinity; they prayed to specific gods for specific purposes, as humans have done before them and since. My (heretical) guess is that, even though theirs is no longer an active religion, their prayers were granted about as often as prayers sent to other forms of divinity.

The Power of Prayer, from a Scientific Perspective

Why is it so common, even in the modern age, across pretty much every human tradition, to pray for help from beings we can't see and which, from an objective point of view, may or may not exist?

There have been some scientific studies on the power of prayer, showing that the more people that are praying for someone's recovery from health, for example, the more likely they are to heal faster than those for whom no one is actively praying (though different studies have shown different results). The more scientifically minded materialists might draw the opposite conclusion from these types of studies: they would say that the unpredictability of prayer shows that it doesn't work!

Prayers sometimes work and sometimes don't— this is a no-no from the scientific, materialist point of view, leading to the negation of the entire concept of prayer! Modern scientists tend to think in stark black-and-white terms: either prayer works or it doesn't work.

But the reality is much more complicated. Anyone who has ever prayed for anything can tell you: sometimes asking for help works and sometimes it doesn't. At least, not in an immediate way. This makes it very difficult to use modern scientific methods (studies, for example) to measure the effect of prayer, because it has as much to do with the sincerity of the one who is praying as with the layers of karma that person has accumulated in this life (and in previous lives)—factors that science has no way to account for!

One thing that studies have consistently shown is that prayer helps the persons praying, and puts them in a better psychological position to solve their own problems—prayer makes it easier for a person in trouble, or just in need, to deal confidently with his or her situation. One could attribute this to the peace of mind that comes from prayer or to the specific internal response one perceives, which can take the form of a voice of a guru, a sudden glow or sense of illumination (which we can usually see around our forehead) or an enhanced ability to discern clues in the world around us that are pointing to the solution.

In short, one thing that materialists and spiritualists can agree on is that praying to an entity we perceive as divine usually puts us in a better mental place to be able to resolve problems and find solutions. For those who are more spiritually-minded, this comes from 'releasing yourself from all responsibility' because you have now transferred the pressure that was weighing you down to something (or someone) larger and more capable than you: surely your little problems are no big deal for the Divine!

Yogananda himself wrote about this process:

> Remember, greater than a million reasonings of the mind is to sit and meditate upon God until you feel calmness within. Then say to the Lord, 'I can't solve my problem alone, even if I thought a zillion different thoughts; but I can solve it by placing it in Your hands, asking first for Your guidance, and then following through by thinking out the various angles for a possible solution.'
>
> God does help those who help themselves. When your mind is calm and filled with faith after praying to God in meditation, you are able to see various answers to your problems; and because your mind is calm, you are capable of picking out the best solution. Follow that solution, and you will meet with success. This is applying the science of religion in your daily life.[6]

But the process of prayer and faith may even be more literal than that. From those who can perceive energy or those who have literally died or/and had near-death experiences (NDEs), we get a more specific description of the power of prayer. NDErs report that when they leave their bodies, they can see prayers as cords of light. This physical energetic aspect of prayer is one that should be explored further.

Two Penniless Boys and a Doubting Thomas

Before we proceed further down the asking-for-help road, let me go through a few more examples from the *Autobiography* that are memorable.

One of these, from the chapter 'The Heart of a Stone Image', involved Yogananda's sister Roma and her husband, who was an ultra-sceptic. I mentioned some of the details in 'Lesson #9: Go Out of Your Way for Little and Big Pilgrimages'. Briefly, Roma recruited Yogananda to help convince her husband, Satish, who thought prayer, meditation and the yogic life were no longer relevant to the modern world, that he was wrong. They undertook a small pilgrimage together to the temple of Goddess Kali in Dakshineshwar, where Satish told Yogananda to make arrangements for their lunch because the temple was known to close at noon.

Yogananda, true to form, spent his time at the temple praying and told Satish that the Divine Mother would provide them their lunch, a notion Satish scoffed at as foolish. Nevertheless, it turned out the prayer was answered, in more ways than one (we will discuss Yogananda's samadhi experience at this temple in 'Lesson #13: Lifting the Veil—The Everlasting Beyond the Illusion').

The main reason I recounted the story again is to point out that Yogananda once again asked for help. In this case, he needed help in convincing his sceptical brother-in-law to live a more spiritual life. It turns out the prayer worked at a practical level, as one of the temple priests, having watched Yogananda meditating all morning, decided to go against temple policy and prepare a meal even though they hadn't arranged for it in advance.

If this seems like a small thing to pray for, it wasn't. Remember, Yogananda wasn't praying for the meal so much as a way to convince Satish. His brother-in-law was so shocked at being provided a meal by the Divine Mother that he did in fact undergo a change of heart. Yogananda wasn't asking for some idle desire to be granted, but for something that would turn out to be part of his larger mission of turning others towards spirituality.

Another story that stood out as one of the most memorable and relevant, especially when I interviewed fans of Yogananda's books, was 'Two Penniless Boys in Brindaban'. In this case, when both Yogananda (then called Mukunda) and his friend Jitendra were returning from their unsuccessful attempt to become monks in Benares, they stopped to visit Mukunda's elder brother Ananta in Agra. Ananta was another avowed sceptic and what he told Mukunda was a variation of what the young monastic aspirant had, no doubt, heard many times while growing up: that he was throwing away his life by trying to become a monk and not getting a 'real job' to support himself. This is perhaps best expressed by Ananta in a statement that we might still commonly hear today: 'Money first; God can come later!'

Ananta, put off by Mukunda's faith that God would 'provide', issued a challenge: if he were to put them on a train to the nearby city of Brindaban (now Vrindavan, UP), without any money, would they be able, with God's providence alone, to spend the whole day, not go hungry and make it back by midnight, all without begging? Ananta mocked Mukunda's faith in divine help: 'What a plight if you were forced to look to the Invisible

Hand for your food and shelter! You would soon be begging on the streets!'[7]

Mukunda accepted the challenge, though his friend Jitendra, who was perhaps more practical, asked for a few rupees before they left and, even as their train was about to reach Brindaban, was ready for a real meal. When Yogananda expressed his disapproval, they had the following exchange on the train:

> 'I see no sign that God is going to supply our next meal!'
> 'Be quiet, doubting Thomas; the Lord is working with us.'
>
> 'Can you also arrange that He hurry? Already I am famished merely at the prospect before us. I left Benares to view the Taj's mausoleum, not to enter my own!'
>
> 'Cheer up, Jitendra! Are we not to have our first glimpse of the sacred wonders of Brindaban? I am in deep joy at thought of treading the ground hallowed by feet of Lord Krishna.'[8]

They were sharing a compartment of the train with a devotional man who could see that the boys were undertaking some kind of pilgrimage to follow in the footsteps of Lord Krishna, and he guessed that they had no money. He called a horse-drawn carriage at the station and led them to a hermitage, where an elderly woman informed them that they had had a princely meal prepared for the royal patrons of the hermitage, who had to cancel their visit at the last minute. The meal was instead made available to the two boys—only Jitendra was amazed. Yogananda then pinched him, saying: 'Doubting Thomas, the Lord works—in a hurry, too!'[9]

More miraculous coincidences occurred during their jaunt in Brindaban, though not without Jitendra losing faith once the meal was done and they were faced with the prospect of getting around town and getting back to Agra with no money. This caused Mukunda to remind his friend that I'm sure we can all relate to at some point in our lives: 'You forget God quickly, now that your stomach is filled'.

A young man who saw Mukunda and Jitendra taking refuge from the supreme heat under a tree asked if he could show them around Brindaban. This young man informed them that he had been meditating on Lord Krishna and saw two young men, one of whom was Yogananda, in a vision. The young man then asked not only to become his disciple but to escort them around town and to buy their train ticket home!

Jitendra wasn't the only one amazed by this turn of events. When they arrived back in Agra, Yogananda's older brother Ananta was also amazed. He pulled Jitendra aside to try to verify Mukunda's account, suspecting that his younger brother was making the whole thing up.

Then, astonishingly, Ananta exclaimed with a new spiritual enthusiasm: 'The law of demand and supply reaches into subtler realms than I had supposed.'[10]

Uncharacteristically, Ananta agreed to be initiated by his younger brother, Mukunda, something that would have been unthinkable in the social hierarchy before this incident.

When the Prayers Align with Your Mission and When They Don't

This story sounds too good to be true. Not only did the Lord provide, but He provided everything the two boys urgently needed just on time. It was as though Yogananda was ordering items from a menu at a Divine restaurant.

The wrong lesson, I think, to draw from this and many other examples in the *Autobiography* is that if you simply pray, all your prayers will be taken care of (though they certainly may be). The real lesson here is to have faith—it is likely that something good will come from your prayer if you are doing things that you have been called upon to do, things that are consistent with the part of your karma that is related to your mission or task in life.

In each of the examples thus far, the things that Yogananda asked for were aligned with his mission to spread yogic teachings among others, but this first required a change of heart from those entirely sceptical souls. In two cases, they were family members whose hearts were closed to the 'ancient wisdom' of their spiritual traditions. The other case was the start of a multi-decade English lecture tour in America that lead to Yogananda's autobiography.

You can see that these stories are all related in some way; in fact, they are all individual threads in the complex tapestry that was to be Yogananda's mission in life. It is as if some Invisible Hand, unshackled by the chains of time, was guiding these incidents not only to benefit the immediate participants in these stories, not only to change the hearts of others, but to weave individual threads in this mission to provide material for Yogananda's book.

Follow the Clues to Find the Treasure

Sometimes we just need guidance in performing everyday activities. At other times, we need guidance on a major decision that will impact our lives and the path we are on. I (and many others I'm sure) have at times thought it would be nice if we could simply see the possible futures that might result from a particular decision, be it a small or big one, including whether it would make us happy or unhappy. But most of us don't possess that kind of omniscience in the real world. We are caught in linear time, something which does not exist outside of this material world.

Nevertheless, I believe we are always receiving guidance in the form of 'clues', little messages about the world around us. However, like in any good treasure hunt, the clues aren't all laid out at once. It would not make for a very interesting film if the famous (and fictional) archaeologist Indiana Jones got his hands on the full, detailed map at the very beginning, would it? Usually, he begins with a single clue. Where does that lead? To the next clue. And then? To the next clue. To find the treasure, like Indiana Jones, you have to follow the breadcrumbs that are placed in front of you.

Only by following the clue can we see where it leads; sometimes it leads backwards because we misinterpreted a previous clue. Younger audiences may remember more recent films such as, *National Treasure,* whose main character, Benjamin Franklin Gates, must find clues on the back of the American Declaration of Independence to locate the Treasure of the Ages (a treasure that goes way back to a time well before the existence of the United States of America). Similarly, the Tomb Raider movies (based on the bestselling video game series) embodies this spirit of following the clues to find the treasure.

In real life, I like to think of these clues as a kind of divine intuition, the Invisible Hand at work. I spoke about how clues can guide us in 'Lesson #2: Sometimes, the Universe Unexpectedly Gives You an Important Task', along with the basic rules of treasure hunting.

When we ask for guidance, we are usually given a clue and not a full answer or resolution. What do these clues look like?

The clues themselves can be quite different, but they usually point us in a direction, like an invisible hand pointing in a direction. Sometimes they are full-blown clues that tell us to 'go here'. Usually, though, they come to us in the form of internal guidance—visions, dreams, hunches, feelings of déjà vu, synchronicity, etc. I go into much more detail in my book *Treasure Hunt*, but Yogananda often talked about how, if we calmed our minds, we could perceive things clearly, Including the thoughts of others.

For example, he received a clue about going to the Himalayas in a vision when he was young, as we saw in 'Lesson #1: You Don't Need to Go to the Himalayas', but he took it perhaps too literally. The vision was of yogis in the Himalayas—in fact, they even explicitly said to him: 'We are the yogis of the Himalayas,' and it showed him a path he could take. The vision came to him while he was in bed, as he fell naturally into a reverie, which is one way a clue might come to us.

Clues are often (but not always) metaphorical and need to be interpreted. By taking this vision too literally, Yogananda spent his childhood trying to run away to the Himalayas, but this vision was a metaphor. This doesn't mean it wasn't important. The vision set the stage for his life as a yogi, and so it was supremely important part of who he was and who he became.

His actual path in life turned out to have the *essence* of what he saw in his visions, but not literally (he wasn't to spend his life meditating in a cave in the Himalayas).

On another occasion, he saw a bevy of white-skinned faces while meditating. The first of these required interpretation—whom did these faces belong to? He realized they were Americans and he interpreted it as a clue. He interpreted it to mean that it was the right time for him to leave his homeland and travel to America. Later, he tells us about visions of several buildings that he didn't recognize, and these ended up being literal clues—about buildings that would house of his spiritual organizations in the future.

Still, sometimes we are unsure if the guidance we are receiving is the right one. In such cases, we should use our logical mind to help validate the clues. By the time Yogananda saw the buildings that he had visions of, he had come a long way, had a clear mind and was able to recognize that a clue from the past was manifesting in the present. In my opinion, while the earlier clue may have been guidance, it is also a reflection of the engine of karma at work in a retroactive way. By seeing the buildings in his vision, he was able, upon recognizing the buildings in the present (i.e., in the future from the time of the vision), to act and secure those buildings as spiritual centres for the organizations in India and the US.

Sometimes clues come to us not just as an internal feeling or vision, but from the world around us. As has been mentioned earlier, the famous psychologist Jung, who also wrote about yoga, introduced to the West the idea of synchronicity—what seems like a coincidence in the external world is linked directly to a thought we have had at some point in the past. Jung called this an 'acausal connection', because the Western scientific method can't figure out the connection. It could be as simple a 'coincidence' as getting a call or message from a friend a day after you think about him or her and the fact that the two of you haven't communicated in a year. A synchronicity, which is also defined as a meaningful coincidence, is usually a clue that a particular internal or external event (or both) are important to the current situation.

In story after story in the *Autobiography*, we find that yogis tend to possess foreknowledge of someone or something that they were destined to meet or experience, having had dreams or visions of those people or experiences. It's as if they constantly sense the future in dreams and daydreams—we all do, and the feelings we have about places and objects and events and people are alerts from our internal monitoring system that tell us 'This is the way to go' or 'This person/place/thing will be important to you later in life. Pay attention.'

The key is to clear your mind so that you can receive these messages. One technique is to pray, to ask the Divine for a clue and then to wait and see what you notice naturally. If you see something in the external world that appears to have resonance with what you were thinking about, you have found a clue, a synchronicity, a confluence between a mental event and an external object.

For example, when I was living in Boston and thinking of moving to California, I didn't want to leave behind my entire life, professional career and the contacts I had built in Boston, and wondered if there could be a way for me to live in both places. It wasn't clear to me how I could do this, or even that it was the right thing to do. Yet, I felt I was being called to California. I had the feeling since my childhood that I would be there someday. Like Yogananda and the Himalayas, I had repeatedly tried to get there, but each time something had come up and the move didn't happen.

It was after meditating and pondering on this question seriously that I received a clue from the outside world. I started to notice mermaids everywhere in New England (the region around Boston). Now, there were many mermaid statues and pictures in New England, which was originally settled by the migration of seafaring citizens of England. The sailors often depicted mermaids on their ships and in their restaurants and pubs. Yet, despite having lived there for ten years, I had never really noticed these mermaids. Suddenly, my mind found itself unmistakably drawn to them each time I passed one in the picturesque towns by the sea that I had visited many times before. This time, I had a funny feeling that this was an important clue.

But it wasn't obvious to me what it meant or what direction it was pointing—it was just an unusual intuition. It had to be interpreted. When I reflected on it, I had a clear intuition. The mermaid, half fish and half human, represented a being that lived in two worlds: the world of humans on land and the world of fish in the water. Mermaids were able to survive in both worlds. There was a sense of certainty in me that I had reached the correct interpretation.

It not only convinced me that I should try to live bi-coastally at the time (i.e., on the East coast of America next to the Atlantic Ocean, where Boston is, and on the West coast next to the Pacific Ocean, where California is). It also served as a powerful metaphor for my own life's work: trying to bridge worlds that rarely interacted with each other. It was during this initial trip to California that I started to write my first book, *Zen Entrepreneurship*, which was about making it in the modern world of business and computer software start-ups while trying to live and act spiritually. In a sense, this clue was about literally living in two worlds, but also in a sense the clue and was metaphorically about the idea of living in different worlds and speaking different languages.

That's often how clues work. We may not get an immediate corporeal person to pop up and help us, like Yogananda did in Brindaban, but we will likely manage to find some kind of guidance. Yoga tells us that if we can quieten our mind, we can perceive these clues more clearly; the quieter the mind, the less effort it will have to put into interpreting the clues.

Illnesses and Health: Karma and Suffering

Many people pray when they find themselves in adverse health situations; sometimes the prayers are granted and at other times they aren't. The subject of illnesses, small or large, is one of the most complicated and interesting ones—on the occasions when we ask for help and don't get it, we are forced to think about the bigger picture of our lives and how our illness does or does not fit into it.

There are a number of stories in the *Autobiography*, including Yogananda's own, which involve healing. The earliest of these describes how Yogananda was cured of Asiatic cholera while praying to a picture of Lahiri Mahasaya. Yogananda's parents were both disciples of Lahiri, and his picture was always accessible in their home. Mukunda contracted the dreaded disease at the age of eight, and the doctors couldn't do anything for him. His mother told him to pray to the picture of Lahiri that was hanging over the bedside, which he did mentally.

> I gazed at his photograph and saw there a blinding light, enveloping my body and the entire room. My nausea and other uncontrollable symptoms disappeared; I was well. At once I felt strong enough to bend over and touch Mother's feet in appreciation of her immeasurable faith in her guru.[11]

There was no doubt in Mukunda's or his mother's mind that the healing was connected to Lahiri Mahasaya: 'Mother pressed her head repeatedly against the little picture. "O Omnipresent Master, I thank thee that thy light hath healed my son!"[12]

Mukunda's family had strong connections to Lahiri, so it was natural for them to pray to him. Yogananda believed that his being taken under the wing of a disciple of Lahiri Mahasaya was foretold to him in visions and was karmically inspired, which only strengthened his ties to this particular lineage.

On the other hand, there are certain kinds of suffering and setbacks for which simply praying isn't enough. Given how close Yogananda was to his mother, there is no doubt that he would have prayed for her health; as he must have for the health of his brother Ananta, who passed away later in his life.

In his mother's case, we see that her early death was an important part of Yogananda's story, and it defined him in many ways. Part of Yogananda's devotion and closeness to the Divine Mother can be sourced to the fact that his mother had died at an early age. We already spoke of how the 'magic amulet' that was given to his mother by another disciple of Lahiri played an almost magical role in helping Yogananda find his own guru.

Sometimes a certain amount of suffering is needed to help us along on our path; it is not always a departure from the path, but can be a part of it. Sometimes, for instance, suffering is what we need in order to resolve some previous karma. We might recover naturally, or via modern medicine, or even through an intercession prompted by a prayer. We'll talk more about this idea of how karma may be related to both setbacks and the evolution of your life in 'Lesson #11: Setbacks May Be A Part of Your Story' and 'Lesson #12: Lessons from Babaji and the Great Engine of Karma'.

LESSON #11

Setbacks May Be A Part of Your Story

The season of failure is the best time for sowing the seeds of success.

— YOGANANDA[1]

A closer examination of Yogananda's life, as revealed in the *Autobiography* itself but even more so by his various biographers,[2] shows that Yogananda, not unlike the rest of us, suffered setbacks in his life and certainly in achieving his life's mission to bring yoga to the West. The reason he was so successful in his mission was not because he didn't suffer setbacks; rather, these setbacks played into his story. At the very least, it was the setbacks that usually had some larger karmic purpose in the story of his life that was difficult for him to see when they occurred.

Sometimes what appears as a setback in our life, something we are not proud of and might even consider a 'failure', is actually a type of assistance. For one thing, a setback can catalyse us into looking for another path, manifesting a reality we were perhaps destined for but have been too blind to see, lost in the winds of samsara. In such cases, it's good to remember the line from the old Rolling Stones song: 'You can't always get what you want ... but if you try sometimes, you might find, you get what you need ...'

Bigger Setbacks and the Story of Your Life

Sometimes the setback is an essential part of our story—like what Yogananda faced when he lost his mother. This can be because the setback takes us down a path we might not have taken, or perhaps it causes us not to take a path we intended to take which could have led us astray from our life's mission.

For this to be true, there would need to be a larger pattern in our lives, a grid of potential timelines that would take us towards one of the many potential futures. Like a train barrelling down the railway lines, the switch rails (called 'point blades') are the decision points that switch us from one railway to another to reach the next stop in the story of our lives.

How do we choose which path to go down? One answer is that we just choose. Another is that we get guidance from other places—from gurus who can see the larger pattern, those that are no longer in the physical world or from the Divine. There is also a different way of looking at it, a scientific point of view—some physicists have suggested that we may be getting information (or 'clues') from these possible futures. Where are these clues coming from? In this case, it would be from our future selves.

In my book *The Simulated Multiverse*, I speculated that perhaps we are constantly sampling possible future timelines, and that we end up choosing the best of all the options, but not until we have 'tried out' different timelines.

This description isn't entirely unsupported by the findings of quantum physics. In fact, there are some physicists who have speculated that time as we think of it doesn't really exist, and that we are constantly getting messages from the future, or rather from what would be *possible* futures. These messages constitute a type of probability wave, and we are constantly reaching out with our minds to ingest this information and make choices. It sounds more mystical than scientific, but it is a serious theory that seeks to make sense of some of the most baffling findings of quantum mechanics, findings that no one has come up with a complete explanation for.

In 'Lesson #1: You Don't Need to Go to the Himalayas', we discussed how Yogananda enrolled in an ashram in Benares and later thought it to be a mistake. While he initially thought he was clearly on his way to becoming a monk when he joined, very soon he realized he was miserable in this ashram for many reasons. One of the main reasons for this was that they didn't approve of him meditating so often, preferring that he spend most of his time doing physical chores. You might say that Yogananda hated this set of priorities and didn't 'fit in'.

The incident of this monastery, which might be viewed as a setback, was actually the kind of setback I'm talking about in this chapter—the kind that leads us down a better path. As we discussed in that lesson, if he hadn't gone to Benares, he wouldn't have had the encounter Sri Yukteswar, who happened to be in Benares that day taking care of family business. In a sense, this misstep was part of his path to find his guru.

A Story of a Modern Setback

One story that reminded me of this episode Yogananda's life, in more recent times, was the story of Chris, a young talented musician and also an enthusiast for Yogananda's work. He decided to become a full-time monk at Yogananda's organization, the SRF.

This isn't a decision that is to be made lightly. Joining a hermitage or monastery entails not pursuing other worldly opportunities—in this case, his singing—and adherence to a certain lifestyle and code of conduct. Just like Mukunda realized he didn't belong in that specific monastery, Chris clearly got the message, after having enrolled, that that he wasn't quite ready for a monk's life.

Chris felt out of place, as if he had made a decision to go someplace he didn't belong. He eventually decided to leave the monastery and go back into the world.

Some might say that Chris' decision to become a monk was 'ill-conceived' or a 'mistake'. When I spoke to him, he was living in the San Francisco Bay Area, making music again and was committed in a romantic relationship. Yet there were subtle signs that a part of him thought he had 'failed' because he hadn't been able to stick to it and be content with the life of a renunciate monk.

This is a common scenario that arises because of expectations we have placed on ourselves—expectations that may have come from parents, family, society, or even from spiritual peers and our own enthusiasm. We make decisions that appear to be setbacks.

I pointed out to him that making music was clearly a part of what he intended to do in this life (he even wrote a song about his monastic adventure)—it was part of his karma and part of his talent for expressing himself. Not all of us are meant to be monks. And not all of us are meant, for that matter, to be musicians (as an example, I have absolutely zero musical ability, a fact that I am not ashamed to admit).

Yet, you could say that going to the monastery was an important way for Chris to sample the life that he 'thought he ought to' have and to use the results of the experience to find perhaps a better fit for his life at the current time. That doesn't rule out the possibility of the monastic life becoming a good fit at some future point for him, but for now he is happier working a new job (which he came by quickly and easily), and continuing to make music while living in the world.

Lahiri Mahasaya taught that 'there is no need to alter one's external life in any significant way to become aware of God's presence'[3] and that we should follow our intuition because it has the solution to many of life's dilemmas.

In these two stories of joining spiritual ashrams, both young men wanted to be monks, made a decision to join a monastery, and both followed their intuition to a different path. In both cases, their intuition told them something was wrong with the current situation. Yet one of them was destined to be a monk in this life (though not a monk living in the Himalayas) and one was not (at least not yet).

Chris is still a devotee of Yogananda and an adherent of the teachings of the SRF. He is just doing it in the way that most of those reading this book are likely to: in the world, not apart from it.

The underlying lesson here is that the things that appear to be setbacks may in fact be part of our story, our karma, our particular quests in the game of life. Yogananda himself expressed this in the statement that I started this chapter with: 'The season of failure is the best time for sowing the seeds of success.'

Yogananda's Big Setbacks in America

Studying Yogananda's life reveals that he was no stranger to setbacks or emotional challenges. It's easy to think, especially with all of the miraculous stories that Yogananda himself narrated in the *Autobiography*, that he had very few struggles and everything proceeded smoothly with him as a result of a blessed life.

This is also a common perception in the world of entrepreneurship, where I spent most of my career—that anyone who has been a successful entrepreneur enjoyed an unbroken line of success from the time they started their company to the time they became rich, fat and happy! This is most definitely not the case; and I can attest to it personally that there are many moments of soul-searching and what I like to call 'trips to the underworld' during the course of an entrepreneurial journey, moments during which you are threatened with not just the failure of your business but personal financial failure and potentially the failure of your reputation as well. Yet, it is part of the spirit of the entrepreneur to be ready to deal with those difficulties—in many ways these setbacks and difficulties make up the interesting parts of our life and career, the parts that teach us the most.

When I interviewed Philip Goldberg, author of *The Life of Yogananda*, for this book, I asked him what he had found most surprising when his research led him beyond the *Autobiography*. Goldberg said he had been most surprised by the many little details he had discovered in letters and interviews that portrayed Yogananda not just as a guru but also a human being:

> He loved to just get people together and go on a picnic, how he loved to joke ... and make meals ... And that he got angry ... there were things that pissed him off and you see it in his letters, you see it in the memoirs of people who knew him wrote. He would get angry, but ... was always quick to be the loving guru afterward ...

Human beings have challenges and setbacks, and Yogananda was no stranger to either. A constant challenge for Yogananda was the struggle of having enough funds to keep his activities going. In Goldberg's biography, you constantly get the sense that Yogananda wished he had 'more money', or that he could simply abandon the responsibilities of running an organization, retreat to the quiet Himalayas and become a wandering monk.

In a sense, Yogananda was an entrepreneur; he did not necessarily treat religion as a business (which some accused him of) but, rather, used business-like techniques to build an organization. He marketed his particular message to the masses in America, adopting new technologies and using the media to his advantage; as a result, he was often lambasted in the press and by traditionalists.

As a software entrepreneur, there have been many moments when I have wished I could just hang it all up and go meditate by the beach or in the mountains, freed of worldly responsibilities, employees, etc. But alas, that wasn't necessarily what fate had in store for me at the time.

Several of Yogananda's biggest setbacks in America were left out of the *Autobiography*, though you can read about them (or watch the documentary about his life, *Awake*) so they aren't exactly secret. One of these involved his good friend and co-collaborator, Swami Dhirananda, and was echoed in other incidents with individuals that Yogananda had come to rely on.

Dhirananda (born Basu Kumar Bagchi) was a close friend of Yogananda's in Calcutta. The Bagchi family had been devotees of Bhaduri Mahasaya (the Levitating Saint) and that's probably how the two first met. Bagchi joined Yogananda, who initiated him as Swami Dhirananda in 1911, and Dhirananda became one of the three swamis who ran and taught at the Ranchi school (along with Yogananda's childhood friend Manamohan Mazumder, who later became Swami Satyananda[4]).

To cut a long story short, Yogananda asked Dhirananda to join him in America and help him with his ever-expanding organization. Not only did Dhirananda help him in Boston (and with a number of early publications), but he eventually became the person Yogananda relied on for the day-to-day teaching in Los Angeles (LA), since Yogananda was often on the road giving classes and publicizing the work.

The topics of meditation and yoga, at least in the West, have always drawn larger numbers of women than men. When Dhirananda was teaching in LA and Yogananda was travelling, a sort of scandal erupted, resulting in many articles charging Yogananda's organization with being a 'love cult' that was teaching American women 'sex techniques'. The event that was cited most frequently involved the husband of one of the women hitting Swami Dhirananda on the nose because he thought untoward things were going on between his wife and the swami.

As is often the case with the press, it conflated the two swamis, playing up the rumour that Yogananda (who was, of course, the better-known one) was the swami who had been bopped on the nose by the irate husband. Headlines like 'Queer Love Cult Lures Many Women' began to appear in the press all over America, in sensational media outlets like those owned by the Hearst family. Although the articles didn't describe any inappropriate behaviour, the innuendo (chanting in dark rooms with incense, for example, seemed to be the worst thing described) and the tone of the headlines ensured that this story caught on like wildfire. The particular narrative that caught on was that Hindu swamis were using nefarious techniques to corrupt American women.

The media firestorm broke while Yogananda was in Miami giving classes, and the outrage of the husbands of the women who had enrolled was such that the Miami police told Yogananda to cancel his lectures and leave the city for 'his own protection'. Yogananda was a fighter and tried to challenge the order in court, but eventually, for his own safety he left Miami. It was never established whether there had been any actual scandalous behaviour behind the irate husband episode and headlines (a subsequent lawsuit was dismissed). However, what is true now about the media was true then as well: it almost doesn't matter what the truth is when the media runs with a story or a narrative.

Goldberg summarizes the undercurrents that defined this period of his life: '[Yogananda] was up against the perfect storm of America's worst defects: media sensationalism, religious bigotry, ethnic stereotyping, paternalism, sexual anxiety, and brazen racism. Yogananda was well aware of the racism he and his fellow countrymen had to contend with ...'[5]

Given that Yogananda is adored by spiritual communities in America today, and that Yogananda rarely mentioned these setbacks in his writings, learning about the setbacks was interesting, to say the least. In some ways, it emphasized to me the point that Yogananda, though he might have been divinely inspired, was human and had to deal with human-level issues just like the rest of us.

The immediate problems resulting from this particular scandal faded as Yogananda simply kept doing what he did best: he kept teaching and spreading his message around the country. Yet it planted the seeds of a bigger scandal, which also involved his long-time friend and colleague, Swami Dhirananda.

In 1929, Dhirananda decided to leave the fold of Yogananda's organization, shedding his monastic name. He not only married an American woman, but also sued Yogananda for 'back wages' and 'royalties on his books', claiming that they had a business partnership and not a traditional swami-disciple relationship.

This ignited another media firestorm, with headlines like 'Swami vs. Swami'. The lawsuit not only put a damper on Yogananda's triumphant trip back to India in 1935, but he was also heartbroken over the betrayal by his close friend, even going so far as to call him a 'Judas' in his letters.[6]

While the lawsuit was eventually settled,[7] there were to be more problems of this nature for Yogananda to deal with, which led to his losing many students (some of whom followed Dhirananda) and he had to rebuild the organization that had taken him a decade to set up. Heartbroken and demoralized, Yogananda took an extended trip to Mexico, where he meditated, prayed and lectured. It is said he even considered abandoning the whole American enterprise and returning to India for good. According to Goldberg, he prayed to 'be free of his worldly duties ... he even beseeched the Divine Mother: Let me go back to India to serve you there.'[8]

While Yogananda did visit India a few years later in what was overall a triumphant trip home, the lawsuit with Dhirananda-Bagchi was ongoing at the time and it cast a pallor over the trip. I see this setback as an interesting part of Yogananda's story—involving as it did a lifelong friend who, as a boy, had meditated at Yogananda's house in Calcutta because he didn't have a space to meditate at his own home. It not only changed Yogananda but may also have prepared him for more challenges to come.

Setbacks put us on a different path than the one we thought we would be travelling on, yet they are often instrumental in helping us complete our life missions. The wisdom gained from setbacks often shapes our destiny in unexpected ways.

Yogananda was forced to regroup and rebuild his organization in America. He also decided upon his return from India that he would spend more time with a smaller number of disciples and less time travelling and lecturing across the country. He spent most of his last fifteen years in southern California. Goldberg again: 'The itinerant spiritual teacher settled more deeply into his dual roles as satguru—a preceptor who guides the spiritual progress of close disciples—and jagadguru—a world teacher who expounds perennial wisdom to the masses.'[9]

With regard to the second role, that of jagadguru, Yogananda took another important decision at this time: to spend more time writing. He even recruited his former editor, Laurie Pratt, who lived in San Francisco, to move to LA and work with him on his books. His close disciples also surprised him by purchasing a seaside piece of land in Encinitas, which became the site where he spent more time in those years and wrote most of the *Autobiography* (see 'Lesson #9: Go Out of Your Way for Little and Big Pilgrimages'), which became his true legacy.

It is fortunate for millions of seekers in the West and the East that he didn't abandon America entirely and go back to India for good. It is unlikely that he would have written his magnum opus, *Autobiography of a Yogi*, certainly not in English to be published in America first, if he had done so.

My Own Big Setback

As I've already said, I believe that big setbacks can sometimes have the unintended effect of moving us from one life path to another, like a switch between two railway lines. This is particularly likely when we have stayed for too long on a path that we should have changed at a certain point in the past. This is what I call a 'course correction' and a good example of it from Yogananda's book was the Tiger Swami's mauling by the tiger (see 'Lesson #3: The Unexpected Lessons of the Tiger Swami'), which led him to explore a different path in life from then on.

Throughout this book, I have tried to weave in examples from my life and others' lives along with those from Yogananda's life. I would like to share another personal story, one that I have not shared in a book before but have alluded to in earlier chapters. This incident also played an important part in why I am writing this book.

In it, we see once again the interplay of setbacks and how that affects our mission and karma in this life. I can assure you that I would not be writing this book today if not for one of the biggest setbacks in my life and career.

It occurred when I was running a start-up accelerator in Boston, Play Labs @ MIT. I was doing what I thought I was meant to do—furthering my career as a technology venture capitalist, helping entrepreneurs and staying attuned to the latest technologies. I liked both the prestige of the position and the outlook it gave me on the industry.

Although I was no longer running an actual start-up, which is what I had done for most of my career until then, running the accelerator came with many of the same challenges and stresses. Like most denizens of Silicon Valley (even though this accelerator was physically located in Boston), I was figuring out what to do next with my career. Somehow, I had convinced myself about the importance of starting and running a much bigger VC fund and that the accelerator was a precursor to this.

I had convinced myself to do this despite the fact that every time I had run a start-up in the past the stress was such that I had assured myself, 'Okay, after this one, I will stop running tech companies and will focus on my other mission in life—to write and to speak and to pursue my own spiritual interests.' Yet each time, I would get caught up with the 'next big thing' in my career.

This isn't just a modern problem, but it is exacerbated in the modern world. I mentioned earlier in this book that I have always had the intuition that I would be an entrepreneur first and then later a writer. But by this stage in my life, I knew that if I ended up starting and running a VC fund, I would be sucked right back into the hustle and bustle of the technology world. It would be a source of additional stress deriving from the need to focus on one thing: making money for my investors.

I suspected (perhaps at the back of my mind) that it wasn't right for me to place so much emphasis on material success, but once you are on the treadmill it's hard to get off—even if you meditate and lead a rich spiritual life, as I believed I had.

It was at that point, just before the summer programme ended, that I started to feel chest pains. Incidentally, one of my partners at Play Labs, Raj, who had been a classmate of mine at MIT, had to be hospitalized that summer due a heart-related illness. Another of our classmates from MIT, Ranjan Das, who was president of SAP India, had passed away a few years earlier. These events only emphasized that all of us were getting to the age at which health in general, and heart health in particular, was becoming very important.

It turned out that my arteries were extremely clogged, no doubt from all the various types of foods that I had eaten with abandon throughout my adult life, and the doctors told me the only option they thought was viable was open heart surgery. If they didn't operate, I was in danger of an imminent heart attack (in fact, it was inconclusive whether I was already having one or not). Anyone who has seen what open heart surgery is knows that it is one of the most serious surgeries that can be performed while you are alive—the chest is literally opened up and the heart is worked on while the person is kept alive using a respirator.

The doctors told me that it would take a few months to fully recover, but I would feel much better and be able to begin cardiac rehabilitation in a month's time. The surgery rendered me unable to finish the Play Labs programme that year. A month or two later, I still wasn't even close to recovering. It turned out they needed to perform two more heart procedures (less invasive than the first open heart surgery, these were stents placed into the arteries without requiring opening up the chest), but even so I could barely walk after these procedures and wasn't recovering nearly as quickly as they had all predicted. Moreover, I had constant chest and shoulder pain that the doctors couldn't explain.

To cut a long story short, over the next year I slowly started to recover, but every time I thought of jumping back into Silicon Valley-type activities, which happened each time I felt well enough, my recovery faltered. It was as if the universe was telling me something—forcibly in this case.

While I had many mystical experiences during this time, I ended up focusing on my writing. I found that I could sit at my desk and write and later take a cab to the local coffee shop and sit there and write for another hour or two. I could no longer put in the kinds of hours that I did before, finding it difficult to stay up late to work, for example.

Interestingly, this was when my writing career started to take off, partly because I was focusing on it (since I couldn't do much else). I was able to publish the book on start-ups that I had been working on erratically for ten years—*Startup Myths and Models: What You Won't Learn in Business School*—which was picked up by a highly prestigious business school publisher (Columbia Business School).[10] More importantly, I finally wrote the book I had been thinking about that integrated Eastern spirituality and mysticism with Western technology: *The Simulation Hypothesis*, which went on to become a bestseller.

The recovery and rebuilding of my life wasn't easy—as I write this, three years after the surgery, I'm still not fully recovered and don't have the energy that I used to have for physical or business activities. But I feel like the path that this setback forced me to be on was the path that I was meant to be on all along—it was only my conscious mind that had interfered and kept me on another path until then. You might say I needed a major course correction.

Asking for Help

Going back to the theme of the previous chapter—asking for help—I spent much time asking for help and guidance from divine sources, especially since the materialist doctors had done all they could to help. They couldn't find anything further wrong with me or my heart, despite my almost constant chest pains and fatigue. I even wondered, many times, if this was a sign that the time had come for me to leave this life.

The answer that I got in my visions was that there was much work ahead of me, and that it wasn't my time yet. This message came through loud and clear in visions while I was half awake and half asleep, during meditation and even in my dreams. Each time the chest symptoms returned, I would rush off to the hospital worried that I was having a heart attack, but then was assured that it was not the case and that there was nothing wrong with my heart at the point. I was eventually led to a new doctor that I could call whenever an episode occurred, and this reassurance was critical to me feeling that I could move on and live life again.

I was struck a few years later, while researching for this book, by how similar the message I got—that I had more work to do and this was not my time—was to the message received by a particular disciple of Lahiri Mahasaya, known as Sri Bhupendra Nath Sanyal Mahasaya, when he was seriously ill.

This story is from Daya Mata's travel diary, written when they visited Sri Sanyal in India, who narrated to them a number of anecdotes from his life that involved Lahiri. In one story, the swami described how, when he had malaria at the age of fifteen or sixteen, his older sister wrote to Lahiri Mahasaya asking if he would be cured. Lahiri replied saying that there was no danger and that he would not die young because he had much work ahead of him.[11]

Another time, Sri Sanyal was deathly sick and he lamented that he wouldn't be able to do more in this life. He received in a dream a clear vision of Lahiri, who told him: 'You're not going to die. You have something more to achieve in this life.'[12] The next morning, said Sri Sanyal, the doctors were surprised to see him greatly recovered.

Miraculous overnight healings are not, however, the only way to get this message across when we have a major setback, like an unexpected illness or surgery. I, for one, got a similar message during my meditations and reveries—that my work was not done, and I had a number of things still to achieve in this life. I should write, write, write, because, though I had written some books, that was the aspect of my karmic life-plan that I hadn't made enough progress on. I was spending too much time on technology and entrepreneurship.

This message was backed up, whether intentionally or not, initially by the fact that I didn't have the energy to continue those worldly pursuits. However, I had just enough energy to write, and within nine months of my surgery, I had published two important books (that was after having published only two books in the previous ten years). It felt like the obstacles to writing and publishing melted away, while the obstacles to other worldly pursuits became stronger.

You might say that the illness and surgery, and the long recovery period, were my wake-up call, forcing me to switch the train to a different track. It was my course correction. To quote a well-known American poet, Robert Frost, 'that has made all the difference'. It is doubtful that I would be writing this book if I hadn't been through that experience.

Conclusion

Though none of us (except perhaps great saints) know the exact moment we will leave this Earth, we should learn to take setbacks in stride. We should think of them as if they contain important messages for us that we might not have been consciously ready for, or were willing to accept if we had simply gone down the same old path without incident. Like the Tiger Swami, Yogananda and countless others, setbacks may in fact be an important part of our path, a clue that we have been spending too much time fighting our 'outer tigers'.

Let me end this chapter with another reminder about how we should take setbacks, no matter how heart-breaking they seem at the time (metaphorically or literally). This quote is from a letter Yogananda wrote to his good friends the Lewises in Boston, who were among his first students when he started teaching in America in 1920:

A life without troubles and vicissitudes is tasteless, insipid. Troubles come, let them come, they will be your stepping stones for your upward climb.[13]

PART V

Seeing the Larger Pattern

To surmount maya was the task assigned to the human race by the millennial prophets ...

Those who cling to the cosmic illusion must accept its essential law of polarity: flow and ebb, rise and fall, day and night, pleasure and pain, good and evil, birth and death.

— YOGANANDA[*]

---

[*] Yogananda, *Autobiography of a Yogi*, 'The Law of Miracles', p. 311.

LESSON #12

Lessons from Babaji and the Great Engine of Karma

'Lahiri, are you still feasting on your dream desires for a golden palace?'
My guru's eyes were twinkling like his own sapphires.
'Wake! All your earthly thirsts are about to be quenched forever.'

— Lahiri Mahasaya's meeting with Babaji[1]

Let's return, for a moment, to the point where this book started from, to the remote Himalayas and the seemingly magical gurus who reside there in both history and legend. Somewhere in the fuzzy middle ground between history and legend lies the colourful landscape we call mythology.

Many myths, like Homer's *Iliad* and *Odyssey* or India's ancient epics like the Mahabharata, have elements of truth in them. However, these tales are also filled with enough fanciful elements and metaphors that it is hard for us, thousands of years removed from the original events, to evaluate the veracity of any particular element.

The lessons in this chapter come to us via Yogananda in the form of stories about Babaji, the almost mythological figure who hovers over the entire *Autobiography*. Rather than recount all the stories about Babaji, I wanted to focus on a few whose lessons form a particular thread through the *Autobiography* without always being explicitly mentioned: the thread of karma.

The stories about Babaji, which are presented as historical fact by Yogananda, are like the most brilliant flowers in an already colourful bouquet. Not only did they stand out for me when I first read the *Autobiography* over twenty years ago, but they also seemed lodged in my memory—I scarcely needed to go back to the book to remember them. You might say they have lived in my mind undimmed ever since my first reading of the book.

I think it's safe to say that anyone who hears or reads these stories will find it hard to forget them too. While it is precisely this memorable quality that may have motivated Yogananda to include them in the first place, from the perspective of a modern reader, they are also among the most fanciful. Depending on who you ask, these stories either serve as validation of the importance of the *Autobiography* in particular (and Yogananda's lineage and teaching as a whole), or they constitute a modern mythology Yogananda introduced to the world that, like all mythology, shouldn't be taken too literally.

For those that don't know about him, Babaji is (according to Yogananda's lineage) a master who lives in the remote Himalayas. He introduced the practice of kriya yoga to

Yogananda's paramguru (or guru's guru), Lahiri Mahasaya, in the middle of the nineteenth century. By itself, that Lahiri had a guru he called Babaji isn't necessarily controversial, even to scientists. Lahiri must have learnt from someone, after all, and the term 'Babaji' is a common form of honorific that might be given to any respected old teacher.

However, modern readers are sure to raise their eyebrows at the claims that Babaji had lived many hundreds (in some versions, thousands of years) in the Himalayas, that he can appear or disappear at will, can foresee events decades before they happen and still lives there today, in the exact same youthful form that he was in when he first became a master. One such passage that claims this:

> The deathless guru bears no marks of age on his body; he appears to be no more than a youth of twenty-five. Fair-skinned, of medium build and height, Babaji's beautiful, strong body radiates a perceptible glow. His eyes are dark, calm, and tender; his long, lustrous hair is copper-colored.[2]

Yogananda compares Babaji to previous avatars such as 'Krishna, Rama, Buddha, and Patanjali'. Unlike many other great liberated souls, who made their impact in a single lifetime, Babaji's mission was to help with the evolution of man over many human lifetimes, throughout this yuga or cycle of the world, which is why he has chosen to stay in bodily form for a much longer period.

Yogananda states that Babaji's purpose in India in the modern age has been to: '... assist prophets in carrying out their special dispensations. He thus qualifies for the scriptural classification of *Mahavatar* (Great Avatar).' This nomenclature has stuck and now he's known popularly throughout the West (and even in India) as Mahavatar Babaji.

According to Yogananda, Babaji said that he initiated Shankara, the founder of the modern swami order, and Kabir, a well-known medieval mystic, into the yogic order. Of course, in more recent history, Babaji taught Lahiri Mahasaya, the householder guru of Benares who met the deathless guru in a cave near Ranikhet in the nineteenth century.

By my calculations, this would make Babaji well over 1,000 years old! Shankara is thought to have lived in the eighth century, Kabir in the fifteenth century, and Lahiri we know lived in the nineteenth century. According to some accounts, Babaji met Christ, which would make him even older—over 2,000 years in the same body!

Most of what Yogananda relates about Babaji was told to him by disciples of Lahiri Mahasaya, including Yogananda's own guru, Sri Yukteswar, and his brother monks, many of whom met the Mahavatar in person only once or twice. Some of the other sightings of Babaji mentioned in the *Autobiography* (including Yukteswar's) occurred in the nineteenth century or early twentieth century. Yogananda's own sighting, which we'll revisit later in this chapter, occurred shortly before he left India in 1920. There are others who claimed to have met Babaji in the second half of the twentieth century as well, though these meetings are not part of the *Autobiography*.

I have referenced Shankara, who is both a well-known historical figure and has also taken on mythological status, in other chapters (such as 'Lesson #9: Go Out of Your Way for Little and Big Pilgrimages'). Kabir is perhaps unique among Indian saints because he's considered both a Sufi saint and a Brahmin saint. Kabir was revered by both Muslims and

Hindus alike (and was equally critical of the traditions of both religions). We'll talk more about Kabir and the universality of yoga in 'Lesson #14: Yoga is For Everyone, East and West'.

What Are We to Make of Babaji in the Modern World?

What are we to make of Yogananda's descriptions of Babaji in the present time? The first question that comes to the modern mind is 'Does Babaji exist?' I asked this question to most of the people that I interviewed for this book, some of whom were devoted disciples of Yogananda, others who were iconoclasts even within Yogananda's lineage, and others who were scholars of religion and took a more dispassionate view.

Most followers of Yogananda presume that the swami was telling the literal truth and that Babaji is still alive today, with a flesh-and-blood body that can be seen by certain chosen disciples, kept forever young by yogic techniques. Others assume that, while Yogananda didn't completely make up the persona of Babaji (Lahiri's other disciples have mentioned seeing Lahiri's guru show up now and then in Benares), perhaps he exaggerated the stories, turning Babaji from an actual historical yogi who lived over a hundred years ago into a modern mythological figure.

For one thing, we know that the name 'Babaji' is really not a name at all. When I first read it, I scratched my head (figuratively, of course), wondering why Yogananda had not used his real name—even I, a desi who was raised in the West with limited fluency in my native Punjabi and a crude but working knowledge of Hindi and Urdu, knew that the term 'Babaji' just meant 'respected old man' or, more formally, 'revered father'.

Two Interesting Questions about Babaji

One question a modern scholar might ask when evaluating the question of whether Babaji is 'real' is: are there other references to this enigmatic superhuman character who walks around the Himalayas for hundreds of years and materializes and dematerializes at will?

I haven't found anything connecting Kabir or Shankara to Babaji directly, outside of Yogananda's autobiography. Neither of them seems to have mentioned this enigmatic figure in their many writings and poems. That said, we do know that, historically, Adi Shankara was a disciple of Govinda Jati, who Yogananda claims was initiated by Babaji in Benares. Yogananda says that Babaji met Shankara there, spoke to him and gave him a kriya initiation as well.

Similarly, Kabir was historically thought to be a disciple of Swami Ramananda, a fourteenth-century devotional saint in Benares.[3] Thus, we could extrapolate the only real connecting line between these three (Shankara, Kabir, Lahiri) was that they were all in Benares—but they also introduced new lineages to old traditions, which distinguished their followers from those that came before.

In the cases of both Kabir and Shankara, Yogananda states that they received yogic initiation but, since they were either primarily part of a different tradition or seeking to reform and/or create a new tradition, it could just be that there was no reason for them to mention Babaji. After all, Yogananda certainly met many more gurus and saints than he profiled in his book—those associations are easily lost to history, even for a guru with a well-documented life story like Yogananda. Or it could be, as Yogananda claimed, that Babaji hadn't wished to be known before his interactions with Lahiri Mahasaya in the nineteenth century.

Again, according to Yogananda, Lahiri said that, about fifty years after his death, a book would come out in the West (because of the interest in yoga) that would tell of the lives of both Lahiri Mahasaya and Babaji for the first time to the general public.

Since Yogananda's book came out (the first edition in 1946, fifty years after Lahiri's death), there have been many references to Babaji in books and online stories, and a number of reported sightings in the twentieth century. There was at least one movie that featured a fictionalized encounter with the Mahavatar Babaji.[4] Yet almost all of these references were made after Yogananda's famous book had not only been published but had made its way around the world, which once again makes it difficult to treat those as completely independent accounts.

Of the other references, one that I found more credible and interesting than many of the others was the work of Sri M. Born to a Muslim family as Mumtaz Ali Khan, he grew up on stories of Sufi saints and had encounters with holy men when he was young, and his adventures, including his meeting with Babaji, are chronicled in his book, *Apprenticed to a Himalayan Master*. In Sri M's case, he called his guru (who he met in the Himalayas) Babaji, but he made it clear that this was Maheshwarnath Babaji, not only a disciple of Mahavatar Babaji (whom he called Sri Guru) but also a contemporary of Lahiri Mahasaya's. In fact, according to Sri M, it was Maheshwarnath who took Lahiri to be initiated by Mahavatar Babaji at the request of the great, seemingly immortal guru.[5] One thing that intrigued me about his descriptions (and you can find many of Sri M's talks online) was his theory of how past-life associations led him to the lineage. In his books, Sri M has claimed to have met Mahavatar Babaji several times in the flesh during the twentieth century, usually in the company of his guru.

Another question we could ask is if there are references to other saints who retain their bodily form for an extended period? Yes, there are many stories of saints that live to well over 100 years of age, such as Baba Lokenath Brahmachari, a Bengali yogi who lived for 160 years and travelled far and wide on foot to places like Russia and Mecca. Trailanga Swami's disciple, Shankari Mai Jiew, who was over 112 years old when he came down from the Himalayas to visit the Ranchi school, where Yogananda and his brother-swami Satchidananda Giri met her. According to the *Autobiography*, she had retrained a youthful appearance and a head of mostly black hair, and she also claimed to have met Babaji while visiting Lahiri in Benares.

Then there is the baffling case of Trailanga Swami himself, who is mentioned in the *Autobiography* as having been a contemporary of Lahiri and meditated with him from time to time. Trailanga Swami, whose age and strange behaviour was discussed in 'Lesson #4: The Many Lessons of the Incomparable Levitating Saint', is rumoured to have lived almost 300 years (and to have weighed some 300 pounds, roughly one pound per year!)[6]

In this context, it is worth mentioning another book that is ostensibly about Babaji: *Babaji and the 18 Siddha Kriya Yoga Tradition*, by a westerner called Marshall Govindan. Govindan had gone to India and studied with Yogi S.A. Ramaiah. Ramaiah claimed that he had met the deathless guru when he was young and had a serious leg injury, which the guru healed and then became his direct disciple and established yet another tributary of kriya yoga in the great river of yoga.[7]

What I found intriguing about this book was that it got into the history of who Babaji was before he became the Mahavatar we know of today, and it linked him to the siddha traditions of south India, with other masters who have stayed in the body for a long period of time. In this tradition, they are known as having attained *soruba samadhi*. This is known as a state of physical immortality achieved by not just realizing the nature of maya and samadhi but also bringing the Divine into the cells of the body, which allows the body to be in perfect health indefinitely.

Govindan claims that Babaji (whom he called Babaji Nagaraj), while a youngster, travelled to south India and studied with Siddha Boganathar and eventually met the equally mythic Siddha Agastyar. Agastyar is a colourful figure of history and legend throughout India, one of the fabled rishis (also spelt Agastya), who was sent to south India to 'balance' the fact that Lord Shiva was in the north, at Mt Kailash. Agastyar is said to have established the Tamil language and existed in his body in the region for 3,000 years; according to some, he continues to exist in the same form today. According to Govindan, it was Agastyar who, upon helping Babaji attain soruba samadhi, directed him 'to go to Badrinath in the upper ranges of the Himalayan mountains and *to become the greatest Siddha the world had ever known*.'[8]

Govindan also provides another example of soruba samadhi. The Siddha Thirumoolar, another south Indian master, was said to have lived for over 3,000 years as well. Thirumoolar was a contemporary of Patanjali's and, while the author of the Yoga Sutras did not mention bodily immortality as one of the siddhis, in his master work, called the *Thirumandiram*, Thirumoolar lists *kayasiddhi*, or the immortal body.[9]

We could go into a discussion of the many other books and yogis since Yogananda that have claimed to have met Babaji. This could be a whole book of its own. However, in this book, it is my goal to focus on the lessons from the *Autobiography* and, in this chapter, on the karmic lessons that we can learn from those stories about Babaji.

Does It Matter If Babaji Existed?

As mentioned earlier, while most of the people I asked believed that Babaji did exist in the physical form as Yogananda described, a few took perhaps the more interesting approach and asked, 'Does it really matter?' Does it matter if Babaji exists in the way we think or is it enough to know that there was a personage who imparted these teachings, starting the particular river of yoga that Yogananda was a part of?

Yogananda was, if nothing else, a very good marketer and a good teacher. The important thing about the stories of Babaji, like many of the other miraculous stories in the book, may lie not so much in whether every detail is correct but, in the essence of the lessons that come through in the stories. Getting this essence across is something the *Autobiography* excels at.

Yogananda wrote what seem like word-by-word accounts of events and conversations many decades after they actually occurred. If you have ever tried to recreate a conversation from even a decade ago, you have probably found yourself having to fill in details based on your own understanding and recollections, resulting in what may or may not be the exact words that were uttered then (unless you have perfect memory). As long as you are able to reproduce the essence of the conversation, you have been successful in presenting that conversation or story to readers.

In my opinion, Yogananda included stories of Babaji (and in fact all the other stories of gurus and miracles) in the *Autobiography* for many reasons:

1. As hooks to draw the reader in;
2. As wrench with which to open our minds to different possibilities;
3. As a way to gain credibility and validate his own lineage;
4. To impress people in a land where yoga was not well-known (i.e., the United States, where the dominant religion was Christianity); and
5. As a colourful way to remember the lessons he was trying to convey.

It is this last point that is perhaps the most important, since the *Autobiography* was meant to inspire and teach lessons through stories, but not necessarily to teach specific techniques. With that in mind, let's move on to the stories about Babaji and some of the lessons we can glean from them.

Yogananda's Encounter with Babaji

Yogananda's own encounter with Babaji was brief and occurred in Calcutta, just before his trip to America. Yogananda had been praying for divine guidance to help with his upcoming trip. In the middle of his prayer session, he heard a knock on the front door and opened the door to see '... a young man in the scanty garb of a renunciate.'

Yogananda was surprised, though, given the frequency with which his prayers are answered in the *Autobiography*, readers may not be. He quickly surmised that this was Babaji answering his prayers, and this was quickly confirmed by the young-looking man: 'Yes, I am Babaji.' He spoke melodiously in Hindi. 'Our Heavenly Father has heard your prayer. He commands me to tell you: Follow the behests of your guru and go to America. Fear not; you will be protected.'[10]

Babaji then confirms that he had foretold to Sri Yukteswar, Yogananda's mission at a Kumbha Mela many years earlier (that story is told in 'Lesson #14: Yoga is For Everyone, East and West'). The immortal guru gave Yogananda his blessing and quickly left, warning the eager young monk that he wouldn't be able to follow him. Yogananda, overcome with emotion and wanting to go with the master, perhaps remembering his boyhood dreams of wandering the Himalayas in the presence of divine masters, tried to follow him, but found he could not.

Whether we take this story at face value or not, it seems to me that part of its purpose and the purpose of the immortal guru's visit to Yogananda in the flesh before his great departure across the oceans was to dispel doubts. In the first place, these were the doubts that Yogananda had about making such a long trip and taking on a task of such immeasurable difficulty (bringing yoga to the materialistic West).

The second set of doubts, and perhaps the larger one that Babaji wanted to address, was the same one I am addressing here: doubts about whether the Mahavatar actually existed in the flesh. Yogananda tells us:

Until now, I have never recounted to anyone this story of my meeting with Babaji. Holding it as the most sacred of my human experiences, I have hidden it in my heart. But the thought occurred to me that readers of this autobiography may be more inclined to believe in the reality of the secluded Babaji and his world interests if I relate that I saw him with my own eyes.[11]

Though Yogananda only told us of one in-the-flesh meeting with Babaji, it seems like the further back you go up the lineage, the more Babaji sightings there are likely to be. Yukteswar and other disciples of Lahiri Mahasaya's reported many sightings (including Ram Gopal, the Sleepless Saint, who saw not only Babaji but also Babaji's sister, Mataji, in the flesh). And of course, Lahiri had many encounters with Babaji, some of which we will go through next.

The Lessons of Babaji and the Great Engine of Karma

At this point in the chapter, I want to shift the focus to lessons about karma that emerge in stories about Babaji, partly because they are, to a certain extent, unique in the *Autobiography*. These stories also connect kriya yoga to the broader world of spiritual thought that emerged from India, of which Yogananda was one of the important modern messengers.

Yogananda rarely talked about karma and past lives directly in his writings like the *Autobiography*, but as this and other stories show, the thread of karma was woven in throughout the book, embedded into many of the stories he told.[12] In fact, when people asked about past lives, he discouraged them from focusing on specific personalities, saying that they were all different aspects of consciousness that had popped up from time to time.

We have already discussed Yogananda's destiny—to be a monk and teacher in this life—which seemed like it had a lot to do with his karma (see 'Lesson #1: You Don't Need to Go to the Himalayas' and 'Lesson #2: Sometimes, the Universe Unexpectedly Gives You an Important Task'). Therefore, it is not surprising that Babaji appeared just before he started his great karmic task.

The First Story: The Chela and the Fire

Next, I want to explore two stories involving Babaji that show, in very different ways, the fulfilment of karma and how this might impact both the setbacks and the triumphs in our lives.

The first story was so vivid that I haven't forgotten it since my first reading of the book. It isn't just the dramatic story but also the underlying lesson that makes it, in my opinion, one of the crown jewels among the stories in the *Autobiography*.

It is a good idea to remember this story when misfortune befalls you or a setback strikes in your life. It shows us the great engine of karma, the law of creation, at work in the world and that it is somewhat like the smaller engine of karma, which creates our nocturnal dreams. We can say that sometimes karma also works in mysterious ways.

This incident was related to Yogananda by Swami Kebalananda, his Sanskrit teacher, who was also a disciple of Babaji's and Lahiri Mahasaya's.

'Two amazing incidents of Babaji's life are known to me,' Kebalananda went on. His disciples were sitting one night around a huge fire which was blazing for a sacred Vedic ceremony. The master suddenly seized a burning log and lightly struck the bare shoulder of a chela[13] who was close to the fire.[14]

'Sir, how cruel!' Lahiri Mahasaya, who was present, made this remonstrance.

Now if the story were to end here, we might also think, just as Lahiri Mahasaya did, that Babaji was indeed being cruel, as we often think that the world, the universe and perhaps even God is being cruel, when seemingly bad things happen in the world around us.

But it's the next part of the story that conveys the underlying lesson, not to be taken lightly or forgotten easily:

'Would you rather have seen him burned to ashes before your eyes, according to the decree of his past karma?'

With these words Babaji placed his healing hand on the chela's disfigured shoulder. 'I have freed you tonight from painful death. The karmic law has been satisfied through your slight suffering by fire.'[15]

The Lessons Contained Therein

This short story, narrated a long time ago, is pregnant with possibilities and lessons that can be unpacked. In fact, notwithstanding the compactness of the story—it is only a few paragraphs long, in the middle of one of the more miraculous chapters of the *Autobiography*—it seems like a whole treatise on karma. I might go so far as to say that understanding the lesson of this one little story is, in the words of William Blake,

To see a World in a Grain of Sand.
And a Heaven in a Wild Flower.
Hold infinity in the palm of your hand.
And Eternity in an hour.

This little story tells us a lot about how the physical world works, how the spiritual side of man works, the illusion of the material world, the nature of suffering, the rules and engine of karma and how we navigate our way through the wheel of samsara. You could also learn about gurus and grace, samsara and nirvana, maya and moksha, miracles and ordinary reality, dreams and wakefulness, and much more.

Let's unpack the karmic lesson here, ignoring for a moment the next part of the story, where Babaji puts his hand on the chela's shoulder and heals it, since that in my opinion is perhaps an afterthought to the main message.

The chela had a karmic debt that had to be paid. What does this mean exactly? According to yogic traditions, karma is the law of cause and effect. Seeds were planted at some point in the past of a particular entity, the 'cause'—a past that could be part of the entity's current life or a previous life—and those seeds grow into the 'effect' in an ongoing process. Something or someone is keeping track of these 'causes', these karmic seeds and, somehow, circumstances are created that ensure the growth of the seed into the 'effect'.

There are exceptions, ways out. Depending on which tradition you subscribe to, there are one or more ways to resolve these karmic debts. Gurus, who have reached a point of divine perfection, can take on the karma of their students. Yogananda talks about this in the context of healing a number of times in the *Autobiography*; his own guru, Sri Yukteswar, is at the centre of some of the stories. Sometimes, gurus can simply rearrange events or cure illnesses. This is usually done in some unseen world, without an explanation of how it's done.

There is also the possibility of achieving realization and liberating yourself—moksha, enlightenment or nirvana. How?

While each tradition will suggest different ways of getting there (including the kriya yoga tradition, which teaches specific techniques that help raise the energy to the crown and experience samadhi), in the end what this really involves is the realization, a direct perception, a knowing, that the world is really just an illusion. One way to do that is to cut karma off at the root by virtue of your actions—both inner and outer actions, attachments and aversions. All the masters tell us that reading about this process isn't enough—you have to practice and then experience it.

Basically, by practicing yoga (using Patanjali's definition here), by causing the cessation of the vrittis, you basically stop creating the karma that is fuelling your path through the three-dimensional world. One way or another, you have to deal with the karma you've already created—energy or divine light can help to clear that karma as well. There are technical terms in the Hindu and Buddhist traditions for the transfer of energy from master to disciple that resolves the samskaras, the hardened vrittis.

But it isn't enough to have your guru do it all for you—at some point, you have to be able to do it yourself, and the courses of action prescribed in the yamas and the niyamas, two of the eight limbs of yoga, are about making sure you don't create new karma.

Now back to the story. It's clear from this story that Babaji could see that dying a fiery death was part of the chela's karma. We don't know exactly why or if it was going to be fulfilled in another lifetime. The story seems to imply that he would have encountered death by fire in that very lifetime but, as was stated earlier, sometimes karma works in mysterious ways.

We also see that there are different ways to fulfil karmic debt. You can see from this story that Babaji found a simpler way, and it may have had to do with the suffering the chela would endure as a result of being burnt. That was perhaps the important part—not that he necessarily dies by fire but that he experiences suffering caused by the fire, in order to satisfy the karmic debt. Once that had been achieved, the seed didn't need to grow into anything bigger. Rather than creating new karma, which could happen in an actual fire, Babaji was able to wash away these effects by healing the chela.

In this story, we see an example of the law of cause and effect and a way of visualizing that karma is actually the force of creation, just as the Bhagavad Gita says. But the story also shows us that karma can be fulfilled in multiple ways and that there are choices to be made about how and when this fulfilment can be attempted.

Quests, Karma and Achievements

Most of us are not all-knowing or all-seeing like Babaji was (at least not yet) and so, it's impossible for us to see the threads that started weaving karmic patterns ages ago. We can only see them when they manifest themselves before us, in the physical pattern of our lives. Yet, in this story, Babaji implies that there is a set of threads that are possibilities, some of which are more likely than others and may have originated as seeds in previous lives.

When something bad happens to us, we react by lamenting our misfortune: how cruel for this terrible thing to happen to us. Yet, we cannot see the invisible threads that were woven by actions and desires in the distant past or the patterns that the threads might form, are forming and are destined to form in our present or our future. Nor can we see the alternative courses of action that might have helped fulfil the destinies of those threads (but caused perhaps even more suffering in others around us).

To modern readers, I recommend thinking of karma as a series of quests or achievements in a video game. The list of quests that we have to achieve in this lifetime comes from a larger list that is stored somewhere in the cloud—the divine cloud in this case! Each time we create more karma, we are simply adding to this database.

For this reason, I like to call karma the Great Engine, because it is like a video game engine that presents us with quests and achievements that we need to 'accept' before being thrust into various situations, complete with other characters and players in the game.[16] Understanding that we may have, at some level, chosen a particular quest from among many different possibilities, even if we are unaware of it, can help to comfort us in times of trouble. That there are divine alternatives to fulfilling this karma, ways to 'level up' and accomplish these quests without going through the grind of the suffering is also an encouraging thought and is tied to what we learnt about setbacks in 'Lesson #11: Setbacks May Be A Part of Your Story'.

The Story of Lahiri and the Palace

The second, perhaps even more dramatic story, about karma and life during Lahiri Mahasaya's first meeting (at least in this life) with Babaji, is thought to have occurred around 1861 (since Lahiri was thirty-three years old and was born in 1828).

At the time, Lahiri was known by his birth name, Shyama Charan Lahiri, and was working as an accountant in a military engineering department of the government when his office received a telegram from the main office with the instruction that he was to be sent to Ranikhet, where a military post was being established. At this point in the nineteenth century, horses and buggies were the only ways to get there, and it took Lahiri thirty days to travel to his new post.

Because his duties at the office were minimal, Lahiri spent a lot of his time wandering the hills of Ranikhet. One day, he encountered a strange young man in the mountains near a cave, who turned out to be his guru, Mahavatar Babaji. Babaji's first words to him were: 'Lahiri, you have come!' The saint addressed him affectionately in Hindi. 'Rest here in this cave. It was I who called you.'

This is the same cave I mentioned earlier, which has been preserved as a spiritual pilgrimage site by the Yogoda Satsanga Society. Babaji asked Lahiri if he remembered the cave or sitting at a particular place in the cave, but Lahiri didn't, at least not at first.

Like all good modern employees, Lahiri said that it was late and he had to go back so he could make it to his office in the morning! At this point, Babaji informed him that the office had been created for him, not the other way around (and in fact, later it was revealed that the telegram summoning Lahiri to Ranikhet had been sent by mistake as there was no good reason for him to be there).

At this point, Babaji 'struck [Lahiri] gently on the forehead. At his magnetic touch, a wondrous current swept through [Lahiri's] brain, releasing the sweet seed-memories of [his] previous life.' Lahiri now remembered his previous life, in which he had meditated with Babaji at that exact spot in the cave. Although Lahiri, after his rebirth, had forgotten about Babaji,

Babaji told him that he had kept a close eye on Lahiri and even sent him messages, fuelling his interest in meditation in this life. One of Lahiri's habits as a child had been to assume the lotus posture while buried in sand, with only his head visible, and Babaji referenced this.

Babaji then instructed him to drink a particular oil and to lie down, which Lahiri did. Memories from his previous life revealed themselves in his mind. A short while later, another of Babaji's disciples appeared and asked if he was ready for the initiation.

It was midnight, but there was a glow in the distance. Lahiri was informed that it was a golden palace that Babaji had constructed in his honour and that the site would be the location of his initiation into kriya yoga.

'Yonder light is the glow of a golden palace, materialized here tonight by the peerless Babaji. In the dim past, you once expressed a desire to enjoy the beauties of a palace. Our master is now satisfying your wish, thus freeing you from the bonds of karma ...'

A vast palace of dazzling gold stood before us. Studded with countless jewels, and set amidst landscaped gardens, it presented a spectacle of unparalleled grandeur. Saints of angelic countenance were stationed by resplendent gates, half-reddened by the glitter of rubies. Diamonds, pearls, sapphires, and emeralds of great size and luster were imbedded in the decorative arches.

I followed my companion into a spacious reception hall. The odor of incense and of roses wafted through the air; dim lamps shed a multicolored glow. Small groups of devotees, some fair, some dark-skinned, chanted musically, or sat in the meditative posture, immersed in an inner peace. A vibrant joy pervaded the atmosphere.

'Feast your eyes; enjoy the artistic splendors of this palace, for it has been brought into being solely in your honor.' My guide smiled sympathetically as I uttered a few ejaculations of wonderment.[17]

This is no small miracle—we are talking about the construction of an actual palace by Babaji, in a story that sounds like it's straight out of the Arabian Nights/Alif Layla. Aladdin had, in fact, asked the jinn to construct a similar resplendent palace! Yet, Yogananda wrote about it in the same matter-of-fact way that he chose to narrate his other miraculous stories, as if he had no doubt that it had happened exactly the way he described it.

For a modern reader, the two questions that arise (once we get past the question of whether the story is true) are likely to be: 1) why and 2) how?

Let's start with why. As mentioned earlier, it was to fulfil Lahiri's wish from the dim past: '... a desire to enjoy beauties of a palace. Our master is now satisfying your wish, thus freeing you from the bonds of karma.'

Note that the karma wasn't the palace itself, but the desire to enjoy a palace. We can assume that it was a strong desire, or else it wouldn't have hardened into one that needed fulfilment. When choosing a site for Lahiri's initiation, Babaji chose a grand site to serve two purposes: the initiation itself and the freeing of Lahiri from a karmic desire. In a sense, Babaji was killing two karmic birds with one stone.

In this and the previous story, Babaji might just have earned a nickname as a 'fulfiller of karmic wishes' or 'liberator from karmic debts'. As Yogananda and other sages have reminded us, reminds us, it is these karmic desires that often bind us to the wheel of reincarnation.

Karma as Desire and the Dream-like Nature of Reality

As an engineer and scientist, I am always wondering how things work—perhaps it is both a blessing and curse of my chosen career path. In exploring the 'how' of this story, we see here, perhaps, an even more obvious but also more subtle demonstration of the workings of karma.

I believe the point of this story, other than to amaze and impress upon us the importance of Lahiri and Babaji's meeting, is to provide an understanding of how our thoughts, our desires, the vrittis, get lodged in our energy field as they harden and have to be resolved eventually.

Did the desire to experience the riches of a palace really need to be worked out in such resplendent physical detail? Couldn't it have been fulfilled in dreams, for example?

The Tibetan Buddhist tradition is instructive in this regard: it proposes the idea of ordinary karmic traces, which can be fulfilled within dreams, and bigger ones, which have to be fulfilled within the physical world. Of course, we can also cut off the karma by releasing the desires and realizing that all of this is a dream, which was Buddha's point.

This story caused me to ask a bigger question: is there a difference between a desire that is fulfilled in a dream and one that is fulfilled in the physical world? In other worlds, is the physical world really just a dream?

When Lahiri expresses amazement at the splendour of the palace and the fact that it appeared so quickly and suddenly, his companion, another disciple of Babaji's, explains it to him. Again, Yogananda describes this in the best way:

> The substance of a dream is held in materialization by the subconscious thought of the dreamer. When that cohesive thought is withdrawn in wakefulness, the dream and its elements dissolve. A man closes his eyes and erects a dream-creation which, on awakening, he effortlessly dematerializes. He follows the divine archetypal pattern. Similarly, when he awakens in cosmic consciousness, he will effortlessly dematerialize the illusions of the cosmic dream.[18]

And later, Babaji asks Lahiri the question that I began this chapter with: 'Lahiri, are you still feasting on your dream desires for a golden palace?' My guru's eyes were twinkling like his own sapphires. 'Wake! All your earthly thirsts are about to be quenched forever.'

At this point, Babaji asks Lahiri to close his eyes and the palace disappeared, emphasizing the metaphor of the dream-like nature of reality. Like our nocturnal dreams, which may seem confusing but are often formed by seeds that are planted throughout the day, karma creates our daytime scenes. Although, in a deviation from the solitary nature of dreams, all of us are engaged in the daytime karma lila together, resulting in a complex interaction of multiple people's karmas (not unlike a massively multiplayer online role-playing game or MMORPG).

I believe this lesson—that the physical world is an illusion created by our desires and our aversions across many lives and that yoga offers a way out—is a central part of the point of this story. In a sense, I think Yogananda, through the story of Lahiri and Babaji, is giving us a modern version of what was said in the Bhagavad Gita: that karma is the creator of the world. This is also what the Buddha was trying to convey when he said:

Know that all phenomena
Are like reflections appearing
In a very clear mirror,
Devoid of inherent existence

Conclusion: Karma, Yoga and the Guru

There are many different lessons contained within the stories of Babaji in the *Autobiography*. I have simply picked two of those stories and chosen to focus on their karmic side—what they can teach us about our thoughts, our desires, our debts and how they bind us, and how the Great Engine of Karma works, manifesting circumstances designed to fulfil our karmic desires (or in a broader sense, desires and aversions, thoughts and emotions). By paying attention to our thoughts, by stilling the whirlpools of thought and emotion, the vrittis, we can stop the engine of creation in its tracks, or even choose different ways of unwinding the long list of things that exists in our database in the sky.

There are many other aspects of these stories I could have focused on. There was a reason, for instance, that Lahiri didn't meet Babaji (in this life) until he was already married and living the life of a householder in his thirties; specifically so that he could show the world that it was okay to live a normal life with a spouse and children and still become a yogi seeking liberation (I talked about this in 'Lesson #8: Practice Every Day, No Matter How Much Time You Have'). This message is even more relevant to modern seekers today than it was in the nineteenth century, when Lahiri returned to Benares and started accepting disciples while still, technically, a householder (with a wife and kids).

In other colourful stories, we can learn that the more spiritually developed you are, the more you are able to perceive beings like Babaji, a point that the Mahavatar Babaji made to Sri Yukteswar when the latter was unable to see the former in the same room with Lahiri because his gaze was not yet 'faultless'. This brings up other questions and a discussion of what it means to be 'in the material world' or not. Presumably this means that there are elements of the physical world that are visible only to some people and not others.

Or we could discuss the incredible story of Ram Gopal, the Sleepless Saint, who was present, along with Lahiri, Babaji and Mataji (the name given to Babaji's sister, but which just translates to revered mother), when Mataji cleverly convinced the Mahavatar Babaji to commit to staying in his body throughout the current age, at least.

But all of these discussions serve to illustrate why *Autobiography of a Yogi* is considered not just an autobiography but a spiritual text—because it is jam-packed with stories and each story is jam-packed with lessons that are open to multiple interpretations and can inspire seekers in different ways, depending on their dispositions. In other words, based on our own individual karma.

LESSON #13

Lifting the Veil—The Everlasting Beyond the Illusion

Vanished the veils of light and shade,
Lifted every vapor of sorrow,
Sailed away all dawns of fleeting joy,
Gone the dim sensory mirage.
Love, hate, health, disease, life, death,
Perished these false shadows on the screen of duality.
Waves of laughter, scyllas of sarcasm, melancholic
whirlpools,
Melting in the vast sea of bliss.
The storm of maya stilled
By magic wand of intuition deep.

— 'Samadhi', a poem by Yogananda[1]

If we accept that the material world is in fact maya, or a carefully crafted illusion, as ancient and modern sages have told us it is, then what is beyond the illusion? When

255

the vrittis (whirlpools of thought and feeling) have been fully stilled, what is left?

Yogananda was very explicit about the answer: a superconscious state in which we can perceive what is beyond the veil, known as 'samadhi'. There are stages of samadhi and there are other ancient terms like 'nirvana' and 'moksha', which, when translated (imperfectly, I might add, since these terms were already difficult to define even in Sanskrit and other ancient tongues) into English, are often grouped under conceptual categories like enlightenment, realization, liberation, etc. Yogananda himself used an English translation of samadhi in the name of his organization, Self-Realization Fellowship.

Another metaphor Yogananda and many other sages have used is that of getting to know God and defining the feeling that occurs beyond the veil as Infinite Bliss or Divine Love. What's beyond isn't just an impersonal universe like the darkness of outer space, but light and feeling at a whole new level, they tell us.

At other times, Yogananda and others use the metaphor of awakening, as if from a dream, or lifting the veil that has been pulled over our eyes. What happens when you wake up in the morning? Not only do you perceive the 'real world' around your body, you remember things that you may have forgotten in the dream state. The dream, which was vivid only a few moments ago, fades into unreality.

What is it that we remember when we 'wake up' from maya? This is a complicated question, but one answer that all the sages tell us is that we understand the law of cause and effect, of karma and its role in keeping us chained to the endless wheel of birth, death and rebirth.

Beyond that, though, it is difficult to describe what lies beyond realization/liberation, which is why metaphors and poetry seem to do a better job than any technical descriptions. All of these metaphors imply the state beyond may be *ineffable*: 'too great or extreme to be expressed or described in words.'[2]

What Is the Experience of Lifting the Veil Like?

In the *Autobiography*, Yogananda tells us that Sri Yukteswar gave him a taste of samadhi and that it had to do with the heart or with feelings of bliss. This happened after Yogananda had (perhaps for the last time!) tried to run away to the Himalayas, where he had an encounter with the Sleepless Saint, Ram Gopal. The saint admonished him, saying that mountains could not be his guru and that he would get better results if he went back to Sri Yukteswar (see 'Lesson #1: You Don't Need to Go to the Himalayas').

Mukunda, back at the Serampore hermitage of his master, had been meditating but was frustrated that he wasn't getting to the point of sensing the Divine Love that his guru and the saints of old talked about. His master called him out on his inability to concentrate, as his thoughts were wandering—his mind 'distributed like leaves in a storm'. This is an expression that anyone who has tried to meditate regularly can grasp quickly; we've all been there!

Sri Yukteswar responded with compassion rather than harshness: 'Poor boy, the mountains couldn't give you what you wanted. ... Your heart's desire shall be fulfilled.'[3] Yukteswar then struck Yogananda gently on his chest above his heart. What happened next is best told in Yogananda's own words:

My body became immovably rooted; breath was drawn out of my lungs as if by some huge magnet. Soul and mind instantly lost their physical bondage, and streamed out like a fluid piercing light from my every pore. The flesh was as though dead, yet in my intense awareness I knew that never before had I been fully alive. My sense of identity was no longer narrowly confined to a body, but embraced the circumambient atoms.[4]

His master had given him a taste of samadhi. What Yogananda describes next is an aspect of the superconscious state that he seems to have experienced multiple times in multiple places throughout his life. We will revisit some of those other experiences in this chapter. One way of describing it is as a panoramic holographic view of what we think is a solid physical world. Yogananda continues:

The whole vicinity lay bare before me. My ordinary frontal vision was now changed to a vast spherical sight, simultaneously all-perceptive. Through the back of my head I saw men strolling far down Rai Ghat Road, and noticed also a white cow who was leisurely approaching. When she reached the space in front of the open ashram gate, I observed her with my two physical eyes. As she passed by, behind the brick wall, I saw her clearly still.[5]

He could see not only everything that was happening all around him, through walls and across distances, but also that the physical world was not so physical at all—it felt like everything was vibrating and made of light:

All objects within my panoramic gaze trembled and vibrated like quick motion pictures. My body, Master's, the pillared courtyard, the furniture and floor, the trees and sunshine, occasionally became violently agitated, until all melted into a luminescent sea; even as sugar crystals, thrown into a glass of water, dissolve after being shaken. The unifying light alternated with materializations of form, the metamorphoses revealing the law of cause and effect in creation.[6]

Perhaps where Yogananda really shines is in his description of the feeling of what he calls God. This light was inextricably linked with the feeling of bliss:

An oceanic joy broke upon calm endless shores of my soul. The Spirit of God, I realized, is exhaustless Bliss; His body is countless tissues of light. A swelling glory within me began to envelop towns, continents, the earth, solar and stellar systems, tenuous nebulae, and floating universes. The entire cosmos, gently luminous, like a city seen afar at night, glimmered within the infinitude of my being. The sharply etched global outlines faded somewhat at the farthest edges; there I could see a mellow radiance, ever-undiminished. It was indescribably subtle; the planetary pictures were formed of a grosser light.[7]

He went on to describe how the entire universe with all its galaxies and constellations was a result of this cosmic light. He felt blissful 'amrita, the nectar of immortality' pulsing through him and hearing voice of God as 'Aum, the vibration of the Cosmic Motor'.

After the experience, Yogananda's breath suddenly returned and he was disappointed to have come out of the macrocosm of ecstasy back to his little microcosm of a body. His breath had stopped during the experience, a known phenomenon that explains why samadhi is referred to as 'the breathless state' by many yogis. In his later years, Yogananda wrote the poem 'Samadhi', an excerpt of which starts this chapter. Poetry and metaphor seem to be the more appropriate ways of conveying the feeling of bliss that comes with this type of experience.

Big E and Little E (or Big S and Little S)

You might say that Yogananda was given the little s, or little samadhi, experience by his guru instead of having achieved it himself. One of my teachers used to call these experiences (usually ones that were much less dramatic than Yogananda's) little Es, or little enlightenments, which may occur along the way to a fuller, more permanent enlightenment.

Nevertheless, when you have experienced the little E (or little S), you have a sense of what it's about, and that does make it easier for you to eventually get there on your own. You might also develop a yearning, as Yogananda did, to return to that state of bliss, which can lead to a neglect of your worldly duties.

This is a lesson that both Sri Yukteswar and Lahiri Mahasaya reinforced repeatedly: you must do the work you are meant to do in the world, fulfilling your karma and not run away into ecstasy and bliss all the time. Lahiri Mahasaya continued to work at his job as a government accountant for many years after his initial enlightenment experience, until he retired on a pension and could be seen thereafter in his drawing room, constantly in a state of samadhi, the breathless state, and receiving spiritual seekers.

Another Tale of a Little Samadhi

When I was interviewing Ryan Kurczak, the disciple of Roy Davis, Ryan told me about a similar experience that Roy had had with his guru, Yogananda himself. One day, when Yogananda was walking by, the young Roy touched Yogananda's feet and asked him, 'Would you give me samadhi?'

'What was that?' asked Yogananda.

Roy repeated his request.

Yogananda looked over at James Lynn, whom Yogananda had given the spiritual name of Rajarsi Janakananda (he was Yogananda's successor as President of SRF). Yogananda considered James to be his most advanced disciple and a Westerner who could reach samadhi.[8]

'He wants samadhi,' said Yogananda to Lynn, to which Lynn replied. 'Bless his heart.'

Later that day, Lynn walked over to Roy and tapped him on the heart. To quote Ryan:

> Mr [Roy] Davis said it was like liquid bliss just poured through his heart. Mr. Davis didn't know what do to, so he ended up going into some gardening shed and sitting there having this experience of enlightenment.[9]

Ryan told me of another anecdote involving Roy Davis and Yogananda that has a bearing on our discussion here. One day, when he was in the Encinitas Hermitage, Yogananda asked Roy if he had any questions for him. Roy hadn't intended to ask any questions, but one popped into his mind: 'How many of the saints that you met in *Autobiography of a Yogi* ... How many of them were fully completely spiritually enlightened?'

Yogananda immediately said, 'Not many. Many of them are content to hang out in the bliss of God communion, and they don't go all the way. They don't go beyond that state.'

Then Yogananda told Roy: 'But you must go all the way!'

Going All the Way

We can deduce from this and what others have said that samadhi is both a state and a process; it is both a journey and a destination!

The sages have told us about different stages of samadhi. The two that most seem to agree on are: savikalpa samadhi, which is the breathless state that Yogananda and other sages talk about when they first achieve samadhi, and nirvikalpa samadhi, which is the state when one has transcended the physical world.

Savikalpa samadhi is a state, which can be entered into by advanced disciples. It is known by its characteristics: sleeplessness, breathless meditation and its incomparable internal quality (feeling the cosmic consciousness or inner bliss). We have also seen that its characteristics may include a 360-degree vision of one's surroundings and knowledge of past lives and other cosmic perceptions.

One of the most important perceptions is one that seems like it is beyond the physical world: to see the source of the physical world and the consciousness of God, often expressed as an incredible light, incredible love that is difficult to describe in words, i.e., it is ineffable.

Speaking of meeting with God, after his initial samadhi experience, Yogananda tells us that he was able to get there himself many times in the next few months. Yet he decided one day to ask his master about when he would actually meet God. Sri Yukteswar informed him that he has already experienced God:

> I am sure you aren't expecting a venerable Personage, adorning a throne in some antiseptic corner of the cosmos! I see, however, that you are imagining that the possession of miraculous powers is knowledge of God. One might have the whole universe, and find the Lord elusive still! Spiritual advancement is not measured by one's outward powers, but only by the depth of his bliss in meditation.[10]

In most traditions, the experience of full enlightenment comes not just with bliss but rather with the destruction of ignorance and mental delusions. While this is consistent with the general understanding of the phenomenon, this also provides a slightly different perspective on it. Mathieu Ricard, a Westerner who studied with the Dalai Lama, has come up with an explanation:

> Enlightenment is an understanding of both the relative mode of existence (the way in which things appear to us) and the ultimate mode of existence (the true nature of these same appearances). This includes our own minds as well as the external world. Such knowledge is the basic antidote to ignorance and suffering.[11]

A more comprehensive definition of nirvikalpa samadhi is as follows: 'In nirvikalpa samadhi, the ego and samskaras (mental or emotional impressions) dissolve, leaving behind only pure consciousness.[12]

Since the states are difficult to put into words, different traditions use different metaphors to talk about God, though most of the descriptions include elements of awe and bliss. The Sufis of Islam use metaphors of love and being drunk with ecstasy. Jesus talked about the 'Kingdom of Heaven'.

Ironically, though this experience is about awakening and awareness, to those relying on existing traditions and texts and descriptions, these metaphors are sometimes reminiscent of the three blind men describing the elephant. Each thinks he has the right description (each blind man describes the elephant from his own perspective as being like a tree trunk, a house, or a snake). But each of them is just trying to describe in words something much larger than the portion they may have experienced.

There are higher stages or states of samadhi that have been described, but if you get too specific, there are disagreements between traditions and sects, so we won't get into those here. We also described, in the previous chapter, the state of soruba samadhi, which confers a state of immortality upon the body, which is a different kind of samadhi but presumably intersects with the other definitions of samadhi in some way.

For most modern seekers, depending on where you are in your own personal path of spiritual growth, one state of samadhi is perhaps enough to think about. It's like how we don't normally need to worry about the different kinds of snow an Eskimo might encounter unless we are planning to go to the far north (or the far south, i.e., Antarctica), but as we move closer, we can start to perceive the differences ourselves.

Ways of Getting There in Various Traditions

Yogananda writes that, while a teacher can give a student an experience of samadhi, they can only do so if the student has achieved a certain level of preparation.

How does one prepare? Since samadhi is the eighth and final limb of yoga according to Patanjali, we can assume that the other seven limbs prepare us for that state: 'Nirvikalpa samadhi occurs spontaneously, and therefore cannot be practised in itself.'[13]

Yogananda describes kriya yoga as the primary (though not the only) way to get there. Other Hindu traditions are very specific about this state and how to get there as well. The techniques usually include moving energy up and down the spine (the shushumna) and to the third eye (or the crown chakra, depending on which authority you are reading), which with practice eventually prepares the subtle channels of the body (the nadis) to be able to experience samadhi when the practitioner is ready. There are of course as many variations on the technique as there are spiritual traditions in the river of yoga.

Yet others, including Ramana Maharshi and many Buddhist teachers, shed light on a slightly different aspect of the whole thing. According to them, samadhi, rather than simply being about bringing up energy, is about the awareness that comes from understanding who you are and the nature of reality and suffering. This relates to the idea of 'anubhava' or insight— while, in the West, yoga and meditation are thought of as simply calming for the mind or the body, the goal is not just to achieve calm, but to perceive what is beyond the calm. That is the insight that leads to realization.

How did Buddha, who had tried many ascetic techniques, achieve enlightenment and become the 'awakened one'? It is said that he simply sat and meditated on his breath and kept asking the questions he had about the nature and origin of suffering. He eventually saw the chain of dependent origination, i.e., what causes the world around us to exist and thus causes the suffering of the world. Eventually he said in the Dhammapada:

> That which is capable of arising
> Is capable of cessation

Buddha said we can look at everything around us and at its causes. The causes are the karmic seeds of the past. Cut out the seeds and you can cut off the results of those seeds. By realizing this, and by not planting any more seeds, we can stop the flow of creation and become 'awakened'.

That agrees with Patanajli's definition of yoga which was codified several hundred years later: *yoga nirodhah chitta vritti*—stop the vrittis and the seeds will stop being planted. Stop planting the seeds and no more trees will grow. Or, to paraphrase Buddha's words: *This* leads to *that*. Stop doing *this* and *that* will stop too.

Another saint whose name came up often in my research is Ramana Maharshi. Yogananda actually met Maharshi during his trip to India and asked him why God would allow suffering in the world. Maharshi, after a little commentary, responded with the questions that were often his responses to these types of questions: 'Who is Suffering? Who is God?'

Eventually he was silent, because he believed that by answering these questions, the questioner arrives at their own realization of the answer. Through these kinds of piercing questions, Maharshi encouraged us to inquire within ourselves, to ask questions. If we meditate on these questions for long enough, we 'realize' what we are seeing is an illusion, created out of our mental delusions.[14]

Maharshi and Buddha (and many others) spoke about achieving samadhi without necessarily talking much about the physical state or about moving energy up the spine. Yet the message is the same: the way to end suffering is to expand our perception beyond the illusion.

The Path of Bliss

Yogananda describes another way of getting to this state of communion, which is less about the mental or energy metaphors and more about compassion and bliss, through union with the Divine Mother, the feminine aspect of divinity. This in yogic terms is referred to as bhakti, or the path of devotion, as opposed to jnana, or the path of wisdom.

Yogananda tells us the story of his visits as a boy to Master Mahasaya, who ran a school for boys where he taught a 'chemistry of love that is not in the textbooks'. Yogananda describes him as being in a constant 'inexhaustible romance with the Beloved.'

The story of their visits to the temple of Kali in Dakshineswar included descriptions of what this feeling was like as they chanted Her name. Yogananda wrote:

> From him I learnt sweetness of God in the aspect of Mother, or Divine Mercy. The childlike saint found little appeal in the Father aspect, or Divine Justice. Stern, exacting, mathematical judgement was alien to his gentle nature.[15]

These experiences were even more potent for young Mukunda, as he had lost his actual mother, and had taken refuge in the Divine Mother often since then, praying to her regularly.

At a 'bioscope' (an older term for a motion picture) screening at Calcutta University, Master Mahasaya, sensing that Mukunda was bored with the picture, gave him a short peek into his future samadhi experience (with a gentle blow to the chest, not unlike how Yukteswar did it years later). Mukunda gained the vision of an omnipresent eye that allowed him to see behind him and all around him, as if he was there but outside his body, seeing others who couldn't see him. Yogananda ends by saying: 'The unique pantomime brought me an inexpressible ecstasy. I drank deep from some blissful fount.'[16]

Yogananda would have a similar experience in that same temple of Kali when he was older and meditating to the Divine Mother, on a trip with his sister Roma and her sceptical husband Satish (which we talked about in 'Lesson #10: Getting Help and Following the Clues').

The path of devotion is one that is universal across most religions, because, as Yogananda tells us, 'God is bliss'. Christian and Islamic mystics are often fond of using the metaphors of the Holy Mother or the Divine Romance with the Beloved (a Sufi metaphor for God) to describe the ineffable nature of divinity. Yogananda tells of the Catholic saint, Therese Neumann, whom he visited in Germany. Neumann reached an ecstatic state through devotion and prayer.

Rumi often spoke, in terms that could have come from Yogananda's description of Master Mahasaya, of the Divine Intoxication that comes with God-union:

The moment I heard my first love story
I started looking for you
Not knowing how blind that was
Lovers don't finally meet somewhere
They're in each other all along[17]

Modern Evidence for Seeing Beyond the Illusion

Until we have experienced it ourselves, we have to trust that there is a state called samadhi and what the sages who have experienced it tell us about death, the bardo (the Tibetan term for the in-between state), karma and rebirth.

In the modern world, the rise of the social sciences provides us with another method by which to acquire knowledge: looking for evidence across multiple sources. If some people tell us they have been to China and describe it, we might not trust them until we speak to others who have also been to China. The more people we are able to have this information corroborated by, the more confident we can be that 1) there is a place called China and 2) we are getting a reasonable description of it, even if the individual descriptions differ in minor ways. While most people are familiar with descriptions of beyond-the-veil consciousness, which can be found in various religions of the world, can we look for examples that are not so culturally dependent and may occur in more modern times?

The advent of modern medicine has led to a rise in the number of cases of people who were thought to be dead for a short period of time but were revived. There have also been many thousands of accounts of what are called near-death experiences or NDEs, reports from those who were thought to be clinically dead but were later revived. Although the term 'I saw my life flash before me' has been around since time immemorial, those who have had NDEs seem to come back with a more vivid description of the afterlife.

I first began to take these accounts seriously when I met Dannion Brinkley, who was struck by lightning in 1975 and was thought to be dead for a short time (he describes this experience in his bestselling book, *Saved by the Light*). He wrote about meeting with Beings of Light that emanated an indescribable love and that took him to a beautiful place, a crystal city. While there, he had a holographic 360-degree panoramic life review of every single action that he had taken in his life. Moreover, he had to re-experience these events from the point of view of other people, people who been affected by his actions. This was an unpleasant experience, since he had been in the military and had literally killed people with guns, and even as a kid had been a bully.

Today the estimates of the number of people who may have had NDEs numbers in the millions, with thousands of them documented. They almost always begin with the person floating up above their body, what's called an out of body experience (or OBE).

There are many common elements in descriptions of NDEs. After an OBE (during which they also experience some of the 360 degree spherical vision that Yogananda described), they often include a visit to a beautiful place (a garden, a crystal city, a beautiful meadow), meeting beings of light (sometimes described as God and at other times as an angel), feeling the ineffable love of God emanating from these beings, seeing colours and sounds that are more vivid than, and do not exist, in the physical world, and becoming privy to the interconnectedness of all things.

Like Yogananda describing the return from the samadhi state, these NDErs tell us that they are almost always unhappy to be back in their bodies, because the sense of love, contentment and knowledge they experienced in the state after death, the bardo, is beyond anything they can describe.

Lesson for Modern Seekers: Karma Yoga and Enlightenment

Many modern seekers practice meditation at home. We may not have a single guru like Yogananda who can walk up to us in the flesh and tap us on the heart, inducing a state of samadhi. Should we still be trying to work on it? And if so, how?

Lahiri Mahasaya was very explicit about this: we should keep living in the world and doing our work in the world, in addition to yoga and the observance of our religious traditions.

Why is it important that we keep doing our work in the world? It is a way of fulfilling our karma. The key is to do it without selfish desires, to not become too attached to the fruits of our actions in the real world. This is the karma yoga that was spoken about in the Bhagavad Gita. Yogananda wrote:

> When your activity centres only on making money for material advantages for yourself and your loved ones, or on any activity with a selfish end, you are going away from God. Thus do most people engage their energies in their attachments and their desires for more and more material acquisitions. But as soon as your active energy is used to seek God, you move toward Him.[18]

Sri Yukteswar was more explicit in telling Yogananda to seek the ecstatic state, but to not let it distract him from his work in the world. In a telling exchange after Yogananda's first experience with cosmic consciousness, his guru warns him not to get 'overdrunk with ecstasy': 'You must not get overdrunk with ecstasy. Much work yet remains for you in the world. Come; let us sweep the balcony floor; then we shall walk by the Ganges.'[19]

And so, perhaps the best way to approach awakening is to deepen our spiritual practice, our sadhana, while we keep doing what are here to do in the world, but in a different state of mind. Even if we don't go 'all the way', each step we take is a step closer to the Beloved, as the Sufis would say.

LESSON #14

Yoga is For Everyone, East and West

Yoga cannot know a barrier of East and West any more than does the healing and equitable light of the sun. So long as man possesses a mind with its restless thoughts, so long will there be a universal need for yoga ...

— YOGANANDA[1]

I am neither in temple nor in mosque: I am neither in Kaaba nor in Kailash

— KABIR[2]

'East is East and West is West, and never shall the twain meet', wrote Rudyard Kipling, whom I quoted in the introduction to this book. Yet, by the time that Yogananda arrived in the US in 1920, the enormous gulf between the two parts of the world had already been narrowed. The pervasive influence of the British Empire, the age of colonialism, not to mention some of America's greatest nineteenth-century philosophers like Ralph Waldo Emerson, had made sure that the West was not a complete stranger to ancient Indian philosophy.

Towards the end of the nineteenth century, Swami Vivekananda had travelled to America and lectured all around the country, becoming one of the first Indian swamis to gain popularity there.[3] Swami Vivekananda didn't, however, live and settle in the West as Yogananda did; he returned to India after his tour, which was considered a great success.

Still, despite the occasional bridge between the cultures, we might say that a big chasm continued to exist between the two countries when Yogananda arrived. Most ordinary Americans knew little about India or yoga, other than rumours and caricatures of swamis and yogis. Yet the interest in Yogananda's lectures throughout the country, evidenced by his many sold-out appearances at theatres across America (some lectures had over a thousand attendees!), demonstrated that, even then, there was a hunger for the spirituality of the East. Moreover, Yogananda's timing was good: the decade of the 1920s, called the roaring twenties, was a time of prosperity and breaking of traditional taboos, which made the culture ripe for new types of spiritual exploration.

Similarly, in the India of the time, Yogananda was raised on clichéd stories about the materialism of the West. He wrote:

I had heard many stories about the materialistic Western atmosphere, one very different from the spiritual background of India, pervaded with the centuried aura of saints. 'An Oriental teacher who will dare the Western airs,' I thought, 'must be hardy beyond the trials of any Himalayan cold!'[4]

This final chapter is about a message Yogananda tried to convey throughout his book and in his life's work: yoga is for everyone. A related lesson is that yoga can be a bridge between the modernity of the West and the spiritual insights of the East. The West needs yoga to provide a stable foundation beneath their frenetic activity as much as India and the East need modern science. Another important aspect of his message was that yoga can be a bridge between different religions, because you can practice yoga (not just the asanas, but all the limbs of yoga), no matter which religion you belong to or how/who you worship.

Today, East Is West and West Is East

In the global exchange of information that was made possible first by books, then by TV and now by computers and the internet, such distinctions as 'East' and 'West' are perhaps not as relevant as they once were. Today, in the software industry, for example, I am just as likely to work with engineers from Bangalore, Lahore or Beijing as I am with engineers in San Francisco or project managers from New York.

At the same time, the interest in yoga and meditation have grown so much over the last few decades that they are probably as common today in some parts of the US as Christian churches are in other parts of the country.

Similarly, to say that India (or any country in the East) is spiritual and the West is more materialistic is perhaps no longer an accurate statement. You will find as much materialism in the streets and universities of Mumbai (Lahore, Shanghai or Hong Kong) as you will find in New York or Los Angeles (and in some cases, perhaps even more).

It is this continual desire for more, a hallmark of materialism, that transcends any national boundaries. An acknowledgement of this is at the heart of Indian spirituality: the desire for more is what produces the chains of karma, binding us and making us come back again and again. In this sense, the desire for more is alive and well all over the world, as is the production of karma!

For this reason, the basic lessons and messages of Yogananda, who hailed from the East but lived, taught and wrote his famous book for the West, are needed in his homeland today as much as they were in the US during his lifetime. In 'Lesson #8: Practice Every Day, No Matter How Much Time You Have', I mentioned the pizza effect, which talks about an idea that travels back to its homeland after being transformed by its encounter with another civilization. Yogananda's teachings, though they were always available in some ancient forms in India, were packaged and put together in a format that would benefit modern people all over the world, including in his homeland.

The Journey of Yogananda Started Before Yogananda

It turns out that Yogananda's journey from East to West had a karma that, like many things, extends further back, even before his memory. Yogananda came from a very specific lineage and, in the *Autobiography*, he revealed that his travel to the US was no accident, but an extension of the interest of the founder of that lineage, the seemingly immortal Babaji (see 'Lesson #12: Lessons from Babaji and the Great Engine of Karma').

Babaji, who had an interest in the West, even as far back as the nineteenth century, mentioned this during his first encounter with Sri Yukteswar, in the same month that baby Mukunda had his first birthday. According to Yogananda, it was this discussion about Sri Yukteswar's interest in the West that laid the seeds which would sprout into his own life's work.

Yukteswar met Babaji at the Kumbha Mela, one of the largest religious festivals in the world, in Allahabad in January 1894. By all accounts, a Kumbha Mela, which is held once every twelve years, can be overwhelming and disorganized to say the least, like many gargantuan festivals. A little perturbed by all the activity and unimpressed with many of the countless sadhus he saw wandering around, the young Yukteswar was told by a tall sadhu that a saint wanted to see him.

The saint, sitting under a tree with a group of disciples, turned out to be Babaji, though Yukteswar didn't realize it at the time (demonstrating yet another type of siddhi, the ability to block a particular thought). Yukteswar, not yet a swami, didn't realize that he was meeting his paramguru. It wasn't until Yukteswar carried a message to Lahiri Mahasaya, his own guru, at Babaji's request, that Lahiri told him whom he had met.

During the meeting with Babaji, it was Yukteswar who brought up the need to carry India's wisdom to the West, and the need to bring western science to the East, saying:

Sir ... I have been thinking of the scientific men of the West, greater by far in intelligence than most people congregated here, living in distant Europe and America, professing different creeds, and ignorant of the real values of such melas as the present one. They are the men who could benefit greatly by meetings with India's masters. But, although high in intellectual attainments, many Westerners are wedded to rank materialism. Others, famous in science and philosophy, do not recognize the essential unity in religion. Their creeds serve as insurmountable barriers that threaten to separate them from us forever.[5]

Babaji then informed Yukteswar that he had summoned him because he had felt this desire in the young man's heart and told him what I think is the one of the most important themes of Yogananda's life and book:

'*East and West must establish a golden middle path of activity and spirituality combined*,' he continued. 'India has much to learn from the West in material development; in return, India can teach the universal methods by which the West will be able to base its religious beliefs on the unshakable foundations of yogic science.'[6]

During that conversation, Babaji called Yukteswar 'Swamiji', though Yukteswar objected to this since he wasn't a swami at the time. Babaji told Yukteswar he would send him a disciple to train who would take yoga to the West. This disciple was Yogananda and it was a necessary task because Babaji sensed a growing spiritual hunger in the West—in America and Europe: 'The vibrations there of many spiritually seeking souls come floodlike to me. I perceive potential saints in America and Europe, waiting to be awakened.'[7]

The Role of Religious Unity

One of the tenets of the lineage, beginning with Babaji, through Lahiri Mahasaya and down to Yukteswar and Yogananda, was that yoga was universal and was for everyone, even those belonging to religions other than Hinduism. Lahiri Mahasaya explicitly told his students to continue to worship in their particular religious tradition—whether in terms of how they prayed or the religious texts they read, such as the Koran or the Bible, as I mentioned in 'Lesson #8: Practice Every Day, No Matter How Much Time You Have'.

Yogananda seems to have had a particular fascination with connections between Hinduism and Christianity, and believed that yoga could be that bridge. Yogananda's language in the *Autobiography* is very attuned to the Middle Eastern religions in general and Christianity in particular—with frequent references to Christ, the Gospels and to biblical prophets like Elijah and others.

Today, many spiritual seekers in the West react differently to all the references to Christ and to God in the *Autobiography*, wondering why Yogananda needed to spend so much time backing up his various spiritual assertions about yoga with Biblical passages and references. This fascination with creating a bridge between Vedantic philosophy and Christianity was probably necessary because of the time and place that Yogananda was teaching in: a primarily Christian nation that knew little about the Hinduism or the mystical traditions of India, beyond some of the clichés that prevailed. In a sense, it was tailor-made to introduce the West to yoga.

In fact, when there was a great surge of interest in Indian traditions in the US in the 1960s, Yogananda's book was one of the primary contributors to that, as it was passed around from young person to young person. In fact, my research led me to believe that the *Autobiography* may have been one of the most passed-around books of that generation in mass market paperback form. During this time of revolution, not unlike the 1920s when Yogananda arrived in America, many youngsters were rejecting the beliefs and cultural norms of their parents' generation. In fact, rejecting traditional churches and religious practice in the US was the one of the hallmarks of this counter-culture movement, which began to embrace Eastern mysticism and a new wave of swamis and teachers arrived from India. Many of these youngsters, who made the book a bestseller and one of the most read books of their generation, who were looking to reject their parents' religious beliefs, must have been as mystified as I was when I first read Yogananda's autobiography decades later in the 1990s. Why are there so many references to the Bible and to Christ?

Was he simply tailoring the yogic message for Americans? While that was definitely part of the reason, Yogananda's sincere respect and reverence for the message of Christ and the Bible is apparent to anyone who reads the book. In fact, many of his disciples today put a picture of Christ on their alters along with pictures of Yogananda and his lineage. One of the people I interviewed for this book, Jay, has been a long-time member of the SRF. He grew up in a Jewish family in America. Like many youngsters of his generation, he didn't learn much about Christ or the New Testament and didn't have the desire to learn more. Yet, after he became fascinated by yoga and read Yogananda's book, he became deeply interested in learning more about the Christian Bible and the esoteric or mystical meanings in it. In a sense, although Yogananda was an ambassador for yoga and India in America, his book also served as an ambassador for the core messages of Christianity to others. Yogananda's views on Christ may not be endorsed by either orthodox Christians or Hindus, but that is nothing new—those who live far inland from the shores of oceans of human thoughts and religions often react negatively to those who try to build bridges between the shores.

This idea that Yogananda might be a bridge between these two very large religions was also born at the meeting between Yukteswar and Babaji. Babaji knew that Yukteswar had written a commentary on the Bhagavad Gita, and gave him another task:

> Will you not write a short book on the underlying basic unity between the Christian and Hindu scriptures? Show by parallel references that the inspired sons of God have spoken the same truths, now obscured by men's sectarian differences.[8]

Yukteswar was unsure if he would be able to fulfil such an important task. Babaji reminded Yukteswar not to doubt, that if the task had been assigned to him (and it was, in this case), the Doer of All Actions, the Divine, would ensure that the task could be completed. This is also a good story to remember, along with those in 'Lesson #2: Sometimes, the Universe Unexpectedly Gives You an Important Task', when we are assigned a task that seems daunting and we are unsure that we can complete.

Taking Babaji's assurance as a blessing, Yukteswar finished the task—writing a book comparing passages of the New Testament to the ancient texts of India, the Upanishads, to demonstrate the essential unity of the messages. The ideas Yukteswar expressed in that book, *The Holy Science*, which is still available today, no doubt heavily influenced Yogananda's training and outlook and laid the foundations for his own ability to teach in a Christian nation when yoga was not so well-known.

Kabir and the Muslims and Hindus

Though I was not surprised that Yogananda had much to say about Christianity, given the era that he was teaching in America, I was surprised that he didn't have more to say about Islam. India had, after all, the largest population of Muslims anywhere in the world before the separation of Pakistan and Bangladesh from India after World War II. The gulf between orthodox Hindus and orthodox Muslims, combined with territorial and political differences, has contributed to several wars and great misery, and the animosity continues to this day in many corners of the subcontinent.

Yogananda does mention the Sufi traditions, the mystical side of Islam, in passing at several points in the *Autobiography*. Given his and Yukteswar's assertions about the unity of God and all religions, I expected him to say more, and if his book wasn't written primarily for the West, we might have seen more of this.

One saint that Yogananda mentions several times is Kabir, the medieval poet who was born a Muslim and became a teacher and mystic of renown, and who was claimed by both Hindus and Muslims as a saint. Kabir is interesting because, hundreds of years before Yogananda, he was trying to bridge a fairly significant divide between the two largest religions in India.

Kabir is thought of as one of the more interesting figures to crop up in the annals of Indian spirituality—and that is saying a lot given the wide spectrum of saints that have emerged since antiquity from the fertile soil of India!

I mentioned Kabir in 'Lesson #12: Lessons from Babaji and the Great Engine of Karma', since Yogananda asserted that Kabir had received an initiation from Babaji. While we don't have any other way of validating the Babaji connection, I believe that Kabir's message about the unity of the search for God, expressed in his songs, had the same underlying message as Yogananda's book: yoga is universal and God is beyond any human religion.

Kabir said he was at once the 'child of Allah and of Ram'. He is known to have studied with the Vedantic reformer Ramananda at one point, and with the Sufi Pir Takki of Jhansi later in life. Depending on who you believe, Kabir was either self-taught or received his realization about the connection with God from one of these gurus. Some say that he only became a disciple of Ramananda because no one wanted to learn from a self-taught teacher, and this gave him the credibility that was needed for people to take him seriously as a spiritual master. The same comment is made about his alleged association with Sufi masters!

Although there are still over a million followers of Kabir's teachings in India today, he is best known worldwide perhaps for his mystical poetry, which is considered a blend of Bhakti Movement and Sufi thought. His poetry, like that of Rumi and Mirabai, often use the metaphor of the lover and the beloved for the soul and the Lord waiting to be reunited. One of the first translations of Kabir's poetry into English was in 1914 by the Bengali poet, Rabindranath Tagore, whom Yogananda met and compared notes with on the respective schools they were running at the time.

There are many colourful stories about Kabir. One of the most famous was about his death, sometime after Kabir was banned from Benares for being, essentially a heretic to *both* faiths by teaching the inherent unity of the experience of God. Kabir was also known for criticizing many of the ritualistic forms of religious worship that sects of both religions seemed to favour, a practice that did not ingratiate him with either side.

According to one such story, when Kabir died, his Muslim followers wanted to bury the body per Islamic tradition and his Hindu followers wanted to cremate it per their tradition. After arguing with each other, they agreed to look under the shroud that covered his body. Instead of seeing his body, they saw a collection of flowers. Half the flowers were given to the Hindus to cremate and the other half to the Muslims to bury, thus avoiding conflict and once again emphasizing his core message of love.

Kabir, like Yogananda, taught of the unity of all religions and in his poetry, reminding us that God is nearby if we seek him out and not necessarily in any specific mosque or temple or technique:

> O servant, where dost thou seek Me?
> Lo! I am beside thee.
> I am neither in temple nor in mosque:
> I am neither in Kaaba nor in Kailash:
> Neither am I in rites and ceremonies,
> nor in yoga and renunciation.
> If thou art a true seeker, thou shalt at once see Me: thou shalt
> meet Me in a moment of time.
> Kabir says, 'O Sadhu! God is the breath of all breath.'[9]

The Middle Ground Between Science and Spirituality

Yogananda wrote his lectures (and later his book, *The Science of Religion*) to make the case for the unity of all religions, which was a part of his life task, by demonstrating how yoga could be that science or connective tissues between different faiths.

Just as the unity of all religions was important to Yogananda, so was the need to unify religion and spirituality with science and materialism. A hundred years later, this message is still sorely needed, in both the East and the West, as I know from my own discussions about consciousness and spirituality with scientists. They usually speak very different languages and bridging this divide may even be more challenging in modern times than was the gulf between different religions; at least almost all religions agree that the physical world is not 'all that there is', whereas materialists only believe in which they can see and measure with instruments.

Today, we live in a world of science and technology. Unlike when Yogananda's book came out, there's a good chance you are reading this book in an electronic format, downloaded over the internet to your eBook reader (or even as a digital audiobook). The transformation of print and so many other media into digital technology has made it easier to transmit any kind of information—video, audio, text—to anywhere in the world. This has given us a new shared language, and this technological progress is built upon the understandings of the material world provided by modern science.

Yogananda spent quite a bit of time in his book trying to unify the latest findings of science ('latest' being a relative term of course) to show how these findings were related to what the ancient rishis have told us about God and the nature of reality. He was, for a swami of the time, quite well-informed on the latest scientific discoveries and his book contains discussions of Einstein's theory of relativity and of the findings of quantum mechanics, all used to support the conclusion that everything is based on light and that this may be the fundamental building block of the world, a conclusion that was shared by his direct experience in the various visions he had.

Yogananda spends several chapters on scientists, including India's esteemed scientist J.C. Bose and Luther Burbank in America, both of whom worked on discovering the secrets of biological life (using plants) in the context of the greater physical world that science had started to explain. Yogananda often references recent research that was ongoing. In his book *Journey to Self-Realization*, which is a collection of his talks, he includes one talk from 1938 on the subject of 'everlasting youthfulness'. In it, he references the experiments of a scientist in New York, Robert Becker, who was electrically stimulating cells to get them back to a state in which they could regrow and was testing this method to help frogs and rats regrow limbs. This clearly pre-dated our research into stem cells and, just before writing this book, I read an article about scientists in 2021 trying to do the same thing—experiments to get frogs to regrow legs using stem cells. Far from being ignorant of the latest scientific findings, Yogananda was usually on top of them.

Yogananda was also no stranger to using modern technologies and methods to spread his message—in fact, his jam-packed lectures and correspondence courses were so radical that they upset many traditionalists who believed yoga should be taught to one individual at a time as was done for thousands of years.

As we explored in 'Lesson #7: The World is Like a Movie, a Dream, a Video Game', Yogananda also wasn't afraid to update the metaphors of the rishis based on the latest technologies. He loved to go to the movies and often used the metaphor of God as the light of a cosmic projector, projecting the world onto a movie screen. Unlike the radio, which wasn't new during the time he was writing the *Autobiography*, the television, which worked on similar principles, was relatively new.

Yogananda compared human thoughts with radio and television waves. For example, in the story of the cauliflower robbery, Yukteswar picked up on a certain peasant's desire for cauliflower and somehow sent that peasant a telepathic message informing him that there was cauliflower in a certain room in their hermitage, which Mukunda had failed to lock. Yukteswar explained how this happened to Mukunda, and Yogananda later explained it to the rest of us: we are constantly caught by radio waves of thought surrounding us and only with a clear mind, which results from quieting the thoughts through yoga, can someone figure out exactly where a thought came from or how to send a thought to a specific person.

Obviously, scientific findings have advanced since Yogananda's time and will continue to do so. That is the nature of science: it is never done. The reason for discussing this in the context of this lesson is that, according to Yogananda, science and what he called the 'science of religion' (i.e., yoga) were not in an adversarial relationship.

The discovery of quantum mechanics, which shows us that the outside world and the world we perceive are linked, introduces a twist in the ancient narrative of yoga. If the physical world we perceive is the collapse of the probability wave, which many physicists tell us it is, then it's clear that perception, observation and acts of the mind, have a role to play in making the physical world.

Yogananda's point was that, in the end, science and religion are trying to discover the same things: the underlying truth about the universe. While the sages may have described samadhi and siddhis long ago, Yogananda is quick to place them in the context of what we know about light and the building blocks of matter from physics.

Yet, despite the efforts of Yogananda and many since then, a purely materialistic and mechanistic view of the universe, which often goes hand-in-hand with atheism, is prevalent in many of the world's scientific institutions. In fact, denial of the existence of God is the default position in the West among scientifically minded people and, even in Yogananda's time, a materialistic attitude was starting to take hold in India as the country was modernizing.

Healings occur regularly in the *Autobiography*, usually initiated by a master like Sri Yukteswar or Lahiri Mahasaya. Healing also occurs regularly in the stories all of the religious traditions of the world, by saints of all stripes and colours. However, modern scientists will be quick to point out that we are naïve to believe in these stories, because healing is only done by physical remedies, like medicines. The spiritual or conscious component, while acknowledged only begrudgingly and haltingly in the past few decades by the medical establishment (meditation and yoga can help to reduce stress, which can help to reduce the likelihood of illness or disease), is usually an afterthought in any kind of medical treatment.

Unlike the healing achieved through the use of a drug or a vaccine, the mechanisms by which miraculous healings work their wonders are mysterious and, therefore, from the point of view of the pure materialistic scientist, might as well not exist at worst or are highly suspect at best. Alternatively, what is miraculous is usually classified as a placebo, which serves as a way of discrediting the body's own healing powers, the role of karma and our divine plan in both creating and healing from illnesses.

The lesson for modern seekers today is the same lesson that Yogananda was trying to teach back then. It is a message as sorely needed today as it was 100 years ago: that science and religion need not be in conflict. We should both use modern medicine and pray to the Divine Mother or Divine Father. We should both trust our intuition when it comes to detecting the thoughts of others or detecting Divine will *and* use our cell phones to communicate directly with friends who are hundreds or thousands of miles away. We should meditate, use our intuition, pray for healing *and* trust the findings of modern science.

Too often, one side is used as a club to stifle the other. Five hundred years ago, in the western world, the Catholic Church attempted to stifle Galileo's findings about the planets and the solar system on theological grounds. In those days, science was persecuted, or at least censored by the dominant institution of the day, religion.

Today, the opposite is true: any findings that cannot be explained by our existing models, and might throw into question some basic scientific assumptions, are overlooked or ridiculed on scientific grounds (i.e., unless they can be reproduced at will in controlled circumstances they are 'pseudoscience'). These include topics such as NDEs, past lives, the presence of divinity, the miracles associated with various masters and saints of different religions, and the presence of entities outside of our perception, like ghosts or jinn.

This is not unlike the tales of 'rocks falling from the sky' that were dismissed by European scientists before the nineteenth century because, as per the understanding of the universe of that time, there were no rocks in the sky! So how could rocks possibly be falling from the sky? This was true despite there being hundreds (if not thousands) of years of incidents being reported of rocks falling from the sky.

Only when there was a mass event in which thousands of rocks fell from the sky in the countryside that scientists from Paris were sent to investigate the phenomenon. They eventually were convinced that rocks did indeed fall from the sky—a notion they had ridiculed only a few years earlier. The problem was that science, which is never complete, had the wrong 'cosmological model' of the universe and assumed reality consisted only of that which was possible within the framework of their existing model.

Stories of seemingly miraculous events and divine intercession like the ones in the *Autobiography* and many others that continue to be reported even today show us that, despite the many achievements of science, it is still operating on a false cosmological model: that the physical, visible world is the only world there is.

In a sense, the struggle to bridge the gap between science and religion is a battle that we are still fighting today, perhaps even more so than ever before, in the twenty-first century. As a result, a growing number of us live and work in the modern world and are believers in science but sense that there is something seriously wrong with the cosmological model, the assumptions at the very heart of science today and the manner in which science is taught.

Unfortunately, many scientists still think that science is fighting the last battle; at a time when religious fundamentalists don't believe in science at all and attribute everything to divine spirits or demons, any acknowledgement that there may be other causes and models for natural phenomena will be seen as a weakness in that battle. As long as people are considered either 'anti-sicence' or 'pro-science'—terms that have become tossed around freely and which are considered mutually exclusive—the battle will still rage.

In fact, one of the reasons I wrote my book, *The Simulation Hypothesis: An MIT Computer Scientist Shows Why AI, Quantum Physics and Eastern Mystics Agree We Are in a Video Game*, was that the technological metaphor of the video game provided a vocabulary that could serve as what we in the sociology of science call a 'boundary object'. A boundary object is an object or a concept that can travel across different domains that may not speak the same language and yet be understandable to both.

The metaphor of the video game and the language of computer simulations can be easily used with engineers, scientists, monks, mystics, teenagers and laypersons in almost any context or domain of knowledge. Many former atheists have been forced to admit that, if the world is a simulation (both a metaphor and a mechanism), then anyone and anything outside the simulation will seem like a supernatural being to us—this is effectively an acknowledgement that the cosmological model of a purely physical existence could be wrong.

The British philosopher David Pearce called simulation theory the most interesting development in theology in 2,000 years. I like to say that, rather than being entirely new, it is simply updating the old metaphors of the prophets, sages and saints for a more modern world.

Finding the Middle Way

A related message that is embedded within Yogananda's book and life, though perhaps not stated so explicitly, is that we must find a balance between the organization, efficiency, ambition and mechanization of the Occident and the calmness, spiritual insight and, sometimes even complacency, of the Orient. I have used the older, antiquated colonial terms (occident and orient) deliberately, to describe characteristics that were traditionally ascribed to these cultures of the time (even though, as I've said earlier in this chapter, these characterizations don't really apply in the same way anymore).

Yogananda was no stranger to activity or efficiency. For example, when he returned to India in 1935, and found out that the land for the Ranchi school, which had been donated by the Raj, was to be taken away, he wrote in his letters that he hadn't spent fifteen years immersed in the 'can-do' attitude of the Americans to be fatalistic about outcomes. He mobilized a campaign that would bring in funds from notable personalities in Calcutta and elsewhere, using fund-raising and organizational skills he had perfected while building his organization from scratch in a faraway land.

Even within Europe, whose recorded history goes back further than the USA's (though perhaps not as far back as India's), the American attitude that 'anyone can do anything' is sometimes frowned upon. However, it is a key part of the American dream. In a sense, Yogananda lived the American dream, which envisions immigrants coming to the USA from all over in the world and rising up from humble beginnings to become successful and make an impact. Of course, this American dream is no longer limited geographically to America.

The real lesson here is that both ways of looking at the world, the modern and the ancient, have value. With modernization, efficiency and ambition comes outward success. But it is also easy, as in the case of the West, to put these on an altar and forget about our inward spiritual development. The more external activity we are engaged in, the more mental clutter we have to contend with. The more intensely we desire material success, the more vigorously we create vrittis. Therefore, in the West and in all the areas of the East that have adopted Western attitudes, yoga is needed today more than ever!

What is also needed is a middle way. When Prince Siddhartha, who had meditated for years with ascetics in the forest, decided to give up the ascetic lifestyle, his fellow ascetics, who had followed him there, were aghast. Yet Siddhartha had an insight about a middle way. At one point, Siddhartha overheard a sitar player tell his pupil while stringing his instrument: 'If you pull the string too tight, it will snap. If you leave the string too slack, it won't play.' This story is well-known in India and was even depicted in a Western movie.[10] Though this is most likely a mythical story, it illustrates an important point that Siddhartha made after he became the Buddha: that there is a middle path between tenseness and slackness.

A middle way between East and the West, or between the philosophies ascribed to both, between external activity and inner calm, is needed. This is also what Yogananda encouraged all of us to pursue and embodied in his life and his organizations. It was for the same reason that Babaji encouraged Sri Yukteswar to find parallels between the Upanishads and the Bible, and sent Yogananda to train under Yukteswar, all the way back in 1894, which I quoted earlier but will repeat here for emphasis:

East and West must establish a golden middle path of activity and spirituality combined.[11]

The Final Lesson: Take The Best of East and West

I felt this was best expressed by Yukteswar to Yogananda on the eve of the latter's departure for America a hundred years ago. It holds true today just as it did then. This was in some ways a message not just for Yogananda but for the thousands of new students he would meet in America in person and millions more via his autobiography: 'Forget you were born a Hindu, and don't be an American. Take the best of them both ... Be your true self, a child of God. Seek and incorporate into your being the best qualities of all your brothers, scattered over the earth in various races.'[12]

For me, this lesson is not just emblematic of Yogananda's life and his autobiography. It applies not just to Hindus, Muslims, Christians or Buddhists. It applies to all of us. It is also the core message of the current book as well.

And that is why I want to end with what I call Yogananda's final lesson, which he both wrote about in his autobiography and was an exemplar of in his life.

The lesson: take the best of all the worlds that you find yourself in—Eastern or Western, scientific or religious, frenetic activity or peaceful calm. Let yoga be the metaphorical bridge between all of the realms you visit during this life and beyond!

Afterword

No book exists as an isolated island in the life of an author. Rather, writing a book is like cruising on a river. In the beginning, the author might sense that an island is coming up, but might not know whether that particular island is a place where they will stop and spend a considerable amount of time.

To switch metaphors, before the actual serious business of writing begins, a book usually has a spark, a seed that germinates for some time before it starts a period of visible growth and fruit-bearing. Even when there is nothing to see, growth and development continue in the soil of the author's mind and psyche.

Sometimes, this seed turns into a short (or long) blog post or article; sometimes, it attempts to break out with one (or more) aborted attempts to put down thoughts on paper; at other times, the idea is well-formed but it takes months (or years) of research before the writing phase begins. Eventually every author realizes that he or she must get serious and get down to the business of the writing. This may come through the author's own intuition or inner voice, or from some external source— the encouragement of a friend, colleague, one's spouse, an agent or the deadline of a publisher.

Once that happens, the author has arrived (to go back to our river-and-island metaphor) on the island and is obligated to stay there for some time, becoming completely immersed in the landscape, the texture, the weather and the residents of the island. With this book, the subject matter is Yogananda and his autobiography and the many tributaries of yoga that he touched.

While on the river, before I arrived on this particular island, I had very little knowledge that the island was to be a meaningful stop in the journey of my own writing career. I have been a big fan of Yogananda's autobiography, which has inspired me for several decades. I had even written about my enthusiasm for the classic book in some blog posts and have mentioned his works and philosophy in several of my other books. Nevertheless, I had no plans or even a hunch that I would write a book about this charismatic spiritual leader.

Sometimes, the idea for a book arrives wholesale. J.K. Rowling described sitting in a delayed train from Manchester to London when the idea for the Harry Potter series came to her: 'It was the most incredible feeling ... out of nowhere, it just fell from above.'[1] Rowling went on to describe a feeling of physical excitement, an electric rush of sorts, and she *knew* she was going to write that book. Not only did she have a complete physical description of the titular character but she also knew it was going to be a seven-book series in that instant. In certain indigenous traditions, it is said that the story stalks the storyteller, and when it catches its prey is when the storyteller realizes that they have no choice but to tell the story.

The idea for this book also arrived 'wholesale' to me and evoked a similar response, though my invitation came from a more earthly and less etheric source. As I mentioned in the introduction and in 'Lesson #2: Sometimes, the Universe Unexpectedly Gives You an Important Task', the idea for this book landed in my inbox, unbidden and unexpected, in the form of an email from an editor at Harper Collins India, while I was living in Silicon Valley. Like Rowling, I felt an electric rush when the invitation arrived. Somehow, I knew that I would have to write this book, and circumstances made it possible.

After this 'serious writing phase', when the book is complete, the author gets back on the boat and continues down the river of their career. Although every book continues to have an impact on you for years, during the editing process and after the book is published, when you give talks and interviews, it is impossible to go back to the island and immerse yourself in the way that you did while writing the book. As compensation, though, you have the memory of that experience and develop, after you have departed the island, a better perspective on both the island and your time on it.

During the research and writing phase of the manuscript of *Wisdom of a Yogi*, I immersed myself not just in Yogananda's famous book but also in his other writings (which were plentiful), and recordings of his lectures,[2] so that I could hear his voice. Most importantly, one of the unique aspects of this particular island was that I also immersed myself in Yogananda's biography—not just in any specific book[3] (though Philip Goldberg's biography is excellent) but in his *story*, his journey from being a boy with spiritual dreams to becoming a mature spiritual teacher who left an incredible legacy.

Much of *Autobiography of a Yogi*, which was written at his hermitage overlooking a beach on the Pacific Ocean, concerns Yogananda's early life in India. This includes the years when he was a young boy who dreamt of Himalayan yogis and his time with his master, when he trained to become a member of the swami order himself. In contrast, Yogananda didn't provide anywhere near this level of detail about his time in America, his adopted homeland. In addition to his teachings, I became interested in knowing Yogananda the man, Mukunda Lal Ghosh, and the feelings he might have had travelling around this strange land of mechanization and western values.

It was here in the US that Mukunda transformed from a young swami who barely spoke English into a well-known guru—in fact, today he might be considered a jagadguru, a guru for the whole world. From America, Swami Yogananda inspired millions by exhorting them in his forceful accent to look beyond their physical lives in the 'search for God.' These years included many setbacks, many of which are not mentioned in the *Autobiography*. These ranged from strained relations with some of his closest friends and fellow swamis, to the challenges of being a man with long hair who wore what seemed to be funny clothes in an increasingly modernized and mechanized twentieth-century America. While the swami was welcomed by many (as evidenced by the large crowds at the lectures he gave while crisscrossing the land in trains), he also faced discrimination and the rejection of the 'unknown' by some elements of society that happens in every era.

In a sense, Yogananda was a classic immigrant, and his story mirrors the stories of immigrants from many other countries and the resulting integration of their families and children into this melting pot. One picture of Yogananda that stood out to me was taken in 1920 in Boston; he stands, dressed in an overcoat and a turban, next to a sign that says, 'Free lecture by Swami Yogananda—renowned lecturer, educator and psychologist from India'.

While this picture depicted the challenges he faced in bringing yoga to this new land, it also made me think of the immigrants I knew best: my own parents. My father left the subcontinent on the first flight out after a war, and arrived in Detroit, Michigan, in the 1970s after a brief stint studying in Paris. My mother, with two young kids in tow (myself and my elder brother, aged four and five, respectively), flew from Lahore to the auto capital of the world to join him several years later. Thiers was also a classic immigrant story, repeated by many in their generation that came to America.

This picture of Yogananda in Boston, trying to get his footing, before he had fully settled into his new American life was what we sometimes call 'fresh off the boat' (in his case, he had literally come on a boat, though most immigrants arrive in airplanes nowadays). This picture evoked images of my mother in the early years after our arrival, dressed in her salwar kameez, fresh off the transcontinental flights, speaking little English and facing similar strange stares from the locals.

During the writing of this book, my father passed away. As a tribute and a way of processing the death of the man who brought me to this land and inspired me in so many ways, I wrote an overview of his life, an immigrant who had lived in multiple countries, but whose adopted home, like Yogananda's, was the United States, the place he had spent most of his adult life.[4]

Writing my father's story made me remember the sacrifices that all immigrants make—whether monks like Yogananda or householders like my parents—in finding a new life in a far-away land. The legacies of most immigrants live on in the form of their children, who end up more integrated into the adopted culture than their parents. In fact, those children represent something new: an interesting blend of both cultures, neither completely Eastern nor completely Western.

Immigration from India and South Asia to the US has increased in the decades since Yogananda's death in 1952. Today, we see many executives of South Asian descent in charge of the largest technology companies in the world, including Google and Microsoft, and the children of South Asian immigrants emerging as mainstays in Hollywood. They are even creating new versions of that most American of tales, the superhero tale, that will go on to influence the next generation of children all over the world. While twentieth-century superheroes consisted of young white men whose alter egos became Batman, Superman and Spider-man, in the twenty-first century we see examples like Disney's Ms Marvel, a superhero tale about a young Pakistani-American girl who grows up in New Jersey. I recently watched it with my parents and nephews, and reflected on how different the lives of my nephews would be, growing up in America watching shows with characters that represent, like them, a blend of cultures.

As a Hindu swami, of course, Yogananda had no children. Yet, like most immigrants, his legacy lives on in the products of his many years in America, including his teachings and writings—his literary children. The most important of these is of course, *Autobiography of a Yogi*. Like all immigrant children, Yogananda's book is neither fully Indian nor fully American.

In the *Autobiography*, he had to adapt and explain the classic Vedic spiritual terms in ways that Americans could understand, often by drawing links between them and passages in the Bible and concepts from Christianity.

This can seem a little odd today, because the classic concepts like karma, asanas, meditation, prana and reincarnation are now as well-known in the West as they were in India back in Yogananda's day. In this sense, Yogananda wasn't merely a translator; he was adapting the teachings to a new audience, a modern audience, and he had to use modern metaphors and references to the technologies that were available to the twentieth-century reader in the West.

In this sense, the *Autobiography*, his most consequential child and the repository of his spiritual legacy, is *both* authentically Western and authentically Eastern. It is authentically Western because of the language that he used and the way he tailored his stories to the modern readers of his day; it is more so because Yogananda lived in America much longer than he lived in India. He knew the American culture and not only embraced it but thrived in its optimistic and can-do spirit.

If the book had been written during his years in India for an Indian audience, you can imagine that some portions of it would have been written differently. Yet, it is authentically Eastern because of Yogananda's lineage and tutelage, his place secure in the great spectrum of tributaries that is yoga. This great rush of wisdom from ancient India continues, as it has done in previous centuries, to generate new branches and streams in the great river of yoga. Yogananda was a recipient of one such tributary, originating with the enigmatic Babaji, but he was also the source of many new streams, represented by the various organizations that were founded by his students and the influence his book has had on many other spiritual teachers.

In the many months since I finished writing this book, having completed my island immersion, the river of my career has led me onto many other projects; most notably, embarking on a PhD late in my career, a task that my father had started at the beginning of his career but left unfinished.

To this day, even as I pursue other projects, I still find myself encountering those who have dipped into one or more streams initiated by Yogananda, and his level of influence continues to amaze, surprise and delight me.

Just recently, I was on a podcast and mentioned that my next book would be about Yogananda. The podcaster proceeded to tell me, both on and off the air, how much *Autobiography of a Yogi* meant to him and how glad he was to hear that I'd be bringing out a book about the lessons of the *Autobiography* that was aimed at more modern readers.

When I visited Mountain View recently, the town I was living in when I got the original invitation to write this book, I went downtown, which was just a few blocks from Google's world headquarters. This town, located not far from Stanford University, is considered by some the beating heart of Silicon Valley. Its residents were working on the next technological advancement, as they had been for decades. In the downtown area is a spiritual bookstore appropriately called East–West Books. The bookstore itself is the product of one of these tributaries—it was founded by the Ananda foundation, which was started by one of Yogananda's direct disciples and continues to advance his legacy.

East–West Books is kind of like a spiritual eye of calm in the middle of the storm of technology and materialism that is

Silicon Valley. As soon as I walked in, I was refreshed not only by the sound of a fountain but also by the familiar picture of Yogananda and his autobiography on the top rack of the shelf with the top 100 bestselling books of the past year, near the entrance. Given that the *Autobiography* was published over seventy-five years ago, this fact was remarkable enough—most of the other books on the bestseller shelf had been published much more recently.

Even more amazing to me was the sight, just next to the *Autobiography* on the top shelf, of my previous book, *The Simulation Hypothesis*. This validated two things for me: that Yogananda's lesson and book remains popular and that today's technology-obsessed younger generation may need new metaphors through which to receive the old wisdom.

While I was browsing the shelves, the manager of the bookstore, David, recognized me and started a conversation. I was very familiar with the store because it had been the first bookstore to carry my first book and the first bookstore where I had given an author presentation that was well-received. I had met David when, a few years earlier, he had been part of the Ananda group in Palo Alto that owned the store and was considering selling it because they weren't sure they could run it any longer.

David had managed the store over a decade before that, but hadn't been involved hands-on since then; he had moved on to his other duties, both in the foundation and in his professional life. He was, at the time I met him, in charge of finding a buyer for the store to make sure it stayed alive as it was going through financial and manpower issues. Like many regular visitors, I was afraid that this store would go away as many other bookstores had. This saddened me because East–West was a breath of spiritual fresh air in the middle of a technophilic area.

On that day during my visit, David told me a story I didn't know about that tumultuous time in the store's recent past. Back when the people at Ananda were planning to sell the store, David, who considered Yogananda his guru, asked, while meditating, for guidance from Yogananda on who they should sell the store to. In fact, the name of the bookstore had also been the name of Yogananda's first magazine, published by the Self-Realization Fellowship. During this meditation, the only image David saw was his own. He realized afterwards what it meant: that Ananda should keep the store alive, and that David himself should be the manager, an option he wasn't even considering at the time.

They didn't sell the bookstore, and David jumped in with gusto as the manager. He told me about how the store had not only survived during COVID-19, a time that saw the end of many small retail stores throughout the country and the world, but had thrived and was now doing better than ever.

East–West is not just the name of a great bookstore or Yogananda's old magazine; it is a perfect encapsulation of the philosophy espoused by Yogananda and built into the DNA of his literary masterpiece. In this story of how East-West, the bookstore, was kept alive and well, Yogananda, it seemed, was still doing the work of a guru, lighting the way for future generations.

—Rizwan Virk, Tempe, AZ (December 2022)

Notes

Introduction

1. Isaacson, Walter. *Steve Jobs*. Simon & Shuster (2011), 'To Infinity: The Cloud, The Spaceship and Beyond' [ebook version, p 527]. A representative of the Jobs family told me in an email that they dispute this story that the *Autobiography* was the only book on the iPad.
2. At TechCrunch Disrupt SF 2013, https://youtu.be/4rO_Vs4M29k

Lesson #1: You Don't Need to Go to the Himalayas

1. Paramahansa Yogananda (henceforth Yogananda), *Autobiography of Yogi*, 'My Mothers' Death and the Mystic Amulet', p. 18.
2. Yogananda, *Autobiography of a Yogi*, 'The Sleepless Saint', p. 161.
3. Yogananda, *Autobiography of a Yogi*, 'My Parents and Early Life', p. 10.

4. Yogananda, *Autobiography of a Yogi*, 'My Mothers' Death and the Mystic Amulet', p. 18.

5. Yogananda, *Autobiography of a Yogi*, 'My Mothers' Death and the Mystic Amulet', p. 21.

6. Yogananda, *Autobiography of a Yogi*, 'The Sleepless Saint', pp. 157–58.

7. Mukunda's aunt, after praying in the temple for a week for the recovery of his uncle, found a herb materialized in her hand. She gave the herb to the uncle, who recovered almost immediately.

Lesson #2: Sometimes, the Universe Unexpectedly Gives You an Important Task

1. Yogananda, *Autobiography of a Yogi*, 'The Cauliflower Robbery', p. 177.

2. Jackson, P. (Director). (2001). *The Lord of the Rings: The Fellowship of the Ring* [Film]. New Line Cinema.

Lesson #3: The Unexpected Lessons of the Tiger Swami

1. Yogananda, *Autobiography of a Yogi*, 'The Tiger Swami', p. 47.

2. Ibid., p. 62.

3. Ibid., p. 69.

4. Gladwell's book *Outliers* and the 10,000 hour rule has been referenced in many places, for example: 'Throughout his book, Gladwell repeatedly refers to the "10 000-hour rule," asserting that the key to achieving true expertise in any skill is simply a matter of practicing, albeit in the correct way, for at least 10,000 hours".Wong, N.C. (2015). The 10,000-hour rule. *Canadian Urological Association Journal*, 9 (9–10), 299. https://www.ncbi.nlm.nih.gov/pmc/articles/PMC4662388/

Lesson #4: The Many Lessons of the Incomparable Levitating Saint

1. Yogananda, *Autobiography of a Yogi*, 'The Levitating Saint', Crystal Clarity web version; a slightly revised version appears in the SRF version on p. 73: 'A knowledge of yoga, like the daylight, is free to all who will receive it.'
2. Yogananda, *Autobiography of a Yogi*, 'The Levitating Saint', p. 71.
3. Yogananda, *Autobiography of a Yogi*, 'The Levitating Saint', exact quote from crystal clarity version, slightly revised quote appears in SRF edition on pp. 72–73.
4. Yogananda, *Autobiography of a Yogi*, 'The Levitating Saint', p. 72.
5. Ibid.
6. Ibid., p. 74.
7. Ibid.
8. Ibid., p. 75.
9. Ibid.
10. Ibid., pp. 74–75.
11. Ibid., p. 76.

Lesson #5: The Ancient Arts of Bilocation, Levitation and Telepathy

1. Yogananda, *Autobiography of a Yogi*, 'The Levitating Saint', p. 70.
2. Yogananda, *Autobiography of a Yogi*, 'The Saint with Two Bodies', p. 29.
3. Ibid.
4. Yogananda, *Autobiography of a Yogi*, 'My Master, in Calcutta, Appears in Serampore', p. 216.

5. The specific quote 'almost 1,000 signatures' is directly from an interview by the author with Dr Pasulka in May 2021. She also refers to the 'copious records' of Joseph of Cupertino's levitation in her book, *American Cosmic*. Pasulka, D.W. (2019). *American cosmic: UFOs, religions, technology.* Oxford University Press, p. 217.

6. Yogananda, *Autobiography of a Yogi*, 'The Levitating Saint', p. 71.

Lesson #6: A Karmic Lesson Embedded in a Story About a Jinn

1. Yogananda, *Autobiography of a Yogi*, 'A Mohammedan Wonder-Worker', p. 208.

2. Ibid., pp. 208–09.

3. Ibid.

4. For more on the journey of the story of Aladdin from ancient to modern times, see my article, *The Marvelous and Complicated Journey of Aladdin from Arabic Coffeehouses to NFTs* at https://medium.com/history-of-yesterday/the-marvelous-and-complicated-journey-of-aladdin-from-arabic-coffeehouses-to-nfts-a2e5cb9ec1c.

Lesson #7: The World is Like a Movie, a Dream, a Video Game

1. Yogananda, *Autobiography of a Yogi*, 'The Law of Miracles', p. 314.

2. Yogananda, *The Divine Romance*, 'Reincarnation Is a Series of Dreams Within a Dream', p. 21.

3. Not much is known about the historical Lawapa, who was named after a blanket he carried that was stolen by some local spirits, or Dakinis. His story was preserved in his teaching of

dream yoga to Tilopa, who then taught it to Naropa, who then developed it into one of the six yogas, or six dharmas, which were preserved in Tibetan by Marpa and his student, Tibet's most famous yogi, Milarepa. The six yogas became part of the Kagyu lineage which survives to this day.

4. Quran, English Translation, Pickthall, ch. 29, verse 64, Surah Al-'Ankabut

5. Yogananda, *Autobiography of a Yogi*, 'The Law of Miracles', p. 318.

6. Ibid., p. 319.

7. A phrase that has its origins in the Upanishads:
   'From the unreal lead me to the real.
   From darkness lead me to light.
   From death lead me to immortality.'

8. Yogananda, *Autobiography of a Yogi*, 'The Law of Miracles', p. 318.

9. Ibid., p. 316. (Text in the SRF version was a slight modification of the original quote.)

10. Ibid.

11. The original paper by Bostrom used the term 'post-human' and is available at http://www.simulation-argument.com/ Bostrom, B.N. (2003). 'Are We Living in a Computer Simulation?' *Philosophical Quarterly*, 53(211), pp. 243–255. https://doi.org/10.1111/1467-9213.00309 Specific interpretation and use of the term, 'Simulation Point' from Virk, *The Simulation Hypothesis* (Bayview, 2019).

12. For more on the architecture that would allow us to store our karma in a 'cloud server' and then create quests based on this data, see my book, *The Simulation Hypothesis*.

13. Yogananda, *Autobiography of a Yogi*, 'The Law of Miracles', p. 320.

Lesson #8: Practise Every Day, No Matter How Much Time You Have

1. Yogananda, *Autobiography of a Yogi*, 'I Become A Monk Of The Swami Order', p. 261.
2. Ibid., p. 263.
3. 'If You Practice Yoga, Thank This Man Who Came to the U.S. 100 Years Ago.' *Los Angeles Times*, 19 November, 2020. https://www.latimes.com/science/story/2020-11-19/self-realization-fellowship-paramahansa-yogananda-los-angeles-history.
4. Kriyananda, *Demystifying Patanjali*, The Yoga Sutras (Aphorisms), p. 17.
5. This isn't strictly true with electromagnetic waves according to most scientists, but we are using a metaphor here and not a precise scientific definition.
6. Author's formulation, combining various source translations of Patanjali's verse
7. Yogananda, *Autobiography of a Yogi*, 'I Become a Monk of the Swami Order', p. 262.
8. Ibid., pp. 262–63.
9. Ibid., p. 261.
10. Yogananda, *Autobiography of a Yogi*, 'Materializing a Palace in the Himalayas', p. 365. Yogananda explains in a footnote that the three-fold suffering is mental, physical and spiritual suffering.
11. In one of the strangest case studies of this technique, it was supposedly used by Marpa's son when he fell off a horse and was about to die, to quickly project his consciousness into a nearby pigeon, which flew to India, where he then used the technique to project consciousness to a recently deceased young man's body. The yogi then taught the six yogas in India, including this secret technique, where he became known as the 'pigeon saint'.

12. Yogananda, *Autobiography of a Yogi*, 'The Christlike Life of Lahiri Mahasaya', p. 284. (Though I changed the spelling of namaz to the Punjabi pronunciation I am used to.)

13. Yogananda, *Autobiography of a Yogi*, 'The Christlike Life of Lahiri Mahasaya', p. 284.

14. Chapter II: 40 in the Bhagavad Gita (as quoted in Yogananda, *Autobiography of a Yogi*, 'Materializing a Palace in the Himalayas', p. 277).

15. Yogananda, *Autobiography of a Yogi*, 'Materializing a Palace in the Himalayas', p. 277.

Lesson #9: Go Out of Your Way for Little and Big Pilgrimages

1. Yogananda, *Journey to Self-Realization*, p. 252.

2. Yogananda, *Autobiography of a Yogi*, 'Therese Newman, Catholic Stigmatist', p. 427.

3. There are various versions of this mythology, several that reference Adam and the fall from Heaven are: https://www.britannica.com/topic/Black-Stone-of-Mecca, https://www.newworldencyclopedia.org/entry/Black_Stone_of_Mecca

4. Yogananda, *Autobiography of a Yogi*, 'We Visit Kashmir', p. 174.

5. According to Philip Goldberg (*The Life of Yogananda, the Story of the First Modern Guru*), based on interviews with those who knew Yogananda and reading his letters of the period.

6. Yogananda, *Autobiography of a Yogi*, 'The Heart of a Stone Image', pp. 241, 244.

7. Ibid., p. 244.

8. Yogananda, *Autobiography of a Yogi*, 'We Visit Kashmir', p. 228.

9. Ibid., p. 232.

10. Ibid., p. 233.
11. From a conversation with Muir related by Albert Palmer in *The Mountain Trail and its Message*, 1911, p. 27.

Lesson #10: Getting Help and Following the Clues

1. Yogananda, *Autobiography of a Yogi*, 'The Christlike Life of Lahiri Mahasaya', p. 377.
2. Yogananda, *Autobiography of a Yogi*, 'Babaji, the Yogi-Christ of Modern India', p. 348.
3. Yogananda, *Autobiography of a Yogi*, 'I Go to America', p. 404.
4. Ibid.
5. Ibid.
6. Attributed to Yogananda by SRF, https://m.facebook.com/srflakeshrineofficial/photos/a.238408250247465/787793088642309/
7. Yogananda, *Autobiography of a Yogi*, 'Two Penniless Boys in Brindaban', p. 113.
8. Ibid., p. 115.
9. Ibid., p. 117.
10. Ibid., p. 120.
11. Yogananda, *Autobiography of a Yogi*, 'My Parents and Early Life', p. 10.
12. Ibid.

Lesson #11: Setbacks May Be A Part of Your Story

1. Attributed to *The Law of Success: Using the Power of Spirit to Create Health, Prosperity, and Happiness*, by Yogananda.
2. Including the documentary, *Awake*, about his life, which also has a companion book.
3. https://mydattatreya.com/lahiri-mahasaya/
4. Swami Satyananda also wrote books on Yogananda's life.

5. Goldberg, Philip, *The Life of Yogananda*, 'Travels, Triumphs, and Travails', p. 180.

6. Goldberg, Philip, *The Life of Yogananda*, 'Travels, Triumphs, and Travails', p. 188.

7. Bagchi went on to pursue a PhD in America and became a respected scholar in his new, non-monastic life.

8. Goldberg, Philip, *The Life of Yogananda*, 'Travels, Triumphs, and Travails', p. 189.

9. Goldberg, Philip, *The Life of Yogananda*, 'Heights and Depths', p. 248.

10. And was later published in paperback by HarperCollins India.

11. Daya Mata (born Rachel Faye Wright) was the president and sanghamata of the Self-Realization Fellowship in Los Angeles, California/Yogoda Satsanga Society of India for over fifty-five years. This excerpt of her travel diaries appeared in 1959, and is available online at: https://yoganandasite.wordpress.com/2016/09/21/stories-of-lahiri-mahasaya-from-sri-sanyal-his-great-disciple-daya-mata/

12. https://yoganandasite.wordpress.com/2016/09/21/stories-of-lahiri-mahasaya-from-sri-sanyal-his-great-disciple-daya-mata/

13. Lewis Brenda Rosser, *Treasures Against Time: Paramahansa Yogananda with Doctor and Mrs Lewis*, p. 86.

Lesson #12: Lessons from Babaji and the Great Engine of Karma

1. Yogananda, *Autobiography of a Yogi*, 'Materializing a Palace in the Himalayas', p. 362.

2. Yogananda, *Autobiography of a Yogi*, 'Babaji, Yogi-Christ of Modern India', p. 263.

3. Tinker, H. (1990). *South Asia: A short history* (2nd ed). University of Hawaii Press. pp. 75–77.

4. Another such movie was the 2002 film *Baba*, a Tamil film produced by Rajnikanth. The scene, which is as incredible as Yogananda's stories, is now available on YouTube dubbed in Hindi with English subtitles. There are a number of documentary-type videos on YouTube, though again most of them seem to be based on Yogananda's book.

5. In Yogananda's *Autobiography*, this fellow student of Babaji is identified by Lahiri only as 'my companion' and 'my guide' in the chapter, 'Materializing a Palace in the Himalayas'.

6. You can learn more about Trailanga Swami and Shankari Mai Jiew beyond the *Autobiography*'s account at https://www.trailangaswami.in/

7. Though I couldn't find a specific reference for Govindan's claim of having met the great guru in person, he claims to have been in spiritual contact with him during his many years of practicing kriya yoga and establishing temples dedicated to Babaji, working first under Ramaiah and later on his own. It is to be noted that SRF/YSS doesn't explicitly recognize this tradition as being from the same Babaji.

8. Govindan, *Babaji and the 18 Siddha Kriya Yoga Tradition*, p. 94.

9. Thirumoolar was said to have meditated for 3,000 years, emerging from the meditation once a year to write a stanza. His resulting book, *Thirumandiram*, is a collection of more than 3,000 spiritual verses.

10. Yogananda, *Autobiography of a Yogi*, 'I Come to America', p. 402.

11. Ibid., p. 403.

12. Though he didn't talk about past lives publicly, he often discussed them with his disciples. A chapter in *Paramhansa Yogananda with Personal Reflections & Reminiscences: A Biography* by Swami Kriyananda and some of the works by

other disciples attest to this, mentioning discussions of the past lives of famous figures of the time including Hitler, Churchill, Stalin and many others.

13. A 'chela' is a novice or student or follower of a guru.

14. Yogananda, *Autobiography of a Yogi*, 'Babaji: Yogi-Christ of Modern India', p. 349.

15. Yogananda, *Autobiography of a Yogi*, 'Babaji: Yogi-Christ of Modern India', p. 349.

16. I get into more detail about karma and quests in my book, *The Simulation Hypothesis*, but for our purposes in this book, it is enough to think of video games as a metaphor for how events are created in the world around us.

17. Yogananda, *Autobiography of a Yogi*, 'Materializing a Palace in the Himalayas', p. 360.

18. Ibid., p. 361.

Lesson #13: Lifting the Veil—The Everlasting Beyond the Illusion

1. Yogananda, *Autobiography of a Yogi*, 'An Experience in Cosmic Consciousness', p. 170.

2. Source: Oxford languages, retrieved via Google search.

3. Yogananda, *Autobiography of a Yogi*, 'An Experience in Cosmic Consciousness', p. 166

4. Ibid.

5. Ibid., pp. 166–67.

6. Ibid., p. 167.

7. Ibid.

8. James Lynn was also quite a successful businessman and one of the wealthiest men in the country. He contributed greatly to Yogananda's growing organization, purchasing the land for some of SRF's locations (among other things). There is

a picture of him in the *Autobiography*, in samadhi, titled 'A Westerner in Samadhi.' Lynn became President of SRF/YSS after Yogananda's death, followed by Sri Daya Mata.

9. I heard these directly from Ryan, but I believe they are recounted in Roy Davis's books about his time with Yogananda.

10. Yogananda, *Autobiography of a Yogi*, 'An Experience in Cosmic Consciousness', pp. 171–72.

11. https://www.matthieuricard.org/en/blog/posts/what-does-buddhism-mean-by-enlightenment

12. https://www.yogapedia.com/definition/6166/nirvikalpa-samadhi

13. https://www.yogapedia.com/definition/6166/nirvikalpa-samadhi

14. Yogananda mentions this encounter only briefly at the end of the chapter, 'An Idyll in South India'. Ryan Kurczak reminded me that a fuller account of their encounter was kept by J. Wright, Yogananda's secretary, and perhaps by one of Ramana Maharshi's devotees as well. One such account is available here: http://greatmaster.info/ramanamaharshi/bhagavanreminiscences/reminiscenceramana1-166/

15. Yogananda, *Autobiography of a Yogi*, 'The Blissful Devotee and His Cosmic Romance', p. 92.

16. Ibid., p. 95.

17. Harvey, *Light Upon Light* (Berkeley, California: North Atlantic Books, 1998), p. 79.

18. https://yssofindia.org/meditation/karma-yoga-and-kriya-yoga-harnessing-the-power-of-outer-and-inner-action-for-spiritual-success

19. Yogananda, *Autobiography of a Yogi*, 'An Experience in Cosmic Consciousness', p. 168.

Lesson #14: Yoga is For Everyone, East and West

1. Yogananda, *Autobiography of a Yogi* (1946 edition, as available at crystalclarity.com), 'I Become a Monk of the Swami Order'.
2. A well-known quote from one of the songs of Kabir, available online in many places, including: https://berkleycenter. georgetown.edu/quotes/kabir-songs-of-kabir-on-the-nature-of-god-c-1440-1518
3. Swami Vivekananda, like Yogananda, was born in Bengal, and came to speak in America at a conference, the 1893 World's Parliament of Religions, the same year that Yogananda was born. Yogananda was no doubt very aware of his legacy when he left India almost thirty years later for a similar conference. Vivekananda's work in America paved the way for other swamis, including Yogananda, to make a more lasting impact on the West.
4. In Yogananda's time, the terms 'oriental' and 'occidental' were still prevalent, though they tend not to be so common today. This particular quote: Yogananda, *Autobiography of a Yogi*, 'I Go to America', p. 401.
5. Yogananda, *Autobiography of a Yogi*, 'Babaji's Interest in the West', p. 389.
6. Ibid. For emphasis, I have italicized the first part of the quotation.
7. Ibid., p. 390.
8. Ibid.
9. https://berkleycenter.georgetown.edu/quotes/kabir-songs-of-kabir-on-the-nature-of-god-c-1440-1518
10. Bertolucci, B. (Director). (1994). *Little Buddha* [Film]. Miramax.

11. Yogananda, *Autobiography of a Yogi*, 'Babaji's Interest in the West', p. 390.
12. Sri Yukteswar quoted in Yogananda, *Autobiography of a Yogi*, 'I Come to America', p. 403.

Afterword

1. Doreen Carvajal. (1999, 1 April). 'Children's Book Casts a Spell Over Adults; Young Wizard Is Best Seller And a Copyright Challenge'. *The New York Times*. https://www.nytimes. com/1999/04/01/books/children-s-book-casts-spell-over-adults-young-wizard-best-seller-copyright.htm
2. Available from the Self-Realization Foundation in the US and YSS in India, no doubt.
3. Though Philip Goldberg's biography is excellent, as is the documentary, *Awake*.
4. 'Remembering Yaqub: A Restless World Traveler Who Lived the America Dream', available at: https://rizstanford.medium. com/remembering-yaqub-a-restless-world-traveler-who-lived-the-american-dream-7b2cf02bbddf

Suggestions for Further Reading

Yogananda's Books:

(all references in the endnotes are to these specific editions/printings)

Yogananda, P., and W. Y. Evans-Wentz. *Autobiography of a Yogi.* 12th edition, Twelfth paperbound printing, 1993. Self-Realization Fellowship

———. *Autobiography of a Yogi.* Self-Realization Fellowship, Thirteenth Edition (Hardcover, 1998), later printing, 2015.

Online version of *Autobiography of a Yogi,* based on original 1946 edition: https://www.crystalclarity.com/autobiography-of-a-yogi-yogananda/

Yogananda, Paramahansa. *Man's Eternal Quest: Collected Talks and Essays on Realizing God in Daily Life, Vol. 1.* Self-Realization Fellowship, Second Edition, Fourth Printing, 1992.

———. *The Divine Romance: Collected Talks and Essays on Realizing God in Daily Life, Volume II.* Self-Realization Fellowship Second Edition (2002), Later Printing, 2013.

————. *The Science of Religion.* Self-Realization Fellowship, 1982.

————. *Journey to Self-Realization: Collected Talks and Essays on Realizing God in Daily Life, Vol. III.* Self-Realization Fellowship, First Edition (1987), Later Printing, 2016.

Other Recommended Books

Davis, Roy Eugene. *Paramahansa Yogananda As I Knew Him: Experiences, Observations & Reflections of a Disciple.* 2nd edition. CSA Press, 2018.

Foxen, Anya P. *Biography of a Yogi: Paramahansa Yogananda and the Origins of Modern Yoga.* Oxford University Press, 2017.

Ghosh, Sananda Lal. *Mejda: The Family and Early Life of Paramahansa Yogananda.* Self-Realization Fellowship, 1980.

Goldberg, Philip. *The Life of Yogananda: The Story of the Yogi Who Became the First Modern Guru.* 1st edition. Hay House, 2018.

Govindan, Marshall. *Babaji and the 18 Siddha Kriya Yoga Tradition.* 2nd edition. Kriya Yoga Publication, 1991.

Kurczak, Ryan. *The Essence of Complete Kriya Yoga Practice.* Amazon, 2020.

Sri M. *Apprenticed to a Himalayan Master: A Yogi's Autobiography.* Magenta Press, 2010.

Sri Yukteswar. *The Holy Science: Kaivalya Darsanam.* 7th edition. Self-Realization Fellowship, 1972.

Swami Kriyananda, and Paramahansa Yogananda. *Demystifying Patanjali: The Yoga Sutras (Aphorisms) the Wisdom of Paramhansa Yogananda.* Crystal Clarity Publishers, 2013.

Swami Kriyananda. *Paramhansa Yogananda: A Biography, with Personal Reflections & Reminiscences.* Crystal Clarity Publishers, 2011.

Resources

Organizations and Websites for Further Exploration of Yogananda's Teachings

Self-Realization Fellowship, USA: https://yogananda.org/

Yogoda Satsanga Society of India: https://yssofindia.org/

Ananda: https://www.ananda.org/

Center for Spiritual Enlightenment: https://www.csecenter.org/

Kriya Yoga Online: https://kriyayogaonline.com/

Acknowledgements

A book, though it's written by an author, is often the result of the contributions of many people, only some of whom are explicitly mentioned. Many others who go unmentioned, but definitely contributed to the author's thought process. For this reason, I would like to acknowledge everyone who has encouraged me on my journey as a spiritual seeker and as an author, whether I name them here or not.

In this vein, I'd like to thank several of my initial spiritual teachers and mentors, including Bill Kennedy, James Forgy, Rama, Andrea Seiver, Vywamus and many others.

For this specific book, I'd like to thank both of my editors at HarperCollins India, including the acquiring editor who sent me the original invitation to write it, Sonal Nerurkar, and my eventual editor, Sachin Sharma, for his help, encouragement and collaboration during this process. Also, I'd like to thank the others at HarperCollins who helped bring the book to completion.

I'd like to thank Philip Goldberg, both for his excellent biography of Yogananda and for taking the time not only to speak with me but to introduce me to the various folks who helped me in my journey. The folks at the Self-Realization Fellowship were incredibly helpful while I was researching and writing this book, including Lauren Landress. I want to extend a special thank you to the monastics, who spent time with me and gave me a tour of the Encinitas Hermitage— where Yogananda wrote his famous book—which I was able to visit despite it being closed to visitors during the time of COVID-19, Sister Sarala, Brother Premeshwarananda and Sister Yogamayee.

As we look at the different tributaries of Yogananda's teachings, I would also like to thank folks at the Ananda Foundation, including Nayaswami Jyotish and Lakshman, as well as the folks at East–West Books in Mountain View, California, for the inspiration they provided me along the way—a special thanks to David G. for his story about receiving guidance from Yogananda about the bookstore. At the Center for Spiritual Enlightenment, I would like to thank Yogacharya Ellen Grace O'Brian for her hospitality and for taking the time to meet with me, again during the thick of the pandemic. I would also like to thank Ryan Kurczak of Kriya Yoga Online, for his time and his perspective on kriya yoga.

I would also like to thank all of those who took the time to speak to me of their experiences with *Autobiography of a Yogi*, only some of whom are mentioned in the book. Although I couldn't include all of the wonderful stories I was told, please know that they all played a part in my formulation of what would become this book.

I would also like to thank Ellen McDonough for her support and patience with me through the authorial journey. I would like to thank my parents, who brought me from the East to the West in an immigrant journey that paralleled Yogananda's own journey to his adopted homeland.

Finally, I'd like to thank Swami Yogananda for the gift of his autobiography and for the vision and encouragement he gave me at the Encinitas Hermitage on the Pacific Ocean.

Index

About the Author

Rizwan ('Riz') Virk is a successful entrepreneur, venture capitalist, bestselling author, video game industry pioneer, college professor and indie film producer. He founded Play Labs @ MIT (www.playlabs.tv) and is a venture partner at Griffin Gaming Partners, one of the largest video game venture capital funds in the world. Riz is a graduate of MIT in Computer Science and Stanford's Graduate School of Business in Management, and is currently at the College of Global Futures at Arizona State University, working on his doctorate and teaching as member of the faculty at ASU's Fulton School of Engineering.

Since catching the start-up bug at the age of twenty-three, Riz has been a founder, investor and adviser in many start-ups, including Gameview (DeNA), CambridgeDocs (EMC), Tapjoy, North Bay Solutions, Funzio (GREE), Pocket Gems, Discord, Telltale Games, Theta Labs, Tarform, Upland and 1BillionTech. These start-ups have created software used by thousands of enterprises, and video games with millions of players, such as

Tap Fish, and games based on *Penny Dreadful, Grimm, Game of Thrones, Star Trek* and *The Walking Dead.*

Riz has produced many indie films, including the online phenomenon *Thrive: What On Earth Will It Take?*, *Sirius, Knights of Badassdom, The Outpost* and adaptations of the works of science fiction writers Philip K. Dick and Ursula K. Le Guin.

Riz is the author of *The Simulation Hypothesis, Startup Myths & Models: What You Won't Learn in Business School, The Simulated Multiverse, Zen Entrepreneurship* and *Treasure Hunt.* Riz's writing and start-ups have been featured on Tech Crunch, The Boston Globe, Vox.com, BBC Science Focus, Scientific American, NBCNews.com, Coast-to-Coast AM and the History Channel.

He splits his time between Mountain View (California), Cambridge (Massachusetts) and Tempe (Arizona). His personal and professional sites are www.zenentrepreneur.com and www. bayviewlabs.com. Follow him on Twitter @rizstanford.

DON'T MISS OTHER TITLES BY
RIZWAN VIRK

THE SIMULATION HYPOTHESIS

STARTUP MYTHS & MODELS

ZEN ENTREPRENEURSHIP

TREASURE HUNT

visit
http://www.zenentrepreneur.com/

Made in United States
Troutdale, OR
10/13/2023

13680857R00227